Liberalism, Conservatism, and Hayek's Idea of Spontaneous Order

Liberalism, Conservatism, and Hayek's Idea of Spontaneous Order

Edited by Louis Hunt and Peter McNamara

palgrave
macmillan

First published in 2007 by
PALGRAVE MACMILLAN™
175 Fifth Avenue, New York, N.Y. 10010 and
Houndmills, Basingstoke, Hampshire, England RG21 6XS.
Companies and representatives throughout the world.

PALGRAVE MACMILLAN is the global academic imprint of the Palgrave Macmillan division of St. Martin's Press, LLC and of Palgrave Macmillan Ltd. Macmillan® is a registered trademark in the United States, United Kingdom and other countries. Palgrave is a registered trademark in the European Union and other countries.

ISBN-13: 978-1-4039-8425-8
ISBN-10: 1-4039-8425-5

Library of Congress Cataloging-in-Publication Data

Liberalism, conservatism, and Hayek's idea of spontaneous order / edited by Louis Hunt and Peter McNamara.
    p. cm.
    Includes bibliographical references and index.
    ISBN 1-4039-8425-5 (alk. paper)
    1. Hayek, Friedrich A. von (Friedrich August), 1899–1992—Political and social views. 2. Liberalism—History—20th century. I. Hunt, Louis, 1956– II. McNamara, Peter, 1959–

HB101.H39L53 2007
320.101–dc22

                                                            2007007066

A catalogue record for this book is available from the British Library.

Design by Macmillan India Ltd.

First edition: October 2007

10 9 8 7 6 5 4 3 2 1

Printed in the United States of America.

Contents

Preface

The importance of Hayek's thought to the development of economic theory in the twentieth century is indisputable. Hayek's critique of central planning and his conception of the market as a means for coordinating the dispersed and often tacit knowledge of countless individuals have served as a spur even for those opposed to his advocacy of free markets. Students of Hayek have always recognized that he was more than an economist, that his economic theory was itself part of a more comprehensive intellectual project. Recent scholarship on Hayek has deepened our understanding of the full scope of his theoretical interests. We are now in a better position to evaluate his contribution not just to economics but also to a broad range of disciplines from psychology to political philosophy. Recognizing the breadth of Hayek's thought necessarily raises the question of its unity. To what degree do the various strands of his thought mesh together to form a coherent whole? Is there a central core to his thought or does the breadth of his interests reflect merely a wide-ranging curiosity, perhaps even a lack of clear focus? A considered judgment of Hayek's stature as a thinker depends on resolving the question of the unity and coherence of his intellectual project as a whole.

The authors in this volume, despite their divergent assessments of the success of Hayek's enterprise, all agree that there is an underlying unity of intention in his thought. Hayek means for his various writings to be understood as parts of a greater whole. He warns repeatedly in his work about the dangers not only of studying his own economic theories in abstraction from his broader intellectual concerns but also of treating economics generally as an autonomous discipline unrelated to other disciplines in the sciences and humanities. This volume is intended as a contribution to the dual tasks of broadening the scope of our understanding of Hayek beyond his contributions to economics and of integrating the various aspects of his thought into an intelligible whole.

The chapters in this volume approach these tasks through an exploration of two interconnected themes that arguably form the central axis of Hayek's intellectual project. The first theme is his conception of the Great Society as a model of social and political organization that aims to achieve the greatest possible individual liberty compatible with social order. The Great Society is Hayek's term for his version of a classical liberal polity based on free markets, limited government, and the rule of law. Hayek developed his idea of the Great Society as part of his polemic against social planning in the years after World War II. However, the significance of this political ideal is independent of its historical origins. Conceived in the struggle against socialism and fascism, the idea of the Great Society can still serve as a model of a free society to set against contemporary regressions into economic populism, ethnic nationalism, fundamentalist theocracy, and other forms of what Hayek would not hesitate to call tribalism.

If the first theme outlines an ideal of social and political order, the second describes the means whereby this ideal comes into being. The idea of spontaneous order is Hayek's best-known contribution to contemporary social science, although as a number of chapters demonstrate, it has great relevance for the natural sciences as well. In Hayek's view, spontaneous order—the emergence of complex order as the unintended consequence of individual actions that have no such end in view—is both the origin of the Great Society and its underlying principle. Hayek means by the Great Society a social and political order that has emerged spontaneously through the interaction of individuals going about their everyday business and that sustains itself through the same mechanism. In this sense, the idea of the Great Society and the idea of spontaneous order stand or fall together.

The chapters in this volume assess these two themes in Hayek's thought by comparing his ideas both with other theorists of modern liberal societies and with contemporary developments in the natural and social sciences. They represent a wide range of intellectual and disciplinary approaches. They are also often sharply critical of various aspects of Hayek's position. But they are united in the conviction that a careful study of his intellectual project can help us to understand, and perhaps even suggest some tentative solutions to, our contemporary social and political dilemmas.

We would like to thank the generous support of the Merrill Endowment and the College of Humanities, Arts and Social Sciences at Utah State University, which funded the lecture series held at Utah State University that was the basis for this volume. Our thanks also go to Brandee Halverson, who played a major role in organizing that series. We would also like to thank Constance Hunt and Carol McNamara for their support, encouragement, and patience.

Louis Hunt
Peter McNamara

CHAPTER 1

Introduction: Governing the Great Society

Peter McNamara

This book on liberalism, conservatism, and Friedrich Hayek's idea of spontaneous order raises critical questions regarding the governance of modern societies. The idea of spontaneous order—the idea that beneficial social orders might arise without the direction of some central authority—is Hayek's major contribution to liberal political theory. As the chapters in this volume demonstrate, the idea itself and its political implications are ambiguous. Does the idea of spontaneous order point in the direction of liberalism? Or does it point, contrary to Hayek's own suggestions, in the direction of conservatism? Does the idea of spontaneous order point to a public philosophy that minimizes the role of the state? Or does it presuppose, again contrary to some of Hayek's own suggestions, an already vigorous state? Resolving these ambiguities is clearly critical to the task of governing what Hayek termed the Great Society and especially to the task of formulating a governing ideology or public philosophy. We do not purport here to have resolved these difficulties. Our goal is the more limited one of exploring these ambiguities and their roots in Hayek's thought. One need not accept Hayek's account of either the idea of spontaneous order or the Great Society in full to see the extraordinary significance of his effort to think through the problems of governance in a large, complex, and modern society. Governing the Great Society is a central problem for philosophers, economists, and political scientists today because, whether by choice, evolution, or fate, we live in something like what Hayek termed the Great Society.

My chief goal in this introduction is to sketch Hayek's account of the intellectual, political, and moral landscape of the Great Society. I will focus closely on the argument and indeed the text of Hayek's three-volume work, *Law, Legislation and Liberty,* where he most fully develops his account of the Great Society.[1] In doing so, I also wish to provide a context for the chapters that follow. It is this terrain that our authors will explore and sometimes, it must be said, battle over. Subsequent chapters, outlined at the end of this introduction, will develop in depth the themes of liberalism, conservatism, and the idea of spontaneous order.

Hayek repeatedly emphasizes the historical uniqueness and precarious existence of the Great Society. It is a development of the last three hundred or so years. It is characteristic of only certain parts of the Western world. And, despite certain resemblances with, it is somehow distinct from the concepts other thinkers have used to describe the unprecedented character of modern life and the peculiar political and moral challenges to which it gives rise. The Great Society is not simply a "nation state," an "industrial democracy," a "mass democracy," a "mass society," a "mass culture," or simply "modernity." What precisely did Hayek mean by the Great Society? Hayek had a penchant for neologisms and for using old words, and even ideas, in new ways. It was part of his rhetorical strategy as he makes clear at the very beginning of *The Constitution of Liberty* when he remarks: "If old truths are to retain their hold on men's minds, they must be restated in the language and concepts of successive generations. What at one time are their most effective expressions gradually become so worn with use that they cease to carry a definite meaning."[2] "Great Society," I believe, is another effort on Hayek's part to make "old truths" live again. Hayek claims that when speaking of the Great Society he is speaking of the same concept Adam Smith has in mind when he uses the term "great society" and when Karl Popper speaks of the "Open Society." The contrast with Smith is most instructive.[3] While Hayek cites Smith as a source for his concept, there are interesting differences between Smith's usage of the term and Hayek's. Hayek's use of the term is not so much a distortion as it is a creative interpretation. Smith sometimes speaks of "a" "great society" usually in the context of a discussion of his economic theories. When doing so, Smith means a large society in which economic forces, such as supply and demand and the division of labor, can come into play. The distinguishing feature would seem to be simply size. Both Great Britain and China qualify as examples of a great society.[4] Hayek means something more than simply a large commercial society. He comes close at times to identifying the Great Society with "civilization" or a least a particular type of civilization, "free civilization," and even "our civilization."[5] Apart from its persuasive value, what did Hayek have in mind when he chose "Great Society"? What is the more, the extra thing or things, that distinguishes the Great Society from the market? I will try to answer these and related questions in what follows. Hayek distinguishes the Great Society most clearly from what he terms "tribal society" and it is there that we must begin.

Tribal Society

According to Hayek, life in tribal societies has been the characteristic way of human life for the longest time. Only in the last few thousand years has there been a departure. The Great Society is even more recent. Its existence has been but the blink of an eye in terms of the overall span of human existence. Tribal society is characterized by life in small groups where kinship bonds are strong. The members of tribal societies also have closely shared ideals and interests. In the most primitive of societies, no distinction at all is drawn between interests and ideals, between facts and values. Tribal societies have shared rules, customs, and traditions that are usually unspoken and that have evolved as adaptations to circumstances. Peace prevails in the group because of the identity of interests among members and because of the limited informational requirements needed for the smooth functioning of society. In "face-to-face" societies everyone knows everyone else, everyone knows everyone else's problems, and everyone knows, more or less, the available means for solving these problems. Under such conditions it is quite plausible that one's efforts on behalf of the common good might be both recognized and have their intended consequences.

Hayek's account of these kinds of societies is dark, even repulsive. These are "closed societies" in the most emphatic sense. Tribal societies turn on the distinction between "us" and "them," between friend and enemy. The reverse side of peace within the group is continual warfare with those outside. Continual conflict is the norm and even desirable because it brings friends even closer together. Hayek suggests that these characteristics of tribal societies have deep foundations in human nature. In terms of biology, we have evolved to live in these kinds of societies. Moreover, these "innate" instincts have been reinforced by cultural evolution. Thus, as Hayek explains things, the Great Society must grow not only by conquering harmful customs and traditions that date back to tribal society, but against certain features of human nature itself.

For Hayek, the most horrifying feature of the twentieth century was the resurgence of tribal ways of thinking. Indeed, it is tempting to see much of Hayek's intellectual enterprise as, first, an attempt to explain and, then, to combat these developments. To Hayek, communism, Nazism, and fascism, each in their own way, embraced what, we might call, philosophically sophisticated tribalism. While admiring in some ways the intellect of the Nazi legal theorist Carl Schmitt, Hayek found his friend-foe distinction an appalling reversion to savagery (*LLL,* I, pp. 71, 161–162 n. 19; II, pp. 144, 191 n. 13). Similarly, Hayek saw Marxist communism as a monstrous attempt to impose the economic ways of a tribal society on the modern world.

Hayek saw a less obvious but, in the long term, no less dangerous manifestation of tribalism in movement for "social justice." This was the name he gave to advocacy of government policies to redistribute wealth, income, and opportunity in the name of justice. Hayek's extensive and controversial account of this movement is important in itself, but it is also important for what it tells us, by implication, about tribal society and the distinction between tribal society and the Great Society. The movement for social justice is in part driven by a real sentiment, concern for the truly needy, but this real sentiment becomes, in the circumstances of the Great Society, a cloak for a multitude of other passions and interests that, if pursued, "must produce a totalitarian society" (*LLL,* II, p. 147). Hayek reasons as follows. "Social justice" is an "abuse" of the word justice because in a Great Society there can be no truly social, that is, universally or almost universally held, idea of what the proper distribution of wealth should be (II, p. 62). Invariably, the policies followed under the guise of social justice benefit neither "society" nor the truly needy, but rather some particular interest group.

The idea of social justice strikes at the heart of the Great Society in another way. One of Hayek's most startling claims is that the free market, the paradigmatic spontaneous order, does not necessarily reward merit.[6] It is, he maintains, only meaningful to speak of the justice of the market when speaking of the legal framework within which market activities take place, the "rules of the game." The spontaneous order of the market is, in a fundamental sense, unpredictable. There will be winners and losers, but just who wins and loses is in large part a matter of chance, of being in the right place at the right time. What is important for the market to function is that some win and some lose. Positive feedback (winning) and negative feedback (losing) stimulate changes in individual behavior that lead to overall improvements in economic performance. Reward and merit are, however, not necessarily connected. The activity of speculators is necessary for the smooth functioning of the market. Their outlandish profits are a signal for others to move into a particular area of the market. Yet these profits are not readily intelligible as a reward for honest effort and perseverance. Conversely, the loss sustained by a skilled and diligent worker who just happens to be in an industry that is in decline seems unfair, but is a necessary signal to change the allocation of resources. Hayek remarks that Horatio Alger-type stories that link effort and reward are "probably a misfortune" and that "it bodes ill for the future of the market order that this seems to have become the only defence of it which is understood by the general public" (*LLL,* II, p. 74).

Social justice is, then, a mirage, an illusion. Yet it is a very powerful illusion because it brings into play a variety of dangerous human desires and emotions. Hayek repeatedly identifies many, if not all, of these desires and emotions with tribal society. The social justice movement is a case of "primitive thinking" (*LLL*, I, p. 73; also II, p. 63) specifically in that it fails to see that the workings of the market are those of an impersonal mechanism, a spontaneous order, that cannot truly be brought under the direction of "society." Society, in its collective capacity, does nothing. To say it does is to personify or anthropomorphize society. This made a certain sense when mankind lived in small groups held together by common purposes and with sufficient knowledge to pursue those purposes. Individual merit was plain for everyone to see and it was within the capacities of the group to attempt to match merit and reward. According to Hayek, such thinking no longer makes any sense. Society is no longer held together by common purposes. Each individual has his purposes that he attempts to realize within the rules of justice. Success is partly a matter of skill and, as noted, partly a matter of chance. In truth, no one is or can be responsible for the outcome of the "impersonal mechanism" of the market (*LLL*, II, p. 81).

An awareness of this aspect of the market is a difficult thing for human beings to achieve. It is, in the first place, intellectually very difficult to grasp that there may be order without design or responsibility. Furthermore, certain emotions and desires lead us to resist this insight. First, pride and vanity inspire intellectuals and politicians to believe that they can govern society the way one governs an organization or a tribe. Succumbing to the "synoptic delusion" they believe they have available to them the information required to formulate plans. Such information is not available. Second, the cause of social justice provides an outlet for "moral emotion" (*LLL*, II, p. 66). The undeniable appeal of the idea of social justice to a large degree depends on its ability to call upon a deep reservoir of emotion that, according to Hayek, reflects our cultural and evolutionary heritage, but that is not compatible with the workings of the Great Society. Social justice plays on feelings of solidarity with others and on our felt need to act morally for the common good. But such feelings and actions in the circumstances of the Great Society are perverse. A third but related emotion is our sense of desert and a corresponding tendency to look for someone or something to blame for misfortune. We do good, especially good for others, expecting that somehow it will be good for ourselves. Hayek is worth quoting at length on this point.

> It is certainly tragic to see the failure of the most meritorious efforts of parents to bring up their children, of young men to build a career, or of an explorer

or scientist pursuing a brilliant idea. And we will protest against such a fate although we do not know anyone who is to blame for it, or any way in which such disappointments can be avoided.

It is no different with regard to the general feeling of injustice about the distribution of material goods in a society of free men. Though we are in this case less ready to admit it, our complaints about the outcome of the market as unjust do not really assert that somebody has been unjust; and there is no answer to the question *who* has been unjust. Society has simply become the new deity to which we complain and clamour for redress if it does not fulfil the expectations it has created.

(*LLL*, II, p. 69)

Our sense of desert leads us to ask for something more than a chance to play the game. We believe that we should receive rewards proportionate to our efforts, including our moral efforts. Hayek does not explain the root of our idea of desert. We might speculate that, for Hayek, the sense of desert too was a product of face-to-face tribal communities in which one's contribution to the common good was proportionally rewarded. Whether this is an adequate account of what is surely one of the deepest human longings need not detain us here. If it is not, it only underscores the way in which the Great Society demands a renunciation of these profound longings.

Finally, the workings of the market are difficult to assimilate because we have a tendency to overrate the benefits of "expediency," actions taken with short-term, apparently tangible goals in mind, and to discount the long-term benefits for society as a whole of following "principles."[7] This is not just a matter of shortsightedness. It also reflects our primordial desire to live in a community of shared purposes in which the conflict between principles and expediency dissolves because law can be conceived as a command or means to an end rather than as an abstract rule with no particular or immediate purpose. To summarize: tribal society involves a moral code that emphasizes solidarity with one's community, combined with a strong sense of individual desert, and a bias toward immediate action in the face of problems.

The Great Society

Before drawing out the comparable moral code of the Great Society, it is necessary to review Hayek's account of the growth of the Great Society. It might be more accurate to say that it is necessary to review his *two* accounts of that growth. At the very least, one must say that his account contains two different threads or emphases. The first emphasis is a historical account of the growth of the Great Society in Europe and North America. The second emphasis is an essentially abstract or conjectural history that focuses on the moral basis of the Great Society. Another way of putting the difference is that in the first account he begins with a society that has already made some, perhaps considerable, advance beyond the primitive tribal stage, whereas in the second account he describes the transition from the tribal stage itself. While both accounts employ the logic of cultural evolution, the second account employs it more rigorously.

Hayek's historical account is presented concisely in *The Constitution of Liberty*[8] and more diffusely in the three volumes of *Law, Legislation and Liberty.* Hayek points to Great Britain as the critical nation. Two factors led the British to embrace an idea of law as abstract principle rather than as the mere command of the sovereign. First, the British system of law developed as a common law system in which judges saw their role as discovering the already, in some way, existing law rather than making it. The ancient and medieval natural law traditions were an important factor in the way judges conceived their role as discoverers rather than makers of the law. It was not until late in British history that the idea of either the legislature or the crown as law-making institutions gained ground. Because of the common law system, British law was able to evolve in response to changing circumstances, with judges attempting to articulate already existing rules on the basis of which the parties to the case had formed their expectations. This approach to law made clear the long-term advantages of a system that guarantees through the rule of law a private sphere free from the intrusion of government and in which individuals are free to pursue their own purposes. Rapid economic progress was one favorable consequence. Civil peace was another important consequence as was, in particular, the ability to expand the numbers of people living together in peace. To some degree— Hayek is vague—this approach gained ground not because anyone understood its workings, but because it was simply more successful than other approaches. In other words, the mechanisms of cultural evolution rather than design were at work. Groups with more efficient rules prevail over those with less.

Gradually, however, the basic features of the system became evident to philosophers. This brings us to the second important factor that influenced the development of the Great Society, namely, the moderate character of the British Enlightenment. In Scotland and England thinkers such as Mandeville, Hume, Smith, and Ferguson provided both an explanation and a moral defense of the workings of the Great Society, including the idea of spontaneous order. Hayek draws a sharp contrast between the British and the French enlightenments. The French rejected what Hayek terms the "evolutionary rationalism" of the British in favor of a "constructivist rationalism" that strove to reshape society according to rational plans.[9] While the French strand of the Enlightenment dominated the Continent and combined easily with its absolutist political tradition, Hayek argues that the American experience should be understood as an adaptation of the British system to North American circumstances, rather than as an instance of constructivist rationalism. Hayek's whole account raises many difficult questions of fact and interpretation, but what is of interest at the moment is that the Great Society emerged in a particular nation with a particular cultural tradition in some ways stretching back to antiquity.[10] This tradition, moreover, involved extensive cultural, philosophical, and theological commitments. Just consider, for a moment, what is entailed in the idea of natural law!

Hayek presents his more abstract account of the growth of the Great Society primarily in *Law, Legislation and Liberty*. Here he focuses directly on the transition from tribal society to the Great Society. Tribal society is, to repeat, small, close-knit, united in a set of common beliefs and purposes, and draws a sharp distinction between friend and foe. Tribal society has custom, tradition, and often law, but not in the sense of abstract rules of justice. Different societies will have different customs, traditions, and laws, and will fare better or worse according to how well those practices fit with circumstances. Abstract rules of justice, however, arise from interactions *outside* the tribe. Again Hayek is worth quoting at length.

> It is in the *ius gentium,* the law merchant and the practice of the ports and fairs that we must chiefly seek the steps in the evolution of law which ultimately made an open society possible. *Perhaps* one might even say that the development of universal rules of conduct did not begin within the organized community of the tribe but rather with the first instance of silent barter when a savage placed some offerings at the boundary of the territory of the tribe in the expectation that a return gift would be made in a similar manner, thus beginning a new custom.
>
> (*LLL,* I, p. 82, emphasis added)

Only outside the tribe is it possible to have the experience of interactions not based on shared purposes with others and of the kind that make possible the development of abstract rules of justice. As Hayek explains in another place:

> The moral sentiments which made the open society possible grew up in the towns, the commercial and trading centres, while the feelings of the large numbers were still governed by the parochial sentiments and the xenophobic and fighting attitudes governing the tribal group.
>
> (*LLL,* II, pp. 145–146)

It is the repetition of such interactions and the gradual recognition of the benefits to society and to the individual that lead to the more widespread adoption of the rules that make them possible. This recognition comes about, in keeping with the idea of cultural evolution, more from the experience of success, including success over other groups and societies, than from direct insight into the causes of success.

I am not suggesting that these two accounts—the historical and the abstract—are incompatible. Yet Hayek's hesitation when speaking of the beginnings of abstract rules as occurring outside the tribe—"perhaps"—is significant because it raises the following issue. What is the relation between the customs, traditions, and laws of earlier stages of society to the customs, traditions, and laws that make possible the Great Society? Are these earlier norms simply to be dispensed with at the earliest possible convenience? Or do they in some way create the conditions that eventually lead to the Great Society? Or might they even be in some, perhaps nonobvious way, still necessary for the smooth functioning of the Great Society? Hayek, in places, seems to come down hard in favor of the first possibility. He writes that the successive expansions of individual freedoms leading to the Great Society at first "were all infringements of customary rules—so many falls from grace." How did these infringements become acceptable? The "law-breakers, who were to be path-breakers, certainly did not introduce the new rules because they recognized that they were beneficial to the community, but they simply started some practices advantageous to them which then did prove beneficial to the group in which they prevailed" (*LLL*, III, p. 161). This explanation comports with Hayek's ideas about cultural evolution and spontaneous order, but does it make sense? And does it square with the historical account he gives of the rise of the Great Society in the Anglo-American world?

These same questions emerge from another aspect of Hayek's account of the Great Society. As noted, Hayek himself emphasizes the tension and often direct conflict between the moral code of tribal society and the moral code of the Great Society. But here too he equivocates. The moral code of the Great Society is not, and will not be for the foreseeable future, a replacement for the moral code of tribal society. Once we have outlined his account of the differences between the two moral codes, we will be in a position to state clearly the distinctive moral commitments of the Great Society as envisaged by Hayek.

Hayek explains that with the enlargement of the circle of society, stemming from the obligation to treat others as equals, there also comes a corresponding contraction in the extent of enforceable obligations to others. More fundamentally still, the Great Society brings about a moral revolution in our relationship to others. Not only are deliberate efforts to help others less likely to be successful, they are likely to be less successful than the beneficial indirect effects of the pursuit of our own purposes, self-interest, or, to use the theological term, "calling" (*LLL,* II, p. 145). Lastly, instead of loyalty to a group united for a visible purpose, members of the Great Society must feel obliged to abstract rules. The Great Society, Hayek observes, comes at the "price" of sacrificing many deeply felt emotions, desires, and sentiments (*LLL,* II, p. 147). This is a real rather than an imaginary or temporary price.

> The kind of abstract order on which man has learnt to rely and which has enabled him peacefully to coordinate the efforts of millions, unfortunately cannot be based on such feelings as love which constituted the highest virtue in the small group. Love is a sentiment which only the concrete evokes, and the Great Society has become possible through the individual's efforts being guided not by the aim of helping particular other persons, but the confinement of the pursuit of their purposes by abstract rules.
>
> (*LLL,* II, p. 150)

The shift to the Great Society "leaves an emotional void by depriving men both of satisfying tasks and the assurance of support in the case of need" (*LLL,* II, p. 146). In another place, Hayek speaks of the "inhumanity" of modern life (*LLL,* III, p. 146).

Hayek must remain ambivalent because he does not believe that the emotions, desires, and sentiments that underlie the moral code of the tribal society are not real or that they will disappear anytime soon. He points to the ways they may be accommodated and appeased to some degree within the Great Society, but, he implies, they cannot be satisfied. For example, we may have in addition to the countless more-or-less anonymous interactions we have in the marketplace, a few interactions with neighbors, friends, and family that resemble those of tribal society. But even in this sphere, our obligations are not of the sort, for the most part, that could be demanded, let alone enforced.[11] To take another example, the decentralization of government, through federalism, for example, might make democracy more real and humane by making a coincidence of purposes among citizens more likely.[12] But this too would take place within the context of the Great Society where the scope of politics has been greatly reduced. Hayek believes that any serious attempt to satisfy the yearnings born in tribal society will result in totalitarianism of either a nationalist or socialist kind. This, for Hayek, was the great lesson of the twentieth century.

We are now in a position to state with some precision the moral commitments of the Great Society. These are commitments in the sense that not only must the members of the Great Society hold to these beliefs, but they must also struggle for them against the tide of the times and even against their own sentiments. These moral commitments distinguish the Great Society sharply from tribal society, as also from Smith's "great society." They also indicate the sense in which Hayek believes the Great Society is prescriptive. Membership in the Great Society requires something more than the mere pursuit of one's self-interest within a legal or customary framework that makes exchange possible. It requires a particular mind-set characterized by a particular set of values. First, it requires that we check our emotions, especially our sense of loyalty to whatever group with which we most immediately and, perhaps, naturally identify. Second, we must devote ourselves to abstract rules of justice. This involves taking a long-run perspective. It also involves accepting the distinctive kind of uncertainty that characterizes the Great Society. We just do not know what the long run will bring. A consequence of this outlook is that we individually and collectively ought to reject expedient short-term measures in favor of staying with principles.

The overall moral posture of resignation, dedication, and personal independence has many similarities with Stoicism, as Hayek himself recognized (*LLL*, II, p. 71). It is true, however, that, unlike Stoicism, Hayek's account of the moral commitments of the Great Society has a hopeful, progressive, even utopian streak. This is evident in a number of areas. Hayek believes that social science needs to proceed by providing ideal models, utopias, to guide policy. Precise predictions are impossible and mere explanations are out-of-date before the ink is dry. Policy makers need ideals to guide them. As cause for optimism, Hayek recalls Smith's claim that free trade in Great Britain was a utopian idea and notes that Smith's goal was realized within just 70 years (*LLL*, I, p. 65). Another instance of Hayek's utopianism is his internationalism. Hayek observes that the boundaries of the Great Society are fuzzy. We belong to many communities and networks and to some that spill across national boundaries. Hayek himself looked forward, as the culmination of the Great Society, to a "universal order of peace" in which national boundaries will all but disappear. Hayek acknowledges though that this idea would shock "current morals" (*LLL*, II, p. 148; see also III, pp. 55–56). More generally, for the foreseeable future, members of the Great Society ought to be aware of its precarious existence. It is an exception in terms of the historical record and it is beset by enemies both without and, as Hayek chooses to emphasize, literally within the bosoms of its own members. Such an awareness ought to make us serious advocates for the Great Society. Somehow we must be both stoics and liberal progressives for the indefinite future. Hayek's life and work, at times lonely and always battling for what seems like a lost cause, both exhibits and calls for such extraordinary seriousness in others.

The Great Society, then, is a set of institutional arrangements in which individuals are free to pursue their own purposes subject to the rules of justice. But, in addition, the Great Society is a task or project. Most of its members need not be actively striving for the realization of the project, but they must have the moral resources, "a strong belief in definite principles" (*LLL*, I, p. 61), to resist resolutely projects that will endanger the Great Society. Furthermore, at least some within the Great Society must vigorously make the case for the Great Society in politics, academia, and in the popular culture. What gives rise to these particular moral commitments? What sustains them once they have become established? These questions may be added to those raised above about whether the Great Society grows *out of* or whether it grows *in opposition to* tribal society and whether the moral code of the Great Society has any continuing relationship with that of tribal society. To a large degree, the different interpretations and answers that may be given to these questions account for the diversity of approaches and arguments in the chapters that follow in this volume.

Liberalism, Conservatism, and the Idea of Spontaneous Order

What does it mean to govern the Great Society? Hayek neatly, too neatly in fact, distinguishes two tasks of government (*LLL*, I, p. 131). One task of government is the provision of public services. Hayek includes not only the requirements of a minimal state, such as national defense, but the provision as well of health care, education, social security, and unemployment insurance. Hayek recommends that these social services be provided through competitive mechanisms rather than through government monopolies. The other, more fundamental but seemingly simpler, task of government is the enforcement of rules of justice. Hayek has in mind chiefly laws that protect life, liberty, and property; secure contracts; and protect against fraud. The enforcement of the rules of justice is a more fundamental task in that only in the context of established rules of justice does the proper role of government as limited to the provision of certain services become clear. Our focus here is the rules of justice themselves and their cultural context, rather than their enforcement. The chapters in this volume address both the nature of these rules and their origins.

As I have just noted, Hayek defined the task of governing the Great Society too narrowly. To address this defect we need to take a step back. At its most general level the question is that of what is, or ought to be, the public or governing philosophy of the Great Society. This in turn requires revisiting the issue of Hayek's liberalism.[13] While Hayek was and is often tagged as a conservative, he famously claims in the caustic postscript to *The Constitution of Liberty* that he is emphatically a liberal. The issue of liberalism versus conservatism will appear in many of the chapters that follow.

It is Hayek's idea of spontaneous order that makes him so difficult to characterize. He is a liberal, certainly, but of a peculiar sort. More importantly, it is a serious question whether his idea of spontaneous order does not point in the direction of conservatism rather than his brand of liberalism.

The liberalism versus conservatism issue does not, however, exhaust matters. In the first place, the idea of spontaneous order might seem to have the potential to escape the orbit of both liberalism and conservatism in that, potentially, it is a complete theory of society. Where such an aspiration to completeness might lead is uncertain. Like many scientific insights, it might be as likely to lead to more government intervention in society as it is to lead to a Hayekian "dethronement of politics" (*LLL,* III, p. 149).[14] But another set of issues arises when we move in the other direction and question the adequacy and scope of the idea of spontaneous order. This question takes shape in a number of ways. While the idea of spontaneous order may illuminate the workings of the market to a very great extent, it is less obvious that it is adequate for explaining just how the framework that makes the market possible comes into being. The ambiguities in Hayek's account of the growth of the Great Society mentioned above raise doubts about its completeness and about just how the Great Society generates the moral commitments that sustain it. In response to this problem, a number of chapters assess Hayek's account of the origins of the rules of justice, as well as explore the task of establishing the rules of justice, both in law and in public opinion.

The chapters that follow are divided into two parts. Part I is entitled "Fundamental Themes." It consists of one chapter on the Scottish Enlightenment and the idea of spontaneous order and one chapter on Hayek's rediscovery of that idea. James Otteson reviews the Scottish contribution to the theory of spontaneous order, focusing on Adam Smith's development of a "market model" to explain the emergence of morality. Otteson defends Smith against the charge that the market model is insufficient because it requires support from the outside, say government, to establish moral constraints. He argues that Smith's principle of mutual sympathy provides precisely the mechanism needed to generate moral rules through bargaining. Furthermore, he observes that recent research in biology and psychology supports Smith's view. Otteson believes that Hayek's major insights into morality and economics closely mirror the Scots and especially Smith.

Louis Hunt's chapter takes up the origin and scope of Hayek's idea of spontaneous order. Hunt describes the origins of the idea in the "socialist calculation debate" that focused on the theoretical possibility of an economically efficient socialist economy. In response, Hayek reconceived the economic problem to be one of dealing with the problem of limited and dispersed knowledge, a problem that socialism clearly could not solve. Hayek used this insight to make a broader point about civilization: civilization itself depends on a similar economizing in the use of knowledge. Hunt then places Hayek's description of the growth of civilization in the context of post-Humean debates, especially in Germany, over the limits of human knowledge. Hunt's chapter closes with a question: is there not a tension between Hayek's conservative recognition of the limits of human knowledge and his liberal championing of a dynamic free market? Hunt speculates that Hayek's rediscovery of the idea of spontaneous order failed to take into account the true radicalism of thinkers such as Smith and Hume.

Part II consists of a series of "Critical Reflections" on the themes of liberalism, conservatism, and Hayek's idea of spontaneous order. We begin with Ross Emmett's analysis of "Knight's Challenge." Frank Knight was a leader in the "Chicago School" and shared with Hayek a strong preference *for* free markets and *against* government planning. Yet Knight did not believe, as Hayek did, that social justice is a mirage. Rather, he believed that it was a legitimate subject of public debate. As Emmett puts it, "For Knight a theory of spontaneous order is not enough; liberal democracies also require a vision—a *moral* vision—of what they want their societies to become. Such vision can only be arrived at by discussion, rather than the adaptation of institutions via natural selection." Emmett outlines just what Knight meant when speaking of "government by discussion."

Richard Boyd and James Morrison compare and contrast Hayek's "liberalism" with Michael Oakeshott's "conservatism." They observe that, despite the labels, the two men have a great deal in common: skepticism about whether the methods of natural science apply to the social world; an emphasis on spontaneous orders; and, later in their careers, a recognition of the need for a stable neutral framework of rules in which individuals can pursue their own individual purposes. Boyd and Morrison suggest, however, that it is Oakeshott who most consistently follows through on their shared premise of epistemological skepticism in that Oakeshott is led to question the very idea of progress.

Scott Yenor contrasts Hayek with Hume and finds in Hume both a more complete account of the origins and a more promising defense of the Great Society. Yenor shows that, for Hume, the commercial republic did not arise spontaneously. Using Hume's account of the religious transformation of England, Yenor argues that, unlike Hayek, Hume does not neglect the critical role of "intentional design and statesmanship." This recognition leads Yenor to delve, again using Hume as a guide, into the problematic relationship of religion to the liberal tradition. Finally, Yenor provides a Humean defense of the commercial republic in which he argues that nature itself provides the standard by which moral judgments may be made regarding the goodness of the commercial republic.

Larry Arnhart makes the case for Darwinian conservatism. Arnhart argues that Hayek fails to do justice to his own claim that there are "three sources of values": natural instincts, cultural traditions, and rational deliberation. Hayek stresses only tradition to the neglect of nature and reason, thereby leaving himself open to the charge of relativism. Arnhart focuses on the contribution biology can make to our understanding of society. Rather than seeing a conflict between our natural instincts and the Great Society, Arnhart argues that the instincts, in fact, can only be fulfilled in a society that protects private property, supports families, and limits governmental power. This constitutes an anti-utopian political agenda consistent with what Arnhart describes as the "Tragic Vision" of life. Properly understood and taking into account the advances in modern science, Arnhart believes, we should see Hayek as a conservative.

Gerald Gaus argues that we should view Hayek as a complexity theorist. After identifying the many significant elements of complexity theory in Hayek's thought, Gaus turns to Hayek's central claim regarding governing the Great Society, namely, that we should stick to "principles" and resist the temptation to do what appears "expedient." Stressing the unpredictability of political and economic life, Gaus works through Hayek's case against expediency, buttressing it with recent work from the fields of public policy and the philosophy of economics. He shows that the case against expediency depends, in the end, on the weight we give to the moral rules we hold on to in our decision making. Gaus is, however, troubled by the conservative implications of Hayek's apparent acceptance of cultural evolution as the source of our moral rules and believes that Hayek's evolutionary argument must be scaled back. That said, he thinks this can be done while still maintaining "a qualified rational deference to current moral rules," thereby substantially vindicating Hayek's preference for principles over expediency.

Michael Munger's chapter asks a basic question: what makes cooperation possible among human beings? Munger's answer is that it is not self-interest or even rational self-interest, but "culture." Culture makes possible political cooperation, say in the choice of political institutions, by substantially reducing the costs and difficulties of establishing trust and communication. Munger believes that culture may be understood as a particular kind of Hayekian spontaneous order. Culture is the product of nurture rather than nature. It is a common set of beliefs and practices that have evolved over time and for which there is no obvious rational explanation. One of the critical functions of culture is to distinguish between "friend" and "foe." The mechanisms of group selection act upon different cultures, with some doing better than others, but it is culture that makes it possible for these mechanisms to come into play.

Jerry Muller presents a series of "skeptical reflections" on Hayek's idea of spontaneous order. He argues that Hayek sometimes pushed his genuine insights further than was warranted. Muller believes that spontaneous order cannot bear the explanatory weight Hayek puts on it and that in practice it is, potentially, seriously misleading. Muller points to a number of areas where Hayek, unlike his inspiration, Adam Smith, failed to acknowledge the positive role of government and the negative externalities generated by the market. One other area where Hayek erred, argues Muller, is his equation of spontaneous order and tradition. This equation fails to see the historical truth that traditions suffer discontinuities and have beginnings that are highly nontraditional.

We have not included an epilogue or a conclusion. Governing the Great Society is a big topic and our treatment of it is not exhaustive. Readers will have to draw their own conclusions and devise their own plans for future inquiries, perhaps, bearing in mind Jerry Muller's closing thought that "those who value spontaneous order most should reflect on its limits and prerequisites."

Notes

1. Friedrich A. Hayek, *Law, Legislation and Liberty,* vol. 1, *Rules and Order* (Chicago: University of Chicago Press, 1973), vol. 2, *The Mirage of Social Justice* (Chicago: University of Chicago Press, 1976) and vol. 3, *The Political Order of a Free People* (Chicago: University of Chicago Press, 1979) (hereafter cited as *LLL*). My discussion draws heavily on *LLL,* II, ch. 11. For the purposes of the argument I will make, it is not necessary to refer to *The Fatal Conceit: The Errors of Socialism* (Chicago: University of Chicago Press, 1988). For the difficulties involved in using this last of Hayek's books, see Bruce Caldwell, *Hayek's Challenge: An Intellectual Biography of F. A. Hayek* (Chicago: University of Chicago Press, 2004), pp. 316–319.

2. Friedrich A. Hayek, *The Constitution of Liberty* (Chicago: University of Chicago Press, 1960), p. 1 (hereafter cited as *CL*).

3. *LLL,* pp. 2, 14, 148n. 11. Richard Vernon discusses with insight the general subject, including the contrast with Popper, in "The 'Great Society' and the 'Open Society': Liberalism in Hayek and Popper," *Canadian Journal of Political Science* 9, no. 2 (June 1976): 261–276. Vernon mentions, as does Hayek, the English socialist Graham Wallas's *The Great Society* (1914). Wallas makes one of Hayek's key points: a large society is not a small society writ large. A fundamental change in the relationship between individuals takes place (Vernon, "The 'Great Society,'" p. 265).

4. Smith uses a variety of similar or related terms in *An Inquiry into the Nature and Causes of the Wealth of Nations* (eds. R. H. Campbell and A. S. Skinner [Indianapolis: Liberty Classics, 1981]) (hereafter cited as *WN*) and *The Theory of Moral Sentiments* (eds. D. D. Raphael and A. L. Macfie [Indianapolis: Liberty Classics, 1982]) (hereafter cited as *TMS*): "civilized society," "commercial society," "mercantile republic," "great mercantile republic," "great society of mankind," "great society of intelligent and sensible beings" and, most famously, the "system of natural liberty." Some of these, in terms of meaning, might have suited Hayek better, but Hayek knew a catchy phrase when he saw one! For Smith's use of "great society," see *WN*, I.viii.57 (which means Book I, chapter viii, paragraph 57 of *WN*), II.Intro.6, IV.ii.3, IV.ix.52, V.i.g.12, and *TMS*, VI.ii.2.17. It is, undoubtedly, the reference at *TMS* VI.ii.2.17 where Smith speaks of "the great chess board of human society," that is largely the inspiration (as opposed to the source) for Hayek. For Smith's uses of the other terms mentioned, see, for example, *WN* I.ii.2, I.iv.1, IV.i.28, 29, IV.ix.51, V.i.f.52, V.i.f.30, and *TMS* VI.ii.2.4, VI.iii.3. Smith, of course, had his own moral theory. For its relation to his economic theory, see chapter 2.
5. For example, Hayek, *LLL*, I, 6, 14–15, 33 and see *CL*, ch. 2.
6. This argument is developed in Hayek, *LLL*, II, ch. 10.
7. See Hayek, *LLL*, I, ch. 3 and II, ch. 10 in particular.
8. See Hayek, *CL*, chs. 11–13.
9. See Hayek, *CL*, ch. 4 and Hayek, *LLL*, pp. 8–10, 22–26, 29–34, passim.
10. For example, on the historical accuracy of Hayek's account of the common law, see Ronald Hamowy, *The Political Sociology of Freedom: Adam Ferguson and F. A. Hayek* (Cheltenham: Edward Elgar, 2005), ch. 10.
11. Hayek, *LLL*, II, pp. 149–152.
12. Ibid., III, pp. 146–147.
13. This issue has figured in a number of important books on Hayek. See especially Norman Barry, *Hayek's Economic and Social Philosophy* (London: Macmillan, 1979); John Gray, *Hayek on Liberty*, 3rd ed. (London: Routledge, 1998); Ronald Kley, *Hayek's Political and Social Thought* (Oxford: Oxford University Press, 1995); and Chandran Kukathas, *Hayek and Modern Liberalism* (Oxford: Clarendon, 1988). See also the essays in *Contending with Hayek: On Liberalism, Spontaneous Order and Post-Communist Transition*, ed. Christopher Frei and John Nef (New York: Peter Lang, 1994).
14. For the potential for theory to lead in a number of directions, consider here the discussion of neoclassical economics in chapter 3 of this volume as well as Hayek's critical comments on the "rationalistic laissez faire doctrine" (*CL*, p. 60).

PART I

Fundamental Themes

CHAPTER 2

Unintended Order Explanations in Adam Smith and the Scottish Enlightenment

James R. Otteson

Theories of so-called spontaneous order, or what I prefer to call unintended order, serve principally two ends: explanation and strategy. They were developed during the Scottish Enlightenment as explanations for the large-scale human social systems that were, for perhaps the first time, coming under sustained empirical investigation: language, morality, economics, and law. It began to be seen that these social institutions shared similar characteristics, both in the present day of the eighteenth century and in known human history. One central, common characteristic was their *unintended* nature. The individual actors whose decisions and behaviors gave rise to these institutions did not *intend* to create them. They had intentions, of course, but they were local and micro, not global and macro. They were navigating their way through daily interactions with others, looking for ways, in the phrasing of Adam Smith, merely to better their own conditions. This means that many of their decisions were ad hoc and pragmatic, subject to trial-and-error success and failure. Some of their decisions were based on precedent, both their own and that of others, of what decisions and behaviors had in their past experience succeeded or failed. What the Scots discovered was that historical and anthropological investigation revealed that the individual trial-and-error methods produced larger systems of order that were often, though of course not always, beneficial to everyone concerned.

This discovery led to the second end that unintended-order explanations served: strategies about how behavior should be structured to enable future success. Once the model underlying these explanations could be formally understood, it could be used to analyze virtually the entire range of mankind's activities and, it could be hoped, to enable recommendations about how to make human life better. In particular, if it turned out that systems of order bore the highest correlation to welfare of the relevant participants when the state was limited to a few specific tasks—which is what several of the Scots from this period concluded—then one could infer quite specific legal, economic, and other political recommendations. If, moreover, it turned out that a community's system of commonly shared moral judgments, rules, and attitudes was the result of a "marketplace mechanism" that also tended to establish a high correlation between following its rules and the welfare of the relevant community's members—which again is what several of the Scots concluded—then one could infer the hypothetical imperative that if one wants to be happy, one should give presumptive authority to one's community's long-standing rules of morality and etiquette.

This second aspect of unintended-order explanations—strategy—has another facet as well, and it reflects another of the concerns important to the eighteenth-century Scots: conflict resolution. The seventeenth century was a turbulent time, and the eighteenth century was no walk in the park, especially for the Scots. Thus many of them were keen to discover not only what the causes of social conflict were but also what strategies could be adopted to minimize them, in the hope and belief that everyone would thereby be better off. The economic, political, and legal recommendations that coalesced into what is now called "classical liberalism" arose out of these investigations and with these aims.

My argument here has three parts. First I give a general sketch of the model I claim was being developed during the Scottish Enlightenment for large-scale human social institutions. Then I give a bit more detail about Adam Smith's account in particular, since I view his account as the most sophisticated from the period. Third, and finally, I raise a potential problem with these accounts and hazard a preliminary response to the objection.

The Scots' General Model

Much has been written about unintended-order theories during the Scottish Enlightenment, but with few exceptions these treatments have tended either to give only cursory discussions of the theories themselves or to have merely assumed the existence of such theories. It thus remains largely unexplained why the leading figures of this tradition were developing just such theories and at the same time becoming what we now recognize as classical liberals. I believe that the connection between these two is not accidental, and that they are indeed quite closely linked. The archetypal representative of this line of investigation I believe is, as I mentioned, Adam Smith, but other contributors include Gershom Carmichael, Francis Hutcheson, David Hume, Adam Ferguson, John Millar, and Dugald Stewart, as well as a handful of others. The connection I see between these "unintended-order" explanations and the political worldview they seemed (to the Scots) to imply is captured in the developing appreciation of the nature of *markets*. Thus I call the Scots' explanatory model a *market model*, which already suggests the link between explanation and strategy. The Scots came to understand the systems of unintended order they were studying as the results of marketlike mechanisms that were characterized by several salient features, and this understanding of how human social institutions developed led to the political, economic, and jurisprudential recommendations they came to make.

Now, the Scots were not all of one mind about exactly what were the proper recommendations to make, and, despite the impression my treatment might give, neither were they in complete agreement about how the market model functioned nor were they all even explicitly developing such a model. Differences do exist, then, but when compared, similarities in approaches, methods, and conclusions clearly emerge. What are these similarities?

Local knowledge and local interests. Human beings have a limited and quite narrow scope of knowledge, which influences and determines their interests. They are most familiar with their own circumstances, including their own abilities, desires, and opportunities; they are somewhat less familiar with the circumstances of their closest family members and friends, still less of more distant family and friends, and so on, until we get to the vast majority of people in the world, about whose circumstances they know not at all. If it is true that the person best positioned to make decisions about what someone should do in order to make himself happy is whoever has the most knowledge of the person in question, then, given the fact that each of us is in precisely this same position of possessing only limited, "local" knowledge, it follows that the persons who should make these decisions are the persons in question themselves. I call this the Local Knowledge Argument. One of its implications is that people must have a high level of personal, individual freedom; this will play a significant role in the political positions the Scots come to adopt, not least because it implies that no third party, and certainly no distant legislator, is in a position to make decisions for others about how they should use their talents or resources, or which opportunities they should avail themselves of or not.

Negotiation, cooperation, and unintentional orders. Because resources are scarce, and because people's desires generally outstrip their abilities to procure what they want on their own, negotiation and cooperation are integral parts of human social life. In the areas of morality and etiquette, people try to convince one another that their own behavior and judgments of others' behavior are correct and should be, to use Adam Smith's language, "sympathized" with, just as people in economic arenas try to convince one another to exchange or contract with them on the terms or under the conditions they severally prefer. Now these negotiations are *localized:* the people involved in them frequently have no other purpose than to get the other person or persons involved to agree, exchange, or contract; they are generally not thinking about what precedents they might be setting for future behavior or about how their agreements might affect others. Nevertheless they *are* setting precedents, in part because their behavior does affect others. The precedents affect their own behavior because they are the beginnings of habits that will shape their behavior in the future. They affect others in several ways, one of which is that others too might follow their example and begin to establish habits and customs. Some of these customs will get written into law, and some will come to be considered moral duty, perhaps even the will of God. These are the systems of unintended order.

"Middle way" objectivity. Although obedience to these systems of unintended order may be considered to be required by the will of God, the formation of the rules themselves requires, and indeed depends upon, no such transcendent sanction. Instead, these rules are developed by fallible human beings just trying to make their lives better: this is a pragmatic and thoroughly terrestrial affair. But the rules are nevertheless not that arbitrary. They enjoy a "middle way" objectivity that is based on the joint, often tacit, agreement and beliefs of the people in question; although they are based on the relevant historical tradition of individual decisions, no single person can create or change them on his own. And they are enforced, often ruthlessly, even by people who would, in individual cases, be better off if different rules were in place, and all this without any official or explicit agreement to do so. So the rules are objective in that they exist and are followed, and that transgressions are punished; but they are not—at least not directly—dependent upon the will of God, or on Platonic forms, or any other otherworldly justification.

Self-interest, limited benevolence, and the "familiarity principle." The perennial bugaboo about self-interest must be admitted straightaway: the Scots did indeed believe that human beings are principally driven by self-interest; Hume called it mankind's natural "*selfishness* and *limited generosity*."[1] That said, however, the Scots' notion of "self-interest" was considerably broader than what is often intended by that phrase today. They believed, for example, that included in a person's self-interest were the interests of those he cared about—his family, his friends, and so on. Note, for example, the first sentence of Smith's *Theory of Moral Sentiments* (*TMS*): "How selfish soever man may be supposed, there are evidently some principles in his nature, which interest him in the fortune of others, and render their happiness necessary to him, though he derives nothing from it except the pleasure of seeing it"[2] (*TMS*, 9). Those are *self*-interests because they are the person's alone, and because they frequently ignore or are indifferent to the interests of people outside the person's circle of concern. But that, the Scots believed, is simply a fact of human nature: we care more about ourselves than we do about anyone else, followed closely (and indeed sometimes surpassed) by our immediate family and best friends, followed in turn by other family and friends, then by acquaintances, and then last by strangers. Wishing this were not so will not change the fact, and the Scots believed that accurate social theory, not to mention sane political policy, had to account for this fact. This descending level of benevolence toward others also, not coincidentally, correlates closely with our *familiarity* with them: the more familiar we are with someone, the more likely we are to be concerned about his welfare, and vice versa. I call this the Familiarity Principle.[3] This principle will also figure heavily in the way human social institutions are created and develop over time, as well as the political and economic recommendations the Scots went on to adopt.

General welfare. The Scots were not under any illusion that people in their normal daily course of activities actually care about the "general welfare." Luckily, however, they do not have to. The nature of the unintended systems of order, in particular the way they are created and the way they develop over time, means that they will, in the long run, tend to conduce to the benefit of everyone concerned. "In the long run" must be emphasized. There are numerous—indeed, indefinitely many—ways in which these systems of order can be derailed or corrupted, and hence not every system is actually beneficial. The Scots tended to think that the truly "natural" systems of order would in fact be beneficial, and, conversely, that if a system was not beneficial it was because it had suffered corruption and was hence no longer "natural." And although the Scots tended to think that human nature was fixed and could not itself undergo great changes over time, nevertheless they seemed to have confidence in the ability of moral philosophers to discern the principles of this nature and on that basis to recommend policies and institutions that would increase the chance of such creatures leading relatively happy and peaceful lives. So there could indeed be a *science* of jurisprudence whose ultimate goal is to enable people to be happy.

Those are the central general features of the Scots' market model explaining the creation and development of human social orders. Interestingly, it turns out that this model has been rediscovered in the twentieth century. Robert K. Merton discovered parts of it early in the century while conducting his own studies of human social institutions;[4] and of course Friedrich Hayek in the middle of the century made detailed use of it.[5] This is, by now, quite familiar. What is perhaps less well known is the extent to which researchers more recently in fields such as evolutionary biology and evolutionary psychology; experimental, empirical, and historical economics; linguistics; game theory; and conflict resolution, international relations, and global political strategies have also, often independently, discovered versions of this model and been able to put them to quite fruitful use.[6] Perhaps the Scots were on to something.

A Summary of Smith's Model

Let me now turn to Adam Smith's model in particular. I begin where Smith did, with his *Theory of Moral Sentiments*. There Smith argues that common moral standards result from a marketlike process that takes place in and over specific historical locations. Since human beings live in different times and places, the systems of commonly shared moral standards vary in their details; but since human beings also share, in some specific, relevant respects, a common human nature, their moral systems enjoy significant overlap and on some issues will enjoy near unanimity. The element of human nature most crucial for Smith's account is the desire for mutual sympathy of sentiments. This desire—as Smith says, perhaps the strongest social desire we have (*TMS*, I.i.2.1)—is the sine qua non of his theory. It is what drives us into society, what leads us to moderate our behavior, and what ultimately gives rise to the habits and rules of moral judgment that constitute what I am calling the "system" of commonly shared morality. Although he acknowledges that humans have other desires, Smith rests an enormous part of the burden of his explanation of moral systems on the workings out of this single principle.

Here is how Smith's market mechanism is supposed to work. We are born, Smith thinks, with no morality whatsoever. A baby knows only its own wants. The baby has no notion of a proper (or improper) thing to ask for, of a proper (or improper) way to ask for it or, for that matter, of shame or remorse for having asked for something it should not have; hence the baby attempts to have its wants satisfied simply by alarming its caregiver with howls and cries. Yet in these self-indulgences, the baby is not to blame: it is not yet capable of considering such matters as *propriety* or *others' interests;* and besides, Smith says, it is probably also encouraged in its selfishness by its overly indulgent parent or nurse (*TMS*, I.ii.4.3 and III.3.22).

According to Smith it is not until the baby has become a child and begins playing with its mates that the child has the shocking and jolting experience of realizing that it is not the center of everyone's life, only of its own. Smith writes that this is the child's introduction into the "great school of self-command" (*TMS*, III.3.22): it is on being with others and experiencing them *judging* oneself—even if only implicitly, by, say, not playing with one or simply ignoring one's demands to have one's desires satisfied—that one has the distinct displeasure associated with not sharing a mutual sympathy of sentiments. After the initial jolt, one begins to cast about to find a way to relieve the displeasure, and one eventually hits upon modifying one's sentiments and behavior to more closely match that of one's playmates. And voilà, an exquisite new pleasure is experienced, that of the mutual sympathy of sentiments, and a new and permanent desire for that pleasure has been aroused. From that point on, according to Smith, the child regularly engages in trial-and-error investigations into what behaviors will achieve this sympathy and thus satisfy this desire.

This investigation leads the individual to adopt habits and then rules of behavior and judgment that increase the chance of achieving "mutual sympathy." By the time the child is an adult, he has adopted a wide range of principles of behavior and judgment that he can apply in many different situations. Moreover, at the community level, everyone else is engaging in precisely the same investigation, so that all our disparate sentiments "gravitate" (*WN*, I. vii.15 and I.vii.20) toward a mutually acceptable mean. This is the invisible hand mechanism that Smith thinks generates commonly shared standards of behavior and judgment, indeed a commonly shared *system* of morality.

Moral and Economic Markets

This mechanism is similar to markets in other parts of human social life.[7] Consider economic markets. In Smith's view, an economic market exists wherever people exchange goods or services in an effort to improve their condition (*WN*, i.iii). A newcomer to a market might initially have no idea what his goods or services will command, so he tries more or less arbitrarily chosen exchange methods, rates, and partners, until he hits upon some combination that succeeds. And then he too feels a pleasure—of his *condition being bettered,* which Smith claims in *WN* is our constant, cradle-to-grave motivation.[8]

Here we see several similarities between the Smithian *moral* marketplace and the Smithian *economic* marketplace. First, in both cases, the persons principally concerned initially have little to go on: they must simply try something out. Second, in both cases the persons principally concerned might have been abashed and felt displeasure at having been initially spurned, which is the likely outcome of one's first sallies in either market. Third, just as a person in an economic market might afterwards regret the exchange he made, so too a person might achieve a mutual sympathy with someone, only later to regret, and perhaps be ashamed at, having done so with this person, or to this degree, or over this object. Finally, the process of trial-and-error discovery is supplemented crucially in both cases by an element of *negotiation:* the person principally concerned tries to convince potential mutual sympathizers or exchange partners that the behaviors or judgments, or the goods or services, *should* be sympathized with or exchanged. He offers reasons or arguments; he exhorts, demands, pleas, cajoles, begs, harangues. You and I try to talk each other into sympathizing with one another's sentiments,[9] just as you and I might try to talk each other into selling one of our proffered goods at the other's proffered price. These negotiations take many different forms, they range over an indefinitely wide variety of issues, and they frequently end in failure. Yet even in failure they are instructive; and when they are successful, they establish precedents that both we and others will later on imitate. The precedents become habits, then rules and principles; they then come to constitute a system of rules or principles.

This, roughly, is Smith's account of the genesis both of shared moral standards, which include commonly held conceptions of *propriety* and *merit,* and of shared economic standards, which include commonly accepted prices, conditions of exchange, contracts, and so on. Both systems are turbulent at the micro level and subject to change over time, but both also settle on, or work toward, a modified equilibrium at the macro level:[10] the individual decisions that make up the systems are, on the individual level, often unpredictable and highly variegated, yet they (unintentionally) give rise to a larger system that is relatively coherent and susceptible of general description.

Middle Way Objectivity

The moral standards and the economic standards that arise in the way Smith describes are thus what the philosopher John Searle calls "institutional facts": "they are portions of the real world, objective facts in the world, that are facts only by human agreement."[11] Unlike, say, rocks and trees, these standards have no physical existence; they are, again using Searle's terminology, *ontologically subjective,* meaning that their existence depends on the beliefs and attitudes of particular agents. On the other hand, they are *epistemically objective,* meaning that it is not simply a matter of any single person's opinion whether they exist or not or what their basic features are: their existence and nature are rather a matter of objectively ascertainable facts. For example, it either is or is not the case that polygamy is morally objectionable in one's community. It is not objectionable in Saudi Arabia, though it is objectionable in Selma, Alabama.[12] My own opinion about polygamy is irrelevant to that fact in exactly the same way that my opinion about what a baseball autographed by Babe Ruth is *really* worth is irrelevant to the fact that one currently fetches about $5,000.

This is what I call the "middle way" objectivity that Smithian standards enjoy. In the moral realm, they are not directly dependent on any transcendent, otherworldly sanction, such as God or natural law, and yet they are not merely arbitrary or dependent on any person's individual opinion. Similarly, in the economic realm, prices are not "intrinsic," as Richard Cantillon claimed in his posthumously published *Essay on the Nature of Commerce in General* (1755) (which Smith read), or "just" or "unjust," as St. Thomas Aquinas claimed in his thirteenth-century *Summa Theologica*. Nevertheless, prices are dependent on real factors—such as supply and demand—and no single person can change them just by wanting to. These standards are objective in that they are facts of our social reality. Their objectivity arises because they are the result of this invisible hand process of local (micro) intentions creating general (macro) order. They are also objective, I should add, because they rely on and develop in consequence of a common human nature. A community's moral standards will, Smith says, vary along less important themes—for example, protocols of clothing, forms of greeting and address, and so on.[13] So the complete description of any given community's shared system of morality will, owing to the community's unique historical station, be itself unique. Nonetheless, certain rules will almost, perhaps in fact, invariably obtain because of our shared humanity: for example, rules against murder of innocents, against incest, against theft and trespass, and so on.

So if asked the question why one should follow the moral rules of one's community, Smith would offer several reasons. First, because doing so gives one the best chance of achieving something one greatly desires: mutual sympathy of sentiments. We can know this because of the way we know these systems of order to have arisen, namely, as the result of countless individual attempts to achieve mutual sympathy of sentiments. Whatever rules have survived this long-term trial-and-error selection will have done so because they *worked*. Second, one should follow one's community's rules because that is what others expect of one, and insofar as one cares about their chances of achieving mutual sympathy not only with oneself but also with others who are observing one's conduct—as Smith believes everyone does (remember the opening sentence of *TMS*)—one should increase those chances by doing what is expected of one. Third, one should follow one's community's rules because, ultimately, it is the only way to be happy. This final reason is a hypothetical imperative: if you want to be happy, you should for the most part follow the moral standards of your community.

Now, the "for the most part" is an important qualification: since the moral standards arise on the basis of a marketlike process, innovation—or *moral entrepreneurship*—is an integral element, and hence novel, abnormal, and unexpected behaviors will be part and parcel of its living quality. Sometimes innovation will succeed and sometimes not, sometimes trying something new will be approved and sometimes not, and some new things will be appropriately attempted and some not. Successful moral innovators are those who know or can anticipate such things and thus achieve mutual sympathy of sentiments, just as successful economic entrepreneurs are those who successfully answer analogous questions in economic marketplaces and thus better their conditions. But insofar as happiness depends in substantial part on the formation of deep and strong psychological bonds with others, as Smith contends it does (*TMS,* I.ii.4.1–2 and III.2.1–2), we will have to pursue these social expectations to be happy.

Summary of Smith's Model

We thus have in Smith a sophisticated market-model explanation both of human morality and of economics. Here are the main elements:

Institutional structures. The institutional structures involved in the moral marketplace are those entities that arise or are created to teach, encourage, enforce, or criticize patterns and protocols of moral behavior. Churches, schools, clubs, families, and newspaper editorials all count; preachers; teachers and professors; friends, parents, siblings, and children; and public intellectuals all maintain and develop the structures by simultaneously conveying the relevant information across the institutional structures, using the structures themselves, and enforcing or weakening the structures. In the economic marketplace we have analogous entities: protocols of exchange and contract and of punishment for breaches; agencies for discovering creditworthiness, solvency, and economic soundness, such as Standard and Poor's and Moody's, *Consumer Reports,* and, more generally, reputation;[14] and so on.

Micromotives and macroresults. In the moral realm, all any of us wants is mutual sympathy of sentiments here, now, with this person (these are our "micromotives"); but our attempts to secure it give rise to larger patterns and rules of behavior ("macroresults"). Similarly in economics: all we want is to exchange this for that, here, now, with this person; but again this gives rise to larger patterns of behavior.

Coordination. People have various desires and goals, yet the patterns allow for amazingly complex arrays of order and suborder. Think of protocols of dress for academic talks, for example, versus those for going to the basketball game this weekend. In economics, think of Jewish diamond traders in

New York versus street vendors at the August Edinburgh festival. Go into your local supermarket and consider the diverse array of goods and the untold numbers of people who cooperated to bring it together. This aspect of market interactions was made famous by Leonard Reed's short, 1958 essay "I, Pencil," but it was already brilliantly captured by Smith in the *Wealth of Nations* with his example of the "woollen coat."[15]

Competition. We compete for sympathy with others' sentiments, which leads us to moderate our own sentiments so that they can accord with those of others; this in turn leads us to develop mutually agreeable patterns of behavior. One cannot sympathize with two people whose views are dissimilar, just as one cannot exchange with everyone; hence one must choose, and do so on multiple fronts. Since everyone chooses and since everyone wants the best deal for himself, the result is a mutual ferreting out of good patterns, rigorously subjected to correction from further testing.

The overall good. We can use others' behaviors as precedents and exemplars for ourselves, but they will then become habits and rules only if they work more efficiently than the competing patterns we are aware of. Thus the patterns that ultimately arise, get repeated, and become widespread habits are those that benefit people generally. They are not necessarily the best possible patterns, because there might be as-yet undiscovered patterns that would conduce more greatly than what has been discovered; but if a given pattern has long endured, chances are good that it is because that pattern is conducive to people's attempts to better their conditions. This is the "invisible hand" mechanism Smith describes, and it is a function of the marketlike nature of human social interaction.[16]

Smith, Hayek, and Political Policy

Let me return for a moment to Hayek's development and use of a "spontaneous order" model and its similarities to Smith's market model. Hayek argued that no third party can possess the relevant information to make good decisions about how you or I should husband or expend our resources, or about which opportunities are available to us and, of those, of which we should avail ourselves—in essence, a third party cannot know what you or I ought to do.[17] Why not? What is the allegedly missing information? Hayek claims that others do not—and *cannot*—know which goals and aspirations we have and what their relative rankings to us are; they cannot know exactly what our resources are and what their relative and absolute scarcities are; they cannot know what opportunities are available to us in our particular local circumstances; and they cannot know what our schedule of values is, including what their relative rankings are.

Hayek has become famous for taking this position and is now perhaps its standard-bearer, but each step of his position builds on arguments Smith made some 200 years earlier. Smith makes his case by means of three interlocking arguments. The first is his Local Knowledge Argument: given that everyone has unique knowledge of his own "local" situation, including his goals, desires, and the opportunities available to him, each individual is therefore the person best positioned to make decisions for himself about what courses of action he should take to achieve his goals. Here is the argument in Smith's words: "What is the species of domestick industry which his capital can employ, and of which the produce is likely to be of the greatest value, every individual, it is evident, can, in his local situation, judge much better than any statesman or lawgiver can do for him" (*WN*, IV.ii.10).[18]

The second is the Economizer Argument, which holds that as each of us seeks to better our own condition (however each of us understands that), each of us will, therefore, be led to seek out the most efficient uses of our resources and labor, given our peculiar and unique circumstances, so as to maximize their productive output and return on our investment. Here is this second argument in Smith's words:

> The uniform, constant, and uninterrupted effort of every man to better his condition, the principle from which publick and national, as well as private opulence is originally derived, is frequently powerful enough to maintain the natural progress of things toward improvement, in spite both of the extravagance of government, and of the greatest errors of administration.
> (*WN*, II, p. iii.31)[19]

Third, and finally, is Smith's famous Invisible Hand Argument, which holds that as each of us strives to better our own condition as provided for in the Economizer Argument, each of us thereby simultaneously, though unintentionally, betters the condition of everyone else. This argument is more sophisticated than it seems, and so some delicacy is required to describe it accurately.[20] To begin, Smith's claim is not that people do not act intentionally; rather, it is that they typically act with only their own, local purposes in mind, unconcerned with, and usually unaware of, whatever larger effects their behavior has on unknown others. Now their "local" purposes are not necessarily related exclusively to themselves. They often, indeed for Smith regularly, include concerns about those family and friends about whom each of them cares. Our concern for others fades, Smith thinks, the farther away from, and thus more unknown to, us they are, but our concern for others closer to ourselves Smith thinks is real and undeniable. So we act in attempts to satisfy our own purposes, whatever they are. Because we are "economizers," however, we tend to try to expend the least amount of our energy as possible while at the same time trying to get the largest, richest, or most extensive achievement of our goals as possible. We seek, as it were, the best possible return on our investment of our energies.[21]

This search for efficient use of our energies benefits not only ourselves and those close to us about whom we care (the direct objects of our concern), but also, Smith argues, others, even others totally unknown to us. This happens for at least two reasons. One, when we specialize or concentrate our efforts on a small range of tasks or talents, we usually produce more of it than we can ourselves consume or use, which means we create a surplus that we can trade or sell away—which in turn means that the overall stock of goods and services increases, and their prices thus decrease, for everyone. Two, we seek out behaviors, policies, protocols, forms of contract and trade, and so on that serve our local interests, but others will learn from us and imitate our successes and avoid our failures, thereby saving themselves time and energy, thereby enabling them to go yet further than we did in securing their—and thus, indirectly, everyone else's—ends. Here is Smith's phrasing of this argument:

> As every individual, therefore, endeavours as much as he can [. . .] to direct [his] industry that its produce may be of the greatest value; every individual necessarily labours to render the annual revenue of the society as great as he can. He generally, indeed, neither intends to promote the public interest, nor knows how much he is promoting it. [. . .] [H]e intends only his own security; and by directing that industry in such a manner as its produce may be of the greatest value, he intends only his own gain, and he is in this, as in many other cases, led by an invisible hand to promote an end which was no part of his intention.
>
> (*WN*, IV.ii.9)[22]

It is this that, according to Smith, effects the "universal opulence which extends itself to the lowest ranks of the people" (*WN*, I.i.10); the wealth, that is, does not stay only in the hands of the person generating it or in the hands of the previously or otherwise wealthy. Two centuries later, U. S. President John F. Kennedy would paraphrase Smith's argument by stating that "a rising tide lifts all boats."

Note that the Invisible Hand Argument does not maintain that the unintended social orders that are produced by this invisible hand mechanism *guarantee* beneficial results. People can make unwise, imprudent, irrational, or downright immoral choices, and those choices can lead to habits, protocols, and standards that are not in fact conducive to everyone's best interests. We are fallible creatures, after all—as Smith realizes all too well. But *given* that we are fallible, the argument focuses not on what is ideally best but rather on what is better among what is actually possible. And Smith's argument is that the best way to find that out is by allowing the invisible hand mechanism to work itself out, and by granting the results of this trial-and-error process of winnowing and culling presumptive, if not absolute, authority. This invisible hand mechanism is what Smith describes as "the obvious and simple system of natural liberty." Here is how he concludes the argument:

> All systems either of preference or of restraint, therefore, being thus completely taken away, the obvious and simple system of natural liberty establishes itself of its *own* accord. Every man, as long as he does not violate the laws of justice, is left perfectly free to pursue his own interest his own way, and to bring both his industry and capital into competition with those of any other man, or order of men. The sovereign is completely discharged from a duty, in the attempting to perform which he must always be exposed to innumerable delusions, and for the proper performance of which no human wisdom or knowledge could ever be sufficient; the duty of superintending the industry of private people, and of directing it towards the employments most suitable to the interest of the society.
>
> (*WN*, IV.ix.51).[23]

A Possible Problem

Let me now briefly consider a potential shortcoming of the Smithian "market model." Walter J. Schultz has argued that Smith's "Invisible Hand Claim" fails.[24] Schultz's argument is that if we assume a population of selfish individuals who meet each other only with (1) desires they wish to satisfy and (2) rationality to discover means to their ends, what will ensue is not a spontaneously ordered system of conventions by means of which individual, uncoordinated actions will lead to socially beneficial results.[25] To achieve that desired result it is necessary instead to supplement the initial scenario with several *moral* constraints. Specifically, Schultz argues that the agents in question must both recognize and abide by certain specific "moral" judgments such as fair play and charity. Schultz argues that markets themselves, however, cannot generate these necessary moral constraints, so he concludes that markets alone are insufficient to produce desirable overall social orders. Another way of understanding the problem is by seeing human society as an extremely complex series of Prisoner's Dilemma problems. Without an externally provided motivation, the argument goes, the parties to such exchanges inevitably take the mutually less beneficial options.[26] Schultz's argument thus calls into question not only Smith's argument, but indeed a foundational part of the Scottish Enlightenment project.

Schultz's conclusion captures the sentiments of a number of commentators who criticize economics for allegedly assuming that people are amoral and inhuman utility maximizers.[27] The criticism is that economics cannot fully capture human social life because it systematically excludes from its models people who act out of motives other than selfish ones or who act in ways that they can be reasonably presumed to know conflict with their own (narrowly conceived) interests.

Robert Axelrod has argued, however, that the Prisoner's-Dilemma problems can in fact be overcome by repeated iterations of the exchanges in which the participants gain reputations or in which at least some participants can generate reliable intelligence on the basis of which to make reasonable judgments about people's likely courses of actions. Axelrod argues that this model fits human society well inasmuch as we face in fact a great number of such exchanges over the course of our lifetimes, and thus it is possible that we can develop rules of behavior that will facilitate the exchanges in mutually or overall beneficial ways. After surveying several different types of rules of behavior that one might expect to arise, it turns out, Axelrod argues, that the simple tit-for-tat rule is both the most natural and the most promising, as long as we have some who are willing to take an initial step (of any kind). The tit-for-tat rule creates a system of punishments and rewards in the forms of noncooperation and cooperation that gives even distant people, third-party observers, and even unknown others motivations to follow the rules that are discovered to be to mutual advantage. Axelrod's argument would seem to be a confirmation of the Smithian and Scottish optimism about the invisible hand's generation of systems of unintended order.[28]

But Axelrod's argument has been criticized for arbitrarily limiting the kinds of social exchanges that are likely to take place. If we allow a more diverse description of human motivation, desires, and interests, Ken Binmore, for example, argues that Axelrod's tit-for-tat rule breaks down; it can end up punishing what we want to encourage and vice versa, or it can can lead to Pareto-suboptimal coordination signatures.[29] Binmore's argument is that the iterated scenarios modeled by Axelrod and others were actually irrelevant to true human interaction—either that or, if one wanted to defend Axelrod's results, one would have to undertake to defend the limitations Axelrod placed on agents' motivations as well as the assumptions Axelrod made about the likely content of agents' desires and ends. And that will inevitably, Binmore argues, introduce not the selfish economizer model of agency that obtains in classical and neoclassical economics but rather an agent who is both self-interested and altruistic. In particular, without assuming some widespread natural altruistic motivation among agents, there will be no way to (1) prevent everyone, or at least enough to destroy the functionality of the system, from trying to free ride on each other; (2) ensure that people will follow generally beneficial rules when following them would sacrifice or be prejudicial to their individual interests in particular cases; or (3) provide sufficient certainty among agents that others will not similarly defect from the rules.[30]

Return now to Schultz. Schultz claims that market mechanisms require in fact several additional supplements to function in the way most free-market economists believe they can. Among these supplements are the assumptions that the agents have an inherent sense of right and wrong, a sense that corresponds closely to the rules that would be conducive to widespread market cooperation, and that the agents must have reliable knowledge about the motivations and characters of others with whom they would cooperate. It is precisely to fill these two lacunae that Schultz and others—such as Samuel Fleischacker and Cass Sunstein[31]—argue that the state and particular state agencies are required. Their conclusion is that the state must provide significant incentives to develop the proper moral sensibilities to increase the chances of rule following, and it must monitor both individuals and corporate entities, measure their relative rule-following performance, and report it publicly. It is furthermore argued, or rather presumed in the argument, that markets cannot themselves generate the requisite moral constraints.

I think the critics are right to suggest that a fuller conception of human nature is required for markets to be able to do what their proponents claim they can, including, in particular, allocating resources in Pareto-superior, if not Pareto-optimal, ways. I also suggest, however, that a mechanism for generating the relevant features of human nature that the "homo economicus" conception of human nature leaves out—principally, a genuine altruism and a functioning desire and commitment, even if unconscious, to follow the socially beneficial rules—is in fact provided in Smith's account of the market model. The mechanism that Smith's model provides that satisfies this palpable need is the desire for mutual sympathy of sentiments. In the Smithian account, we do not only want to satisfy our own narrowly conceived ends: we are also interested in the "fortunes of others" close to us. Even more than this, because, in Smith's account, we desire mutual sympathy of sentiments, we do in fact care what others think of our conduct.

As it turns out, modern researchers have rediscovered this apparent fact about human nature, and it has startled them (and changed the direction of evolutionary psychology). Reflecting their various perspectives, it has been called an "irrational" sacrificing of one's own interests (Robert H. Frank), "conformism" to the thoughts and judgments of others (Boyd and Richerson), an "exchange organ" (Barkow, Cosmides, and Tooby) that drives us to seek out social situations of reciprocal exchange, and a "sympathy knob" that can be dialed up or down by training and environment (Pinker).[32] Thus the knowledge that others would disapprove of our free riding, breaching contracts, reneging on promises, or making exceptions for ourselves from rules of behavior by which we expect others to live acts as a surprisingly effective disincentive to engage in such practices, and an incentive to pay our own way, keep our promises, honor our contracts, and abide by general rules. The crucial point is that these are *natural* incentives, that is, present without the aid of third-party intervention. Hence even if Schultz, Binmore, and others are correct that self-interest is not enough by itself to generate stable and beneficial social orders—and I think they have a point—it is nevertheless hasty to conclude that market-based systems of order generated by invisible hand mechanisms cannot themselves generate the kind of moral norms required for stable social interaction.

More would have to be said, of course, to properly flesh out this proposed solution to a significant obstacle to widespread social coordination. But allow me to close by saying that if my proposed solution turns out to be adequate, it will mean that this fuller market model of human social orders is more powerful than it is often given credit for. It also means that by working out the explanatory model of human social interaction generally, the Scots, and Adam Smith in particular, were constructing something like a grand unification theory for the study of human sociality. That would mean they were on to something indeed.

Notes

1. David Hume, *A Treatise of Human Nature*, ed. L. A. Selby-Bigge and L. P. H. Nidditch (Oxford: Clarendon Press, 1978), p. 494; italics in the original.

2. All references to Adam Smith are to the Glasgow editions of his works, with the now-standard abbreviations: TMS is *The Theory of Moral Sentiments*, WN is *An Inquiry into the Nature and Causes of the Wealth of Nations*, LJ is *Lectures on Jurisprudence*. This quotation is from TMS I.i.1.1, which means part I, section I, chapter 1, paragraph 1 of *The Theory of Moral Sentiments*. Other references will employ similar notation.

3. See James R. Otteson, *Adam Smith's Marketplace of Life* (Cambridge: Cambridge University Press, 2002), ch. 5.

4. See, for example, Robert K. Merton's "The Unanticipated Consequences of Purposive Social Action," *American Sociological Review* 1, no. 6 (December 1936): 894–904, http://www.compilerpress.atfreeweb.com/Anno%20Merton%20Uninte nded.htm (accessed October 5, 2006).

5. Hayek uses and discusses this notion in many works. One central location is his *Constitution of Liberty* (Chicago: University of Chicago Press, 1960), especially chs. 2–4. I return later to similarities between Smith and Hayek.

6. Examples include: in evolutionary biology and psychology, Jerome H. Barkow, Leda Cosmides, and John Tooby, eds. *The Adapted Mind: Evolutionary Psychology and the Generation of Culture* (New York: Oxford, 1992), Charles Darwin, *The Origin of Species* (1859; New York: Gramercy, 1979), Matt Ridley, *The Origins of Virtue* (New York: Penguin, 1996), Elliot Sober and David Sloan Wilson, *Unto Others: The Evolution and Psychology of Unselfish Behavior* (Cambridge: Harvard University Press, 1998), Edward O. Wilson, *Consilience: The Unity of Knowledge* (New York: Vintage, 1998), and Robert Wright, *The Moral Animal: Why We Are the Way We Are* (London: Abacus, 1994); in economics, Friedrich Hayek, *Individualism and Economic Order* (Chicago: University of Chicago Press, 1948), Lorenzo Infantino, *Ignorance and Liberty* (London: Routledge, 2003), Deepak Lal, *Reviving the Invisible Hand: The Case for Classical Liberalism in the Twenty-First Century.* (Princeton: Princeton University Press, 2006) and *Unintended Consequences: The Impact of Factor Endowments, Culture, and Politics on Long-Run Economic Performance* (Cambridge: MIT, 2001), Vernon Smith, *Bargaining and Market Behavior: Essays in Experimental Economics,* 2nd ed. (Cambridge: Cambridge University Press, 2005), and Viktor Vanberg, *Rules and Choice in Economics* (London: Routledge, 1994); in linguistics, Guy Deutscher, *The Unfolding of Language: An Evolutionary Tour of Mankind's Greatest Invention.* (New York: Henry Holt, 2005) and Rudi Keller, *On Language Change: The Invisible Hand in Language* (London: Routledge, 1994); in game theory, Ken Binmore, *Natural Justice* (New York: Oxford University Press, 2005), Brian Skyrms, *The Stag Hunt and the Evolution of Social Structure* (Cambridge: Cambridge University Press, 2004), and Michael Suk-Young Chwe, *Rational Ritual,* 2nd ed. (Princeton: Princeton University Press, 2003); and in conflict resolution, political strategy, and political theory, Robert Axelrod, *The Complexity of Cooperation: Agent-Based Models of Competition and Collaboration* (Princeton: Princeton University Press, 1997) and *The Evolution of Cooperation* (New York: Basic Books, 1984), James R. Otteson, *Actual Ethics* (Cambridge: Cambridge University Press, 2006) and Peyton H. Young, *Individual Strategy and Social Structure: An Evolutionary Theory of Institutions* (Princeton: Princeton University Press, 2001).

7. For further discussion of these similarities, see Otteson, *Adam Smith's Marketplace of Life,* esp. ch. 7.

8. Smith, *WN,* II.iii.28; see also I.viii.44, II.i.30, II.iii.31, II.iii.36, II.v.37, III.iii.12, IV.ii.4, IV.ii.8, IV.v.b.43, and IV.9.28. Cp. Smith, *LJ,* A.vi.145.

9. See Smith, *TMS,* I.i.2.1, I.i.3.1–3, I.i.4, and VII.iv.6.

10. I adapt the "micro" and "macro" terminology from Thomas C. Schelling, *Micromotives and Macrobehavior* (New York: Norton, 1978).

11. John Searle, *The Construction of Social Reality* (New York: Free Press, 1997), p. 1 and passim.

12. I take this example from Max Hocutt, *Grounded Ethics: The Empirical Bases of Normative Judgments* (New Brunswick: Transaction, 2000), ch. 14.

13. Smith, *TMS,* V.2.1, V.2.7–9.

14. See Hayek's chapter "The Meaning of Competition" in *Individualism and Economic Order* on the role reputation plays in markets. See also Axelrod, *Evolution of Cooperation*, ch. 8.

15. Smith, *WN*, I.i.11.

16. Schelling, *Micromotives and Macrobehavior*, pp. 31–33, argues that the practice of sending Christmas cards is a counterexample. He claims that no one actually wants to send Christmas cards, but because various institutional pressures are already in place—no one wants to be the only one not to send them out, appearing thereby to be rude and inconsiderate—everyone sends them out nonetheless. If he is right, this would be an example of an "invisible hand" explanation producing a large-scale system of order that does not produce general benefits. But how can Schelling be so sure that people really do not like sending out or receiving Christmas cards? My guess—though it is only a guess—is that if it were true that no one liked the practice, then it would fade, like, for example, the wearing of powdered wigs.

17. See Hayek, *Constitution of Liberty*, chs. 1 and 2.

18. Smith continues: "The statesman, who should attempt to direct private people in what manner they ought to employ their capitals, would not only load himself with a most unnecessary attention, but assume an authority which could safely be trusted, not only to no single person, but to no council or senate whatever, and which would nowhere be so dangerous as in the hands of a man who had folly and presumption enough to fancy himself fit to exercise it" (*WN* IV.ii.10). Other statements of the Local Knowledge Argument can be found throughout *WN*. See, for example, *WN* I.i.8, IV.v.b.16, IV.v.b.25, and IV.ix.51.

19. Smith also writes: "But though the profusion of government must, undoubtedly, have retarded the natural progress of England towards wealth and improvement, it has not been able to stop it. The annual produce of its land and labour is, undoubtedly, much greater at present than it was either at the restoration or at the revolution. The capital, therefore, annually employed in cultivating this land, and in maintaining this labour, must likewise be much greater. In the midst of all the exactions of government, this capital has been silently and gradually accumulated by *the private frugality and good conduct of individuals, by their universal, continual, and uninterrupted effort to better their own condition*. It is this effort, protected by law and allowed by liberty to exert itself in the manner that is most advantageous, which has maintained the progress of England towards opulence and improvement in almost all former times, and which, it is to be hoped, will do so in all future times" (*WN* II.iii.36; my italics). This argument too can be found throughout the *Wealth of Nations*. See, for example, *WN* I. viii.44, I.x.c.14, II.i.30, II.iii.28, II.iii.31, II.v.37, III.iii.12, IV.ii.4, IV.ii.8, IV. v.b.43, IV.ix.28, and V.i.b.18. See also Smith, *LJ* (A), vi.145.

20. Many commentators get it wrong. Emma Rothschild, for example, describes the "invisible hand" passage in *WN* as an "ironic joke," failing to understand, apparently, the Invisible Hand Argument's centrality in so much of Smith's analysis of human social life. See Emma Rothschild, *Economic Sentiments: Adam Smith,*

Condorcet, and the Enlightenment (Cambridge: Harvard, 2001), ch. 5; for sustained demonstrations of the centrality of the notion, see Otteson, *Adam Smith's Marketplace of Life* and *Adam Smith*. (London: Continuum, forthcoming).

21. I emphasize that the Economizer Argument does not hold that everyone always and without exception so seeks to economize: that would be obviously false, since there are many cases of people deliberately taking harder ways. Think, for example, of serious athletes. The argument's claim speaks, rather, to overall tendencies. Even for people who would rather bicycle to work than drive, for example, in most other areas of their lives they will economize on their energies—perhaps in part to make sure they have the energy to bicycle!

22. Smith continues: "Nor is it always the worse for the society that it was no part of it [that is, his intention]. By pursuing his own interest he frequently promotes that of the society much more effectually than when he really intends to promote it. I have never known much good done by those who affected to trade for the publick good" (ibid.). Smith repeats variants of this argument throughout *WN* as well. See, for example, *WN* Introduction.8, II.Introduction.4, II. iii.39, IV.ii.4, IV.v.b.25, and IV.vii.c.88.

23. In his 1793 *Account of the Life and Writings of Adam Smith, LL.D.*, Dugald Stewart speaks of a manuscript of Smith's, now unfortunately lost, that Stewart reports as stating, "Little else is requisite to carry a state to the highest degree of opulence from the lowest barbarism, but peace, easy taxes, and a tolerable administration of justice; all the rest being brought about by the natural course of things. All governments which thwart this natural course, which force things into another channel, or which endeavour to arrest the progress of society at a particular point, are unnatural, and to support themselves are obliged to be oppressive and tyrannical" (*Essays on Philosophical Subjects*, ed. W. P. D. Wightman and J. C. Bryce [Indianapolis: Liberty Classics, 1982], IV.25). See also the striking "man of system" passage in Smith, *TMS*, VI.ii.2.17–18.

24. Walter J. Schultz, *The Moral Conditions of Economic Efficiency* (Cambridge: Cambridge University Press, 2001), ch. 4.

25. In his characteristically complex way, Schultz puts it thus: "Every equilibrium allocation is Pareto optimal if and only if (1) There exists a normative social practice such that (i) Property rights for each commodity, a right to true information, a right to welfare, and a right to autonomy are held by each agent, and (ii) Each agent has some sufficient internal incentive to comply with these rights, and (iii) There exists some responsibility scheme, and (2) There exists some set of price conventions, and (3) There exist conventions and normative constraints for commodifying desire and for rectifying the results of accidental and intentional externalities. These are the moral conditions of economic efficiency" (p. 105).

26. See Peter Danielson, "Competition among Cooperators: Altruism and Reciprocity," *Proceedings of the National Academy of Science* 99, no. 3 (May 14, 2002): 7237–7242.

27. On this topic, see, for example, Guido Erreygers, ed. *Economics and Interdisciplinary Exchange* (London: Routledge, 2001); Bruna Ingrao, "Economic

Life in Nineteenth-Century Novels: What Economists Might Learn from Literature," in Erreygers, *Economics and Interdisciplinary Exchange;* and Margaret Schabas, review of *Economics and Interdisciplinary Exchange,* ed. Guido Erreygers, *History of Political Economy* 35, no. 3 (September 2003): 602–603.

28. See Axelrod, *Evolution of Cooperation;* Robert Axelrod and Robert Keohane, "Achieving Cooperation under Anarchy: Strategies and Institutions," *World Politics* 37, no. 1 (October 1985): 226–254; and Axelrod, *Complexity of Cooperation.*

29. Ken Binmore, *Game Theory and the Social Contract,* vol. 1, *Playing Fair* (Cambridge, MA: MIT Press, 1994).

30. For further discussion, see Axelrod and Keohane, "Achieving Cooperation"; Axelrod, *Complexity of Cooperation;* and Danielson, "Competition among Cooperators."

31. See Samuel Fleischacker, *A Third Concept of Liberty: Judgment and Freedom in Kant and Adam Smith* (Princeton, NJ: Princeton University Press, 1999), ch. 10, and Cass Sunstein, *Free Markets and Social Justice* (New York: Oxford University Press, 1997), chs. 1 and 2.

32. Robert H. Frank, *Passions within Reason* (New York: Norton, 1988); Robert Boyd and Peter Richerson, "Culture and Cooperation," in *Beyond Self-Interest,* ed. Jane Mansbridge (Chicago: University of Chicago Press, 1990); Barkow, Cosmides, and Tooby, *The Adapted Mind;* and Steven Pinker, *The Blank Slate: The Modern Denial of Human Nature* (New York: Penguin, 2003). See also Richard Alexander, *The Biology of Moral Systems* (Hawthorne, NY: Aldine de Gruyter, 1997); Ridley, *Origins of Virtue;* Peter Singer, *The Expanding Circle: Ethics and Sociobiology* (New York: Farrar, Straus, and Giroux, 1981); Edward O. Wilson, *Consilience;* and James Q. Wilson, *The Moral Sense* (New York: Free Press, 1997).

CHAPTER 3

The Origin and Scope of Hayek's Idea of Spontaneous Order

Louis Hunt

Introduction

The idea of spontaneous order straddles the disputed divide between the natural and the social sciences. It encompasses phenomena as diverse as the evolution of species, the architecture of a termite nest, the organization of the market economy, and the development of the Internet.[1] The insight captured in the idea of spontaneous order is that complex organization can emerge from the interaction of more basic entities following relatively simple rules of action or behavior. The phrase "spontaneous order" implies that such complex organization is not the result of deliberate design or the unfolding of some predetermined plan but the unintended consequence of actions that do not directly aim at its production. The idea of spontaneous order applies to those phenomena that exhibit the appearance of deliberate design without being the product of any designing intelligence.

Darwin's theory of evolution by means of natural selection and the "invisible-hand" account of the market in classical political economy are paradigmatic examples in the natural and social sciences respectively of this conception of spontaneous order. Pre-Darwinian naturalists ascribed the complexity of natural organisms and the remarkable "fit" between organisms and their environment to the design of a creator God. Darwin's argument in *On the Origin of Species* that such "perfection of structure and coadaptation" could be accounted for by the interaction between the random variation of traits and the winnowing of such traits through natural selection deconstructed the notion of design into a series of more elementary, undesigned processes.[2] Neither the random generation of traits nor the effects of natural selection on the transmission of such traits to succeeding generations aim at any particular goal and yet they give rise to phenomena that are profoundly suggestive of intelligent design. Darwin's theory undermines our common-sense, anthropomorphic view that intelligent design requires some form of conscious centralized control.

The account of the market as a spontaneous order found in the writings of the classical economists is the exemplary model in the social sciences of this idea of decentralized design. Unlike the case of natural organisms and their environment, however, the market economy does not immediately suggest to the untutored eye the presence of intelligent design. Most of the partici-pants in the market process have no understanding of the functioning of the market as a whole nor do they need to have such understanding for the market to function. When Adam Smith and other early economists turned their attention to the market economy, however, they discovered a systematic whole that rivaled the complex order of the solar system as laid out in Newton's *Principia*. Smith's phrase the "invisible hand" encapsulates the astonishing manner in which the market coordinates the activities of count-less individuals without the need for any central control. The idea of the "invisible hand" is, of course, not meant to be an explanation of the coor-dinating role of the market, but rather a succinct metaphor for the process itself. The market behaves, in Smith's words, "as if" the conjunction of supply and demand had been brought about by the invisible hand of some benevolent deity with the power to survey the operations of the market as a whole. In fact, as Smith argues, such market coordination is the result not of the benevolent designs of an omniscient deity but of the interaction of self-interested individuals pursuing their own gain without any necessary concern for the good of the whole. As in the case of Darwin's theory of evolution, the market, in Smith's account, proves to be more intelligent than its component parts.

In this chapter, I propose to examine the idea of spontaneous order through a consideration of the thought of its most prominent exponent in the twentieth century, Friedrich A. Hayek. Although Hayek did not invent the term "spontaneous order," he provides the clearest and most coherent attempt to develop a social and political theory on the basis of this idea.[3] Hayek himself traces the idea of spontaneous order at least as far back as the writings of Bernard Mandeville at the beginning of the eighteenth cen-tury, but I will concentrate in this chapter on the origin and scope of the idea in Hayek's own thought. The first part of the chapter looks at Hayek's contribution to the Socialist Calculation debate in the 1930s as the point of departure for his later reflections on the market as a spontaneous order. The second part examines more closely what Hayek means by calling the market a spontaneous order. The concluding part of the chapter considers some objections to Hayek's idea of spontaneous order.

The Socialist Calculation Debate and the Origin of Hayek's Idea of Spontaneous Order

The earliest intimations of Hayek's mature view of the market as a spontaneous order can be found in his contributions to the Socialist Calculation debate. This debate centered on the question of whether economic calculation, and thus rational economic planning, was possible in a socialist society. The original impetus for this debate was an article by the Austrian economist Ludwig von Mises on "Economic Calculation in a Socialist Community" (*Die Wirtschaftsrechnung in sozialistischen Gemeinwesen*) first published in 1920 in the *Archiv für Sozialwissenschaft und Sozialpolitik*.[4] This article was then incorporated in Mises's major work, *Socialism: An Economic and Sociological Analysis* (*Die Gemeinwirtschaft*), which first appeared in 1922.[5] Mises's critique of the possibility of economic calculation under socialism was directed primarily at the attempt, under "war communism" in the Soviet Union, to abolish monetary exchange and the price system, thus instituting a "natural economy," that is, an economy in which all transactions would be "transactions in kind."[6] Mises argued that in the absence of monetary prices for factors of production, economic managers would not be able to allocate resources rationally.

As the debate developed in the 1920s and 1930s, the majority of socialist economists abandoned the idea of a moneyless economy as unworkable and argued instead for some combination of collective ownership of the means of production with a monetary market for consumer goods. The market socialist model of socialism was bolstered by the arguments of many neoclassical economists that the problem of economic calculation in a socialist economy was in principle no different from that of calculation in a capitalist economy. Culminating in the work of the Polish economist Oskar Lange, the market socialists argued that a central planning board could coordinate supply and demand as (or even more) effectively than the unfettered market.[7] It is this later version of the argument for central planning that Hayek takes issue with in his critique of socialism. Hayek argues that the defense of market socialism on the basis of neoclassical principles misunderstands the fundamental problem to which markets are the solution, and is thus led to the mistaken conclusion that a central planning board could replace the market.[8]

The purpose of this chapter is not to review the twists and turns of the Socialist Calculation debate, but to show how Hayek's conception of the market as a spontaneous order emerged out of what he took to be the defects of a planned economy, both in its earlier Marxist form and its later neoclassical version.[9] To explain what is distinctive about Hayek's approach to this problem, however, I must discuss briefly how it differed from that of Mises. This difference is sometimes described as that between a theoretical critique of the *logical* possibility of collectivist economic planning (Mises) and a critique of its *practical feasibility* (Hayek). The implication of this way of formulating the difference between their positions is that Hayek was forced to retreat from Mises's more radical claim that central planning is conceptually incoherent to the more limited claim that, given human beings' finite cognitive capacities, central planning is practically infeasible. This latter position is then open to the charge that it rests on a merely technical deficiency, a deficiency that may be remedied by advances in technology. For example, if the difficulty facing a planning board is merely one of processing a large amount of data and calculating a large number of complex equations, then this objection is rendered moot by the development of computers.[10] While it is true that at times both Hayek and Mises (writing before the development of computers) rely on such "technical" objections to the possibility of economic calculation under socialism, these objections clearly do not go the heart of the problem.

Just as much as Mises, Hayek wants to argue that there is a conceptual or logical problem in the very idea of a planned economy, but the target of his critique is different from Mises's. Mises had directed his fire against a conception of the planned economy that derived directly from Marx's view that the "anarchy of production" under capitalism must be replaced by the same kind of conscious control over production one (allegedly) finds in the modern firm. In agreement with some modern theories of the firm, Marx viewed capitalist firms as "islands of conscious power" in a sea of anarchic competition.[11] This original Marxist vision of centralized planning anticipates the economy as a whole being run in a manner similar to a capitalist firm. Marx makes this argument in the context of his distinction between the division of labor in society and the division of labor in manufacture (or the "workshop").

> Division of labour within the workshop implies the undisputed authority of the capitalist over men, who are merely the members of a total mechanism which belongs to him. The division of labour within society brings into contact independent producers of commodities, who acknowledge no authority other than that of competition, of the coercion exerted by the pressure of their reciprocal interests, just as in the animal kingdom the "war of all against all" more or less preserves the conditions of existence of every species. The same bourgeois consciousness which celebrates the division of labour in the workshop . . . as an organization of labour that increases its productive power, denounces with equal vigour every conscious attempt to control and regulate the process of production socially . . . It is very characteristic that the enthusiastic apologists of the factory

system have nothing more damning to urge against a general organization of labour in society than that it would turn the whole of society into a factory.[12]

In effect, Marx argues that a socialist economy can achieve the same (or greater) productivity than a capitalist economy—without the wastefulness and periodic booms and bust of the market—by emulating the command model of the capitalist firm. The burden of Mises's critique of socialism is to show that it is impossible to emulate capitalism's economic productivity without retaining the "anarchic" character of rivalry between competing economic agents. In Mises's view, the centralized economic planning *within* a firm is essentially guided by the expectations of profit and loss due to rivalry with other firms in a competitive market. While recognizing that misallocations of resources do occur in a dynamic capitalist economy, Mises argues that such misallocations are constantly being corrected by the competitive process itself. However, if society as a whole is one giant firm, there is no way its "managers" can correct their mistakes, or even rationally plan to avoid making them in the first place. As Don Lavoie notes,

> Mises's argument, if valid, implies that the tendencies toward concentration and centralization that Marx believed would proceed until it was possible to subsume all of production under a central plan have in fact a logical limit. Centralization of any given firm cannot continue beyond the point where the knowledge generated by the rivalrous bidding of its competitors is sufficient to rationally guide its economic calculation. Were the firm to centralize any further it would increasingly find itself "in the dark" concerning the proper production evaluations it should attach to the factors of production under its control.[13]

Hayek's argument addresses a different sort of claim. The proponents of market socialism, or what Hayek called the "competitive solution" to the problem of economic calculation under socialism, wanted to combine collective ownership and management of the "means of production" with private markets for consumer goods. Moreover, the defenders of market socialism based their claim for the greater efficacy of central planning on an argument, going back to Friedrich Wieser and Enrico Barone, of the "formal similarity" of the problem of economic calculation under capitalism and socialism from the standpoint of neoclassical economics.[14] This argument of formal similarity was sufficiently persuasive to most economists of a neoclassical bent that even those who were strongly opposed to socialism on moral or political grounds, such as Frank Knight and Joseph Schumpeter, accepted its validity.[15]

The realization that the intellectual framework of neoclassical economics lent itself all too readily to the project of a planned economy led Hayek to embark on a philosophical reconsideration of the assumptions of the neoclassical tradition. In particular, it forced Hayek to call into question the assumptions of perfect knowledge and of static analysis inherent in the original neoclassical model of the market.[16] Hayek admits that, if these assumptions are granted, then there is no difficulty in principle with the project of managing the economy through a central planning board. The practical difficulty of solving a large number of complex equations remains, but this is a *technical* rather than an *economic* problem. A genuinely economic problem only arises, in Hayek's view, when one recognizes that the knowledge one most needs for rational economic planning—knowledge of the particular needs, wants, and abilities of the innumerable individuals who make up a complex modern society—is not, and cannot in principle, be given to any single mind (not even if it is embodied in silicon rather than carbon). Such knowledge exists, according to Hayek, only in a dispersed and partially tacit form, in the minds (and practical skills) of countless individuals. To treat such data as already given (and given once and for all) to a single mind, whether the fictitious Walrasian "auctioneer" of general equilibrium theory, or the computer bank of a central planning board, is to assume away the very problem economics sets out to solve.[17]

In Hayek's view, the main function of the price system is to convey such dispersed and partially tacit knowledge to other members of society without requiring anyone to have (*per impossible*) comprehensive knowledge of the system as a whole. In this sense, the price system takes the place at the level of society of the kind of planning that an individual might properly engage in to achieve his goals. As Hayek puts this point,

> Fundamentally, in a system in which the knowledge of the relevant facts is dispersed among many people, prices can act to co-ordinate the separate actions of different people in the same way as subjective values help the individual to co-ordinate the parts of his plan.[18]

Hayek gives the example in this passage of how a rise in the price of tin can convey to consumers the need to economize on the use of tin, or develop alternatives to such use, without the need for such consumers to know *why* tin is now scarce (whether it be because a new use for tin has been discovered, or a source of tin has disappeared). The price system economizes on the amount of knowledge that an individual needs in order to act in concert with others. The potential consumer of tin does not need to know that the tin mines are no longer producing ore because there has been a miners' strike, or that scientists have developed a profitable new compound with tin, in order to make a rational allocation of his resources. Moreover, his decision will in turn affect the prices of other goods, alerting other consumers and producers that they need to change their allocation of resources. Information spreads through the market via prices without there being any one mind or agency to which this information as a whole is given.

> The whole [of society] acts as one market, not because any of its members survey the whole field, but because their limited fields of vision sufficiently overlap so that through many intermediaries the relevant information is communicated to all.[19]

In section 6 of "The Use of Knowledge in Society," Hayek argues that his account of the informational role of the price system shows not only that the market does a better job of coordinating the economic activities of disparate individuals than any planning board could hope to do, but also that it illustrates a much larger point about the dependence of civilization itself on similar unconscious and spontaneous processes. In other words, Hayek argues not only that the market itself is most appropriately conceptualized as a spontaneous order, but also that understanding how the market functions *as* a spontaneous order will cast light on the evolution and structure of other social and political institutions. Although Hayek does not develop this point at great length here, it can be seen as the germ of the social and political theories he later develops in such works as *The Constitution of Liberty; Law, Legislation and Liberty;* and *The Fatal Conceit: The Errors of Socialism.* It is worth quoting the central passage from this section:

> [T]hose who clamor for "conscious direction"—and who cannot believe that anything which has evolved without design (and even without our understanding it) should solve problems which we should not be able to solve consciously—should remember this: The problem is precisely how to extend the span of our utilization of resources beyond the span of the control of any one mind; and, therefore, how to dispense with the need of conscious control and how to provide inducements which will make the individuals do the desirable things without anyone having to tell them what to do.
>
> The problem . . . is by no means peculiar to economics but arises in connection with nearly all truly social phenomena, with language and with most of our cultural inheritance, and constitutes really the central theoretical problem of all social science.[20]

The Market as a Model of Spontaneous Order

The fundamental criterion for classifying anything as an instance of spontaneous order is that it exhibit the appearance of deliberate and intelligent design without being the product of a designing intelligence. The market is the paradigm case of spontaneous order among social institutions because it best satisfies this criterion. The market functions in many ways as if it were the product of design—as the "invisible hand" metaphor implies—and yet, far from being the product of deliberate intention, the market developed historically, and still largely functions, however imperfectly, without the aid of direct conscious human control. The most striking feature of the market is that it appears to work without anyone needing to know why it works. It is this feature of the market that, in Hayek's view, reveals the more general dependence of civilization on institutions that are neither the product of rational design nor fully comprehensible by human reason.

However, as Hayek suggests in a number of places in his writings, this very character of the market as an instance of "design without a designer" is also one of the principal sources of frustration with the market order and thus of the desire to replace it with a planned economy. On this point, Hayek writes in "The Use of Knowledge in Society,"

> I am convinced that if [the market] were the result of deliberate human design, and if the people guided by the price changes understood that their decisions have significance far beyond their immediate aim, this mechanism would have been acclaimed as one of the greatest triumphs of the human mind. Its misfortune is the double one that it is not the product of human design and that the people guided by it do not know why they are made to do what they do.[21]

The conception of the market economy as a spontaneous order that is on the whole best left to its own devices is thus a two-edged sword on Hayek's interpretation. On the one hand, the development of modern economic theory from Smith's simple model of supply and demand to the mathematical sophistication of contemporary general equilibrium analysis is a testament to the human capacity to make sense of the unimaginable complexity of economic life. To this degree, the development of economics as a discipline appears to be in line with the aspirations of modern science generally to master nature (including human nature) for the "relief of man's estate." It can be seen as belonging to the intellectual tradition of what Hayek calls "constructivist rationalism."[22] On the other hand, the result of such theoretical understanding is to suggest that there are insuperable limits placed on the human capacity to *control* the conditions of social and political life. Insofar as economic science shows that the market is truly a spontaneous order, we must recognize that one of the fundamental conditions of the existence of a progressive society is neither under direct human control nor fully comprehensible by those who benefit from it. This conclusion means abandoning the "constructivist" hopes of the radical Enlightenment that science can directly control social forces in the same way that it aspires through the development of technology to control nature.

This last point suggests that Hayek's quarrel in the Socialist Calculation debate is not merely (or even primarily) with economic planners but with the discipline of economics itself insofar as it mistakenly understands itself to be a form of social engineering. In Hayek's view, most economists (including most contemporary advocates of free markets) have learned the wrong lesson from the development of economics as a social science. Misled by scientistic prejudices and by the prevalence in economics of models derived from nineteenth-century mechanics, they have conceived of their discipline as a technique for extending knowledge, and thus—in accordance with Bacon's dictum that "knowledge is power"—control, over larger and larger domains of society. This conception of economics is clearly implicit in the increasingly strident claims made by many economists that economics should be *the* architectonic discipline in the social sciences. In Hayek's view, however, economics is merely a part (although a crucially important part) of a larger inquiry into the *limits* of our knowledge about the conditions of social life. This inquiry is not so much scientific as philosophic in character. It is an attempt, to use language deliberately reminiscent of both Socrates and Kant, to discover the nature of our ignorance concerning the conditions of social life.

Hayek sketches this alternative conception of the nature of economics and of social science generally in the beginning of chapter 2 of his major work in social and political theory, *The Constitution of Liberty.* He begins by noting that the "Socratic maxim that the recognition of our ignorance is the beginning of wisdom has profound significance for our understanding of society."[23] This is so because it is a defining feature of civilization, in Hayek's view, that it be possible for the individual to benefit from knowledge that he does not himself possess. "Most of the advantages of social life, especially in the advanced forms which we call 'civilization,' rests on the fact that the individual benefits from more knowledge than he is aware of."[24]

Hayek's emphasis on the degree to which the complex social structures of civilized societies allow individuals to benefit from such dispersed knowledge turns on its head Rousseau's well-known complaint about the weakness of individuals in civilized societies compared with the members of tribal societies. Rousseau argues in the *Second Discourse* that if you strip an average "civilized" man of the advantages he derives from the tools of his civilization (i.e., from the products of scientific and technical knowledge that he himself does not possess), he will be helpless in comparison with a typical "savage."[25] In Rousseau's view, one of the fundamental roots of modern "alienation" is the tendency of human beings in modern market societies to become dependent on the very tools they have created to liberate themselves from the bondage of nature. Civilization is bought at the price of weakening the independence and wholeness of the individual. From a Hayekian perspective, however, what Rousseau's comparison really shows is that the "savage" social and political state is as far as one can go on the premise that all knowledge must be present in the mind of the person using it. The separation of knowledge from the immediate insight of the individual, its dispersal among various individuals and institutions of society, is the very condition of civilized life.

Hayek goes on to note that this necessary ignorance about the conditions of civilized life has not received the attention it deserves in the social sciences, in large part because it goes against the grain of the technocratic, engineering model of science dominant in these disciplines. The goal of science in this technocratic view is to extend the range of human knowledge, not to trace its limits. This lack of knowledge of their own ignorance has encouraged social scientists to develop utopian schemes of social improvement that presuppose that "rulers" (or scientific "administrators") possess perfect knowledge of the conditions of social life. The critical task of Hayek's own social and political theory is thus analogous to that engaged in by Kant in his epistemological critique of the pretensions of early modern rationalism to know by direct intellectual insight the true nature of "things in themselves." With clear reference to Kant's inquiry in the *Critique of Pure Reason* into the "conditions of possible experience," Hayek describes the character of his own inquiry in the following terms:

> If we are to understand how society works, we must attempt to define the general nature and range of our ignorance concerning it. Though we cannot see in the dark, we must be able to trace the limits of the dark areas.[26]

It is obviously not possible in the limited scope of a single chapter to trace all the ramifications of this theme in Hayek's thought. But it is worth briefly comparing Hayek's social epistemology of the limits of our knowledge with Kant's transcendental inquiry into the conditions of human knowledge to bring out the relevance of these epistemological concerns for Hayek's account of the market as a spontaneous order.

In his *Critique of Pure Reason*, Kant argued that the limits of human knowledge are set by the basic structure of the human mind. In Kant's view, the human mind is characterized by a fundamental dualism between discursive reason and receptive sense-perception. The human mind is ineluctably dependent for its cognitive operations on the deliverances of the senses. To this degree, Kant is in agreement with the British empiricist tradition that the ultimate source of the *content* of our knowledge is sense-perception. The *form* of our knowledge, however, is not given in sense-perception, but provided by the a priori structure of the human mind. Kant argues that the human mind necessarily subsumes the raw data of the senses under both the "forms of intuition," space and time, as well as "the categories of the understanding," such as cause and effect, that give rise to the ordered structure of both ordinary experience and scientific inquiry. But since both the forms of intuition and the categories of our understanding apply only to the data supplied by the senses, they can provide us with no knowledge of what transcends possible experience. For Kant, the human mind is a bright, but narrow, light that can illuminate only what falls within its limited purview. The ultimate nature of reality, the "thing in itself," in Kant's language, must remain forever in the dark.

Hayek's social epistemology builds on the Kantian notion sketched above that human reason is limited in its capacity to know the ultimate nature of reality and yet able through a kind of self-examination to determine the extent of its own limitations. He rejects, however, the Kantian view that the human mind has a fixed a priori structure independent of history or social development. As Hayek puts this point:

> Man did not simply impose upon the world a pattern created by his mind. His mind is itself a system that constantly changes as a result of his endeavor to adapt himself to his surroundings . . .
> The conception of man deliberately building his civilization stems from an erroneous intellectualism that regards human reason as something standing outside nature and possessed of knowledge and reasoning capacity independent of experience. But the growth of the human mind is part of the growth of civilization.[27]

A full account of Hayek's social epistemology would require a detailed examination of his major work on psychology, *The Sensory Order*.[28] It is possible, however, to make some progress in understanding this argument by seeing it as an attempt to incorporate Kantian insights about the limitations of human knowledge into a broadly naturalistic and evolutionary framework. Unlike Kant, Hayek does not view the mind as something that transcends either nature or history. Indeed, it is arguable that Kant's conception of the "fixed" a priori character of the mind's categories is a residue of the very dogmatic metaphysics he set out to overthrow. Certainly, the course of post-Kantian thought in Germany, culminating in Hegel's *Phenomenology of Spirit*, saw its task as that of demonstrating the culturally relative and historically changing character of the basic categories of human experience. Following Darwin rather than Hegel, Hayek suggests that the basic categories of human thought emerge through a process of cultural adaptation.[29] Moreover, unlike Kant, who locates the human mind in a kind of transcendental "no-man's land," identical neither with the physical brain nor with any underlying spiritual substance, Hayek argues that the human mind is in part a physical system embodied in the brain, in part a cultural artifact dispersed among a variety of cultural and social institutions.

Thus, in Hayek's view, human intelligence itself exemplifies the dispersed and partly tacit character of spontaneous order. In his essay, "The Connectionist Mind: A Study of Hayekian Psychology," Barry Smith argues that Hayek's account of the synaptic organization of the brain in *The Sensory Order* strikingly anticipates the "connectionist" or "parallel-processing" model of the mind in contemporary cognitive science.[30] Unlike the more orthodox model of the mind in cognitive science as a symbol-processor that treats explicit "rule-following" and the conscious manipulation of symbols as the mark of intelligence, connectionist accounts of the mind are better able to model the kind of tacit awareness that is exemplified, for instance, in facial recognition and other forms of pattern recognition. This model of the mind lends support to a crucial aspect of Hayek's case for the superiority of the market over central planning, which is that much of the knowledge relevant for economic decisions exists only in a tacit form and cannot, even in principle, be formalized in terms of explicit rules.

Hayek's account of the mind is similar not only to connectionist models of the mind in cognitive science but also to the "externalist" position in contemporary philosophy of mind. "Externalism" is the view that our cognitive capacities depend not only on the functioning of the brain but on a wide variety of external media and tools. From this "externalist" perspective, the dispersed character of the mind as a spontaneous order is exemplified by libraries (or more contemporary media of information storage such as compact discs). The brain of an individual has a relatively limited capacity to store and process information, but that capacity can be indefinitely extended by the development of external media. Without the capacity to embody knowledge in such external media, progress in the sciences would necessarily be limited to what an individual could learn and retain in a single lifetime. Moreover, progress in the sciences often consists in extending the range of activities one can engage in *without thinking about them* by developing algorithms or tools that allow such activities to be done mechanically. A simple example of this would be the use of a calculator to extract square roots. A calculator is nothing more than the embodiment of human intelligence in electronic form, which, by economizing on the amount of conscious mental effort one must invest in such routine calculation, allows one to pay more attention to higher-order intellectual operations.

Hayek's theory of the mind as a spontaneous order suggests that the market must be understood as both an effect and a cause of the human mind. It is an effect of the human mind insofar as it is an emergent result of the interaction of the separate plans of countless individuals. It is a cause insofar as the result of such interaction embodies patterns of intelligent collective behavior that in turn influence individuals in their plan making. Indeed, given Hayek's "externalist" view of the mind as constituted not just by the brain but by the external cultural artifacts the brain has at its disposal, one might say that the market is itself an extension of the mind of the modern human being. It is partly for this reason that Hayek tends to regard criticism of the market as a form of atavism.[31] To attack the market is to attack a central faculty of the modern mind. To call for its replacement by a central planning authority because it appears to lack central direction is like suggesting that we should burn all the libraries because the knowledge in them is not contained in a single brain. If most modern social scientists find it difficult to conceive of the market in Hayek's terms as an embodiment of mind, it is in part because they are still under the (largely unconscious) sway of the Cartesian tradition of thinking of the mind as a unified and transparently self-conscious subject. One of the merits of Hayek's account of the market is that it demonstrates in a specific case that intelligence does not require the unity and explicit self-awareness of the Cartesian ego but can be embodied in a dispersed and partly tacit system.

Spontaneous Order, Reason, and Tradition

Hayek's account of the market as a spontaneous order has provoked a wide range of critical responses. In this concluding section, I will examine a difficulty with Hayek's project that has not, in my view, received sufficient attention in critical literature: the dependence of the market order on the willingness of individuals to accept as *binding* on themselves traditions and social practices that are necessarily resistant to rational explanation and justification.

As we have seen, Hayek argues that central planning is impossible because of two distinct but related features of the market: the knowledge required for such planning is dispersed among a countless number of individuals and at least some of that knowledge is tacit knowledge, or "know-how," which cannot, in principle, be formulated in terms of explicit rules. Both of these features of the market imply that the market rests on institutions and practices that must be accepted by those who benefit from them without rational justification. Indeed, Hayek suggests that the demand for such justification, insofar as it brings to light the unplanned, historically contingent, character of the institutions on which civilization rests, potentially poses a threat to that civilization. Moreover, even the capacity for rational inquiry and progress in the sciences proves to be dependent on the willingness to accept some "irrational" traditions. Progress itself cannot be planned but must be allowed to develop of its own accord. Hayek connects both of these points in the following passage from *The Constitution of Liberty:*

> The rationalist who desires to subject everything to human reason is thus faced with a real dilemma. The use of reason aims at control and predictability. But the process of the advance of reason rests on freedom and the unpredictability of human action . . . for advance to take place, the social process from which the growth of reason emerges must remain free from its control.
>
> There can be little doubt that man owes some of his greatest successes in the past to the fact that he has *not* been able to control his social life. His continued advance may well depend on his *deliberately* refraining from exercising controls which are now in his power . . . We are not far from the point where the deliberately organized forces of society may destroy those spontaneous forces which have made advance possible.[32]

As the above passage suggests, Hayek's project faces some daunting obstacles. He must, first and foremost, persuade modern, scientifically minded intellectuals, who have inherited from the Enlightenment the pernicious opposition between scientific rationality and irrational traditions, of the necessity to accept some traditions as authoritative without rational justification. This requires showing that the conception of reason as autonomous from tradition developed within the radical Enlightenment is one-sided and ultimately self-undermining. In this respect, Hayek's project is similar to Edmund Burke's defense in the *Reflections on the Revolution in France* of the latent wisdom contained in the common prejudices of a people against the corrosive rationalism of the French philosophés as well as to Hans-Georg Gadamer's critique in *Truth and Method* of the Enlightenment as "prejudice against prejudice."[33] Like Burke and Gadamer, Hayek does not mean to deny the possibility of subjecting tradition to any form of rational criticism but rather to argue that such criticism can never be "global," that it must always rest on the acceptance of a broader framework of unexamined traditions. In other words, Hayek's position rests on a critique of the Cartesian view that in order to establish the sciences on a certain foundation one must first reject as false everything of which one can entertain any doubt at all. Hayek's conception of the market as a spontaneous order is "anti-Cartesian," or "anti-foundationalist," to use contemporary jargon, insofar as it insists that there can be no fixed standpoint from which one may survey the market as a whole and subject it to direct rational control.

Unlike Burke and Gadamer, however, Hayek, at least in *The Constitution of Liberty*, is unsympathetic to many features of traditionalist conservatism. In the Postscript to *The Constitution of Liberty*, which bears the apt title "Why I am not a Conservative," Hayek outlines his disagreements with the conservative tradition. While acknowledging a real affinity between his own conception of spontaneous order and the emphasis on "spontaneously grown institutions" in the work of such conservative (or even reactionary) thinkers as "Coleridge, Bonald, De Maistre, Justus Möser [and] Donoso Cortès," Hayek emphasizes his sharp disagreement with this tradition in three crucial respects.[34] First, Hayek argues against the moral paternalism inherent in the conservative tradition. This moral paternalism rests ultimately on the view that the majority of human beings are not competent to govern themselves. The conservative position asserts that political authority is natural and that the freedom classical liberals cherish is an illusion. In Hayek's view, this moral standpoint means that conservatives are just as likely as socialists to abuse state power for the sake of allegedly benevolent social and political aims. Second, Hayek argues against what he regards as the dangerous tendency of conservatives to deprecate the importance of moral and political principles. Conservatives tend to regard the appeal to principle as an obstacle to the proper exercise of political authority and prudence. To use Hayek's own words: "To advocate any clear-cut principles of social order is . . . to incur the stigma of being an unpractical doctrinaire."[35] Hayek's defense of the necessity of general principles is that only on their basis can one create a social and political order in which individuals with different moral values can coexist.[36] General principles provide the necessary scaffolding for a free and morally diverse society. Finally, Hayek argues that conservatism is characterized by resistance to innovation and a fear of change as such. Hayek admits that conservatives are often right in their distrust of rapid or revolutionary change, but he thinks that this distrust too often devolves into an unwillingness to let spontaneous social forces take their own course. In sum, Hayek sees an unintended convergence between traditional conservatives and socialist planners in their common desire to control the unruly process of social and political change.

Hayek's liberal commitment to individual freedom, governance by general principles, and openness to change does pose a problem, however, for his defense of spontaneous order. In the first place, it is not clear why someone who adheres to these three features of the classical liberal tradition *should* accept the results of spontaneous order as binding on himself. In particular, the combination of individual freedom and governance by general principles—what Locke, in the *Second Treatise* calls "a standing Rule to live by, common to everyone of that Society"—points more to the social contract tradition than it does to the idea of spontaneous order.[37] From the social contract perspective, government is the result of individuals freely choosing to accept certain rules as binding on themselves and, to a lesser degree, their posterity. The first task of government is to construct a workable constitutional order—a process that involves choice and deliberation rather than an acceptance of tradition. Like Burke, Hayek may argue that such constitutional reform is never as radical as it seems, that it tends to be successful precisely to the degree that it draws upon the spontaneous forces already present in society, but it is still the case that such constitution building requires more deliberate design than Hayek is prepared to admit.[38]

Hayek's strong belief in progress also is in some tension with his theory of spontaneous order. While the underlying dynamics of society may be constantly changing, at any given moment one's attitude to the particular social and political configuration one finds oneself in must be conservative. Precisely because the source of change is spontaneous and undirected, it is important not to interfere with this change through untimely human intervention. Hayek's practical advice will necessarily be quietist. It can consist in little more than the admonition to be patient and let the dynamics of spontaneous order work themselves out. But this advice is likely to be more attractive to conservative defenders of the status quo than to the innovative and progressive individuals he hopes to attract away from socialism to his defense of the market economy.[39] It seems more likely that they would apply to Hayek's own position, the criticism he levels at traditional conservatism:

> [B]y its very nature it cannot offer an alternative to the direction in which we are moving . . . It has, for this reason, inevitably been the fate of conservatism to be dragged along a path not of its own choosing.[40]

In the second place, apart from the normative question of whether the results of spontaneous order have any moral force from a liberal perspective, there is also the positive question of whether modern liberals—imbued as they are with the principles (or prejudices) of individual freedom and the demand for rational justification—*can* accept the results of spontaneous order as binding on themselves. As we saw in the long passage quoted above, Hayek himself argues that the progress of civilization may depend on our ability *deliberately* to refrain from interfering with the spontaneous course of our civilization. The problem, of course, hinges on the word "deliberately." We must now consciously, intentionally, refrain from doing something that in earlier, less-enlightened epochs, we would not have regarded as either possible or desirable. Nonintervention in the spontaneous course of human history must now be a deliberate policy.

It is unclear, however, whether such self-restraint is any longer possible for modern human beings. To be sure, the collapse of communism has taken the luster off the idea of central planning, and no serious economist today would argue for anything like a Soviet-style command economy. In this respect, Hayek's position in the Socialist Calculation debate has enjoyed a belated triumph. But his deeper project of employing a Kantian critique of our capacity to know the conditions of social and political life as a way of constraining the Promethean aspirations of modern science to control and shape the destiny of humanity has had little effect. The debates surrounding such issues as human cloning, intervention in the human genome, and the extension of the human life span suggest that "constructive rationalism" is still the dominant standpoint in both the natural and the social sciences.

With this last point in mind, we must conclude that Hayek's defense of spontaneous order is more conservative than he wants to admit in the Postscript to *The Constitution of Liberty* and more pessimistic in its implications for the future. For if Hayek is right that civilization requires the acceptance of institutions that are neither deliberately constructed nor rationally justifiable, and if the progress of civilization inevitably gives rise to an attitude that is inimical to anything that is not deliberately constructed or rationally justifiable, it seems that the progress of civilization necessarily culminates in its own subversion. There can be little doubt, however, that this last conclusion is too strong. For, in agreement with the conservative tradition from which he tries to distance himself in the Postscript to *The Constitution of Liberty*, Hayek recognizes that the majority of human beings, even in the most liberal and progressive of societies, derive their moral and political orientation not from rational reflection but from custom, habit, and tradition. It is perhaps for this reason that Hayek—a professed agnostic—has a few kind words to say about the role of religion as a "Guardian of Tradition" in his last work, *The Fatal Conceit:*

> We owe it partly to mystical and religious beliefs, and, I believe, particularly to the main monotheistic ones. That beneficial traditions have been preserved and transmitted . . . This means that, like it or not, we owe the persistence of certain practices, and the civilization that resulted from them, in part to support from beliefs which are not true —or verifiable or testable—in the same sense as are scientific statements, and which certainly are not the result of rational argumentation.[41]

The above passage suggests, however, that Hayek has underestimated the possible tension between the stability of social institutions such as religion and the spontaneous order of the market. Hayek's defense of religion as a bulwark of the market order is highly paradoxical in light of the strongly antireligious, and specifically anti-Christian, intentions of such prominent early defenders of the market as David Hume and Adam Smith. Both men defended what they called "commercial society" not only because of its greater capacity to produce wealth, but also because of its tendency to redirect the attention of human beings from "other-worldly" to "this-worldly" concerns. While Hume and Smith would agree with Hayek's view that human reason is a limited and fallible instrument, they would certainly balk at the suggestion that civilization requires the acceptance of institutions that are wholly opaque to reason. Hayek's evolutionary naturalism seems to have led him ultimately to embrace the necessity of a religious support for morality. This conclusion is at odds with the view of both Hume and Smith that religious beliefs and practices sometimes conflict with moral decency and generally tend to undermine the prospects for a commercial society.

In conclusion, I would suggest that Hayek's impressive defense of the market as a spontaneous order and his allied criticism of the intellectual tradition of "constructive rationalism" underestimates the extent to which the market itself is a rationalist project and thus subject to the same potentially self-undermining tendencies Hayek diagnoses in modern social science generally. In historical terms, this means disputing Hayek's often-repeated claim that there is a clear-cut distinction between a radical (or "French") and a moderate (or "Scottish") Enlightenment.[42] Thinkers such as Hume and Smith were just as concerned as the French philosophés with social and political transformation, even if they thought such transformation would be better achieved through the indirect means of commerce and education than through the direct exercise of state power. Moreover, the avowed or implied object of such social and political transformation was to weaken the hold of the very "irrational" customs and traditions that Hayek argues are crucial to the maintenance of a free society. This analysis suggests that there is a fundamental tension in Hayek's defense of the market.

In the light of our earlier discussion, this tension can be characterized as one between the conservative and the classical liberal tendencies in Hayek's thought. Hayek's "epistemological" defense of the superiority of the market over central planning in terms of our limited knowledge of society as a whole paradoxically increases the importance of cherishing and preserving traditional customs and institutions. For these customs and institutions are the guideposts we use to navigate the darkness of our ignorance about the true conditions of social and political life. To use a Burkean phrase, these customs and institutions are the "precipitate" of an anonymous collective wisdom that the individual would be foolish to jettison for the unsteady light of his own reason. In this respect, Hayek conceives of the market as simply one of a number of different social and political institutions that have arisen spontaneously in response to the exigencies of human life. This may be fair enough as a description of the market in the eighteenth, or even the nineteenth century, but, as many observers have noted, the market in contemporary advanced industrial societies appears to be expanding rapidly at the expense of other social and political institutions. One does not have to be a Marxist, or believe in collective planning, to share Jürgen Habermas's concern about the tendency of the market to "colonize" almost every aspect of modern society. Faced with this growing imbalance between the market and other social and political institutions, it seems that one can either embrace the market and all its works or attempt to defend the moral necessity of traditional institutions, but it is hard to see how one can, as Hayek's theory of the market as a spontaneous order requires, do both at once.

Notes

1. There are good overviews of the various claims made on behalf of spontaneous order explanations in Steven Johnson, *Emergence: The Connected Lives of Ants, Brains, Cities, and Software* (New York: Scribner, 2001) and Steven Strogatz, *Sync: The Emerging Science of Spontaneous Order* (New York: Hyperion Books, 2003).
2. Charles Darwin, *On the Origin of Species* (Cambridge, MA: Harvard University Press, 1964), p. 3.
3. The term "spontaneous order" seems to have been coined by Michael Polanyi in his essay, "The Growth of Thought in Society," *Economica* 8 (November 1941): 428–456. Cf. Straun Jacobs, "Michael Polanyi's Theory of Spontaneous Orders," *Review of Austrian Economics* 11, nos. 1–2 (1999): 111–127.
4. An English translation of this article is available in Friedrich A. Hayek, ed., *Collectivist Economic Planning: Critical Studies on the Possibilities of Socialism* (London: Routledge, 1935), pp. 87–103.
5. Ludwig von Mises, *Socialism: An Economic and Sociological Analysis,* trans. J. Kahane (Indianapolis: Liberty Classics, 1981).
6. The phrase "natural economy" comes from a book by Otto Neurath, *Durch die Kriegswirtschaft zur Naturalwirtschaft* (*From the War Economy to the Natural Economy*). Neurath would later become a prominent member of the "Vienna Circle" of logical positivists. On Neurath's role in this debate, see Bruce Caldwell, *Hayek's Challenge: An Intellectual Biography* (Chicago: University of Chicago Press, 2004), pp. 113–119 and 428–429.
7. See Oskar Lange, "On the Economic Theory of Socialism," in *On the Economic Theory of Socialism,* ed. Benjamin Lippincott (New York: McGraw-Hill, 1964), pp. 55–143.
8. Hayek's main essays in this controversy have been reprinted in Friedrich A. Hayek, *Individualism and Economic Order* (Chicago: University of Chicago Press, 1948), pp. 119–208.

9. The most comprehensive account of this debate is in Don Lavoie, *Rivalry and Central Planning: The Socialist Calculation Debate Reconsidered* (Cambridge: Cambridge University Press, 1985). There are good overviews of the issues in this debate in Peter Boettke, "Economic Calculation: The Austrian Contribution to Political Economy," in *Calculation and Coordination* (London and New York: Routledge, 2001), pp. 29–46; and Bruce Caldwell, "Hayek and Socialism," *Journal of Economic Literature* 35 (December 1997): 1856–1890.

10. Cf. Don Lavoie, "Computation, Incentives, and Discovery: The Cognitive Function of Markets in Market Socialism," *Annals of the American Academy of Political and Social Science* 507 (1990): 72–79.

11. Cf. Ronald Coase, *The Firm, the Market, and the Law* (Chicago: University of Chicago Press, 1990), p. 35. Coase takes the phrase "islands of conscious power" from D. H. Robertson, *The Control of Industry* (London: Nisbet, 1928), p. 85.

12. Karl Marx, *Capital,* volume 1, trans. Ben Fowkes (New York: Vintage Books, 1977), pp. 476–477.

13. Lavoie, *Rivalry and Central Planning,* p. 62n13.

14. Ibid., pp. 79–84.

15. Cf. Joseph Schumpeter, *History of Economic Analysis* (New York: Oxford University Press, 1954), pp. 986–990.

16. The new information-theoretic approach to economics, pioneered by Stiglitz and Grossman, is an attempt to incorporate Hayek's emphasis on imperfect information into the framework of neoclassical economics. For a good survey of this approach relevant to the themes of this paper, see Joseph E. Stiglitz, *Whither Socialism?* (Cambridge, MA: MIT Press, 1994). For an Austrian assessment of this approach, which argues that it does not do justice to the radical character of Hayek's critique, see Esteban F. Thomsen, *Prices and Knowledge: A Market-Process Perspective* (London and New York: Routledge, 1992), pp. 29–62. Gerald P. O'Driscoll, Jr. and Mario J. Rizzo, *The Economics of Time and Ignorance* (London and New York: Routledge, 1996) engage in a sustained critique of the static assumptions of neoclassical economics from an Austrian perspective.

17. This is the main point of Hayek's famous essay, originally published in 1945, "The Use of Knowledge in Society" reprinted in Friedrich A. Hayek, *Individualism and Economic Order* (Chicago: University of Chicago Press, 1948), pp. 77–91. Stiglitz, *Whither Socialism?* pp. 1–82, provides an effective critique from an information-theoretic perspective of the assumptions common to both neoclassical economics and market socialism.

18. Hayek, "The Use of Knowledge in Society," *Individualism and Economic Order,* p. 85.

19. Ibid., p. 86.

20. Ibid., pp. 87–88.

21. Ibid., p. 87. Cf. Friedrich A. Hayek, *The Constitution of Liberty* (Chicago: University of Chicago Press, 1960), p. 25: "[O]ur attitude, when we discover how little we know of what makes us co-operate, is, on the whole, one of resentment rather than of wonder or curiosity. Much of our occasional impetuous

desire to smash the whole entangling machinery of civilization is due to this inability of man to understand what he is doing."

22. Hayek gives a critical account of the tradition of "constructive rationalism" in the studies collected in *The Counter-Revolution of Science* (Indianapolis: Liberty Press, 1979).

23. Hayek, *The Constitution of Liberty,* p. 22.

24. Ibid.

25. Rousseau, *The Discourses and Other Early Political Writings,* ed. and trans. Victor Gourevitch (Cambridge: Cambridge University Press, 1997), p. 135.

26. Hayek, *The Constitution of Liberty,* p. 23.

27. Ibid., pp. 23–24.

28. Friedrich A. Hayek, *The Sensory Order* (Chicago: University of Chicago Press, 1952).

29. Hayek's thought owes a great debt to Darwinism, but he is critical of the attempt to apply Darwinian logic directly to the explanation of social phenomena, as was attempted, for example, by the early sociobiologists. The most important difference between cultural and biological evolution, in Hayek's view, is that the former works through "group selection," while most biologists (with the exception of an increasingly influential minority) deny that group selection operates on biological species. As Hayek puts it in *The Fatal Conceit: The Errors of Socialism* (Chicago: University of Chicago Press, 1988), p. 25: "Cultural evolution *simulates* Lamarckism," that is, it works by means of the transmission of acquired characteristics, rather than by means of the natural selection of random variations characteristic of the standard model of biological evolution.

30. Barry Smith, "The Connectionist Mind: A Study in Hayekian Psychology," in *Hayek: Economist and Social Philosopher: A Critical Retrospective,* ed. S. F. Frowen, (London: Macmillan, 1976), pp. 9–29.

31. Cf. Hayek, *The Fatal Conceit,* pp. 19–20.

32. Ibid., p. 38. My italics.

33. Edmund Burke, *Reflections on the Revolution in France* (Indianapolis: Hackett, 1987), p. 76. Hans-Georg Gadamer, *Truth and Method* (New York: Continuum, 1993), pp. 270–277. For a comparison between Burke and Gadamer on this point, see Louis Hunt, "Principle and Prejudice: Burke, Kant and Habermas on the Conditions of Practical Reason," *History of Political Thought* 23, no. 1 (Spring 2002): 130–132.

34. Hayek, *The Constitution of Liberty,* pp. 397–411.

35. Hayek, *Individualism and Economic Order,* p. 1.

36. Hayek, *The Constitution of Liberty,* pp. 401–402.

37. John Locke, *Two Treatises of Government* (Cambridge: Cambridge University Press, 1988), p. 284.

38. For an interesting argument that constitutional reform and spontaneous order are compatible, based on a comparison between Hayek and James Buchanan's "constitutional political economy," see Karen I. Vaughn, "Can Democratic Society Reform Itself? The Limits of Constructive Change," in *The Market*

Process: Essays in Contemporary Austrian Economics, ed. Peter Boettke and David Prychitko (Cheltenham: Edward Elgar, 1994), pp. 229–243.

39. Cf. Hayek, *The Constitution of Liberty,* pp. 410–411: "In a world where the chief need is once more, as it was at the beginning of the nineteenth century, to free the process of spontaneous growth from the obstacles and encumbrances that human folly has erected, his hopes must rest on persuading and gaining the support of those who by disposition are 'progressives,' those who, though they may now be seeking change in the wrong direction, are at least willing to examine critically the existing and to change it wherever necessary."

40. Ibid., p. 398.

41. Hayek, *The Fatal Conceit,* pp. 136–137. Cf. Hayek, *The Constitution of Liberty,* p. 155, where a similar point is made in passing.

42. This distinction is developed at length in the essay "Individualism: True and False," in Hayek, *Individualism and Economic Order,* pp. 1–32.

PART II

Critical Reflections

CHAPTER 4

Knight's Challenge (to Hayek): Spontaneous Order Is Not Enough for Governing a Liberal Society

Ross B. Emmett

The classical liberal must . . . remain a constructivist, at least in some limited sense.

James M. Buchanan[1]

When the noted Chicago economist Frank H. Knight first read F. A. Hayek's *The Road to Serfdom* (1944), he advised the University of Chicago Press (the book's eventual U.S. publisher) that the book was "well stated, compact and conclusive." Although he noted that "the position defended is in accord with my conviction before reading this work," he went on to comment on some of the book's "limitations," including Hayek's inadequate recognition of "the necessity, as well as political inevitability, of a wide range of governmental activity in relation to economic life in the future." Hayek, he wrote, "deals only with the simpler fallacies, unreasonable demands and romantic prejudices" of the "popular clamor" for government control, while failing to discuss the difficult problems "set by the serious shortcomings" of capitalism as it actually existed in the United States. In short, Knight cautioned the university's press about publishing the work, saying, "I doubt whether it would have a very wide market in this country, or would change the position of many readers."[2]

Well, Knight always did doubt the predictive capabilities of social scientists, including himself! However, despite the success that *The Road to Serfdom* had, Knight's doubts about Hayek's intellectual project—now known to us as "The Abuse of Reason" project[3]—lingered. Thus, when he read Hayek's *Constitution of Liberty* (1960) shortly after its publication, Knight's first comments were that "the book disappoints as a treatment of freedom. This reader finds no serious effort even to state clearly the practical problem of . . . free society."[4]

The problem with Hayek's project, as Knight saw it, lay in the inadequacy of its conceptualization of both cultural evolution *and* free society. The former inadequacy led Hayek to offer what Knight understood to be a reductionist account of cultural evolution, specifically with regard to the emergence of the cultural complexities of free, democratic societies, while the latter made his arguments inappropriate to the practical social problems facing those very societies. To make matters worse, Knight went on to argue that Hayek's "mirage of social justice" was no mirage at all.[5] Indeed, a free society faced with solving practical problems inevitably had to resolve conflicting notions of distributive justice as well as conflicts between the pursuit of justice and the pursuit of other social ideals. Knight claimed that the resolution of such conflicts did not occur in free society only via recourse to existing law. Instead, he argued that governance of a free society was characterized by *discussion,* aimed at changing, and making, law. His critique of Hayek, therefore, echoed remarks he wrote even before reading *The Road to Serfdom:* "Social action," he said in 1941, "is group self-determination. The content or process is rational discussion. . . . Discussion is social problem-solving, and all problem-solving includes (social) discussion."[6]

Knight's challenge to Hayek was to provide an account of the institutions of free society that did not reduce to the evolution of *government by law,* but which allowed for the cultural evolution of *government by discussion* within free societies.[7] The significance of the term "discussion," already hinted at in the quotation above where Knight equated it with both social problem-solving and the process of group self-determination, will become clear in the course of the chapter. But first, we will look at a question some readers will no doubt have: who is Frank Knight, and why are his criticisms of Hayek noteworthy? Once we address that question, we will return to the criticisms Knight made of Hayek's project and use them as a springboard to examine his own accounts of freedom, cultural evolution, and of the role of discussion in a liberal democracy, in order to explain more fully Knight's challenge.

On Frank Knight and the Hayek Project

Outside the economics profession, Knight is recognized as the senior member and philosophical guide of the Chicago school of economics, which supported classical liberalism in America through the rise of Keynesianism during the post-war period and launched the rational choice (or neo-) liberalism of the late twentieth century.[8] As the dean of American anti-Keynesianism, Knight was a logical candidate to lead the American contingent at the first meeting of the Mont Pelerin Society, from which Hayek's agenda for the revival of liberalism sprang.[9] Hence, Knight's lukewarm reception of *The Road to Serfdom* and of Hayek's appointment at the University of Chicago may surprise those who generally (and correctly) associate him with Hayek's side in the postwar debate over capitalism and socialism.[10] The fact is that Knight's work is hard to fit into our preconceived notions of what an opponent of socialism, the New Deal, and Keynes would look like. In consequence, Knight's work, including his criticisms of Hayek, is often overlooked in our tales of social science and social philosophy in the twentieth century.

Inside the economics profession, Knight is remembered primarily for the frequently cited distinction between risk and uncertainty drawn in *Risk, Uncertainty and Profit* (1921) and for his spirited defense of neoclassical theory and the role of markets in economic organization he provided from his position at the University of Chicago.[11] In the latter regard, the education he provided Milton Friedman, George Stigler, James Buchanan, and many others played a large role in the eventual emergence of Chicago economics as a dominant force in economics and American public policy. Yet again, that role has a surprising side, for while it may highlight Knight's importance to the Chicago tradition, it overstates his allegiance to the Chicago approach. To understand the difference, we need only look to *Risk, Uncertainty and Profit*. Defenders of neoclassical theory, including Hayek during his years at the London School of Economics, taught from Knight's book because it provided a clear and systematic exposition of the foundations of price theory. But its importance to the history of price theory leads us to forget that the book ultimately offered a tragic conception of social science and its potential contribution to social action.[12]

The economics profession is also dimly aware of Knight's prior engagement with Hayek, during the 1930s, over the most esoteric of subjects in economic theory—capital. While the substance of their "capital controversy" need not detain us,[13] Knight drew some interesting conclusions from their exchange regarding the prospects for liberalism;[14] these conclusions foreshadow his criticisms of Hayek some 30 years later. During the controversy the two men corresponded about their differences, and Knight believed they were making progress toward a common understanding through the give-and-take of discussion about specific questions and responses. But then Hayek, unbeknownst to Knight, published an article on the theory of capital that made only a passing reference to Knight's criticisms.[15] Knight interpreted the article to mean that Hayek would make little effort to respond directly to the specific objections of Knight and others to Austrian capital theory. In the last letter of their correspondence from this period, Knight highlights a difference between the two men that will emerge again in their respective positions on the nature of liberalism—the role of discussion:

> In the large, I think I understand what the drift of [your response] is, and it serves to emphasize the fundamental problem in my mind these days, which is the question whether there is any profit in the discussion of fundamental issues in economics. . . . In this connection, I recall the observation in your letter [and eventually in the published article], that systematic exposition rather than the meeting of specific questions is the way to "advance knowledge." I am strongly convinced of the opposite.[16]

As we will see, Knight believed the ideal of a free society to be the search for agreement by discussion, which advances in response to "specific questions" or particular problems, rather than a "systematic exposition" of abstract positions. When two individuals who shared both a commitment to free society and the commonality of a professional discipline could not themselves agree on either content or method, Knight feared that the future of liberalism was bleak.

Between the capital controversy of the 1930s and the response to Hayek's project that forms the basis for this chapter, Knight increasingly focused on why the prospects for liberalism were bleak, and what might be done about it. Many aspects of Knight's project parallel those of Hayek's. For example, they both thought socialism was a nonstarter; they were both widely recognized as defenders of market organization in an age devoted to correcting the failures of markets; and they both believed that appeals to scientific authority as the basis for granting scientists and social scientists the right to exercise social control elevated science to a dangerous place within a liberal society. But the extent of the overlap of their projects, and their common cause against the intellectual hold of socialism in the free world, belies their significant differences. For example, where Hayek thought socialist planning would fail because of a knowledge coordination problem, Knight downplayed socialism's economic problems in order to focus on its ethical dilemmas; and he was as concerned about the role of moralism as the basis for appeals for social control as he was about scientism. Thus, by the time Hayek arrived in Chicago in 1950 as a professor in the Committee on Social Thought (CST), the time was ripe for their disagreements to surface again. Perhaps it is only surprising that it took another almost 20 years for Knight's simmering dissatisfaction with Hayek's "systematic exposition" of liberalism to emerge in a published critique.

Knight on Hayek: Identifying the Issues

Frank Knight wrote only two direct critiques of Hayek's work on the liberal tradition: the first a short response to the famous essay "The Intellectuals and Socialism," in which Hayek attempted to account for the intellectuals' tendency to accept socialism;[17] and the second a review of Hayek's *Constitution of Liberty*.[18] For our purposes, the first critique serves little purpose. So we will focus on the second critique and will take the short précis mentioned at the beginning of this chapter as a synopsis of his argument.

> Hayek, on close reading, disappoints as a treatment of freedom. This reader finds no serious effort even to state clearly the practical problems of personal freedom or free society. The book "straddles" on the philosophical problem of freedom versus universal causality (pp. 72, 73). "Of course" human acts are caused, "largely," but as certainly, not completely. How far does not matter, since animal behavior is based on release of potential energy, in which there is almost no quantitative relation between cause and effect; "trigger action" may multiply an effect indefinitely. Furthermore, it seems rather pointless to discuss personal freedom apart from control of means of acting, and opportunity to act, and an interest in action, as is done here. More serious—man is a social being, and freedom in society rests on agreement on forms and terms of association, that is, free agreement on the laws, or "government by discussion." This concept is not mentioned, as far as one notices. (The word "agree" does occur [pp. 314, 315] but is not on solving a problem.) The book, apart from historical content (which this writer lacks the learning to criticize in detail), is propaganda for "government by law" but against law "making"—law should be left, or "almost," to spontaneous change in tradition, (like language; which is barely mentioned [pp. 24, 57, 59, 434n.] but not developed or the analogy pressed). Of course a large and basic element in law—its premises, the mores—does have that character and so is beyond the reach of social action (except by vague reflex influence of "jural law").
>
> In a recent lecture at the University of Chicago—repeated from a tape recording—Hayek attacked the idea of social economic justice. He held that we are committed to the enterprise organization and must take what it brings, working without political interference. The substance of this is absurd, but it is right to reject the ideal of social justice. It is hopelessly undefinable, meaningless; and there is some prospect of agreement on concrete *in*justices, and on procedures to lessen them.[19]

Looking at this summary, we notice immediately that Knight does not formulate a statement of the Hayekian position to which he is going to respond. Instead, he outlines objections to specific parts of Hayek's argument, suggesting that they fall short of some already specified understanding of liberalism. In this regard, Hayek is treated like most of Knight's intellectual opponents: first, he identified the issues he saw as important, usually in his own terms, and then, he proceeded to criticize the opponent for not understanding the issue the same way he did. Because Knight's analysis always examines the tension between competing principles, while others often proceeded by identifying a core set of principles—a general position, if you will—from which the issues at hand can be approached, Knight generally found ample fodder for criticism. The earlier distinction we saw Knight make between "systematic exposition" and responding to "specific problems" is indicative of his general philosophical approach.

However, the summary quoted above also makes it clear that, for Knight, the core of Hayek's argument is the evolution of institutions by spontaneous order rather than rational design. Hayek's thesis is that liberalism is divided into two traditions: "one empirical and unsystematic, the other speculative and rationalistic—the first based on traditions and institutions which had spontaneously grown up and were imperfectly understood, the second aiming at the construction of an utopia."[20] As we will see, Knight rejects Hayek's division of the liberal tradition, arguing that it implies that spontaneous order emerges without *discussion*. For Knight, a theory of spontaneous order is not enough; liberal democracies also require a vision—a *moral* vision—of what they want their societies to become. Such visions can only be arrived at by discussion, rather than the adaptation of institutions via natural selection.

Turning to his specific objections, Knight identified three problems with *The Constitution of Liberty*. In the review essay that he developed from this abstract, Knight picked up and expanded on the second and third of these. The first problem—the one not developed further in the review essay—was Hayek's disappointing treatment of the practical aspects of the problem of personal freedom of action. The second issue was Hayek's tendency to talk about "government by law," rather than "government by discussion," as Knight was wont to do. The final issue was Hayek's attack on the notion of "social justice." Because Knight did not expand on the first issue, the focus of this chapter will be the second and third issues, although any discussion of Knight's theory of liberalism will inevitably include mention of his views on freedom. But in order to make sense of his criticisms of Hayek, we must first explore Knight's understanding of the cultural evolution of liberalism and see the central role he attributes to discussion. In the process, we will also find that, for Knight, if discussion is to be more than mere talk, it must embody our common pursuit of social ideals, including a notion of social justice.

Knight on Human Nature, Cultural Evolution, and the Liberal Revolution

From the mid-1930s, Knight, like Hayek, increasingly turned his attention from issues of economic theory to those of social philosophy. But while Hayek moved toward psychology and evolutionary theory, Knight moved toward history and ethics, fields that had played a role in his economics as well. The point of his historical account of the emergence of liberalism was that it had been won against all odds, and was now in danger of being suppressed by those seeking power in the name of either morality or science.[21] "The danger now, in the world and in the West, is that freedom will be thrown away, for a promise or hope of justice but with an actual result of neither justice nor freedom, and very likely the suicide of civilization in war without rules."[22] If we learn anything from the history of liberalism, it is that freedom must constantly be fought for, and it faces powerful opposition.

The historical account of liberalism, and its probable future, that Knight provided is built upon his argument that human nature "is a manifold paradox": "The essential fact would be that human nature as we know it— the nature of man sufficiently advanced or civilized to think and talk about his own nature—is a tissue of paradox."[23] Rather than articulating a set of common elements that define "human nature," Knight thought that every aspect of our nature comes in paradoxical combinations: we are rational, but the content of our rationality is context-dependent; we need stability and order, but crave novelty and take risks; we have to cooperate in order to exist, but want others to cooperate more with us than we do with them; we are as inhumane to others as we are humane; and we turn everything serious into a game. Because we are the product of the specific choices we have made in resolving these paradoxes, our history is essential to our nature. Knight often quoted Ortega y Gasset: "Man has no nature, what he has is . . . history."

To explain the changes that occur within the history of human societies, Knight focused on "emergent novelty."[24] "What to my mind is most important in the long sweep of change is the recurring emergence of novelty, with the new generally not replacing the old but superimposed upon it, giving rise to ever-increasing complexity."[25] The complexity that emerges from human evolution requires a pluralistic, and nonreductionist, explanation of human activity. Knight did not use pluralism as some do today to deny the authority of the sciences or to reject anthropological accounts. Physical, biological, and anthropological accounts of human activity are necessary, but not sufficient, to explain the complexity of human society. Human activity is more complex than animal activity because our cultural evolution has produced another layer of novelty: the social association of individuals who make deliberative choices in pursuit of purposes that are known to them. A complete social scientific explanation requires additional levels of analysis:

> [M]an must be described in terms of at least five fundamental kinds of entity or being. He is (*a*) a physical mechanism; (*b*) a biological organism, with characteristics extending from those of the lowest plant to the highest animal in the biological scale; (*c*) a social animal in the traditional-institutional sense; (*d*) a consciously, deliberatively purposive individual; and concomitantly, (*e*) a social being in the unique sense of an association of such individuals. . . .
> It is evident that at least the first three of these types of existence can each be the subject matter of a distinct positive science or group of such sciences. . . . It is also evident that all these sciences must in a sense take account of the social nature of man. Yet they are not social sciences. . . . The study of actual or possible society must involve a large congeries of special positive sciences, more or less effectively interrelated, co-ordinated, and unified, according to the actual possibilities of such an achievement. . . . But such study must also involve other sciences not of the positive sort, or only partly so. . . . It must involve social science in a distinctive sense, the nature of which must be considered in the light of the nature of the human individual as the real unit.[26]

Paradox, complexity, and emergence are themes common to non-Darwinian theories of evolution[27] over the past 30 years, but Knight's use of them in the 1950s and 1960s predates their rediscovery in science and philosophy by at least a decade. The complexity that leads to the uniquely human path of evolution begins, for Knight, with the emergence of "culture." Biological and physical processes controlled some of the stages that brought about the introduction of the human species, but once humans were able to "think and talk about [their] own nature," human evolution proceeded on different terms.[28]

> The essence of the emergent view is that "stages" of evolution introduced categorical novelties, somehow (usually) superposed upon what existed previously (rather than a replacement) but not to be accounted for in terms of the same concepts. A brief sketch may ignore the earlier breaks, even the appearance of organic life; but it must note the supreme discontinuity, the emergence of consciousness. This clearly cannot be explained in "physical" terms, nor in those of the main accepted theory of organic evolution—the chance occurrence of "mutations" and natural selection of those highly exceptional ones which happen to be favorable for the survival and increase of a species. Thus new strains arose, sometimes becoming distinct varieties, and occasionally new species. In the human species, when it was established, this

had not occurred. There is much prejudice to the contrary, but truth-seeking students are dropping the conception of races of man, since no one can list them, or name any one that will be generally accepted as valid. The next emergent to be stress is "culture" (in the anthropological meaning).[29]

Taking a sideswipe at the common eugenics argument of his day, Knight rejected the notion that biology differentiated the human species via some form of natural selection.[30] Rather, human diversity is the product of cultural evolution, which as we have just seen, is itself the emergent property of our biological and physical attributes. Our physical, biological, and anthropological features are similar enough to be universal to the human species; we differ at the fourth and fifth levels identified earlier—the purposes that make us individuals and the forms of deliberation that characterize our social associations.

Because culture is a "complex of social institutions,"[31] one might mistake Knight's theory of cultural evolution as similar to Hayek's, with "natural selection" across institutions functioning as the mechanism of cultural evolution. But Knight rejected biological and institutional theories of natural selection because human society is not explainable solely in terms of the evolution of institutions: human society is also an association of purposive, deliberating individuals. We cannot account for their actions without considering their history as individuals and associations of individuals.

Freedom, or "creative activity" is the "essential fact" about individuals,[32] but human freedom itself is never free. Freedom is culturally located in a complex of social institutions. Our culture, then, is as much a fact of our nature as our freedom. Freedom is always limited by that institutional complex, which arranges the choices available to us, the expectations we strive to fulfill, the hopes we seek to satisfy. For Knight, our socially located nature means that the terms on which novel human action is taken, and novel institutions are created, are set by the culture from which they emerge. But modern societies have evolved into social associations of free individuals who deliberate and discuss the actions and institutions that limit their freedom. In Knight's analysis, discussion is an integral part of cultural evolution.

Thus, cultural evolution for Knight is the process by which novel institutional forms emerge from the deliberation of, and discussion among, free, purposive individuals within specific cultural contexts. Emergent novelty, for Knight, is in constant tension with rules, laws, and institutions. Rules and institutions create the order that is essential to the perpetuation of social organization, but they also constrain the emergence of new laws and institutions. Cultural evolution is generated by the tension between the

creative activity of individuals and the order provided by the existing institutional complex.

> The supreme paradox of man, in our civilization, is that he is an individual—
> unique, creative, and dynamic—yet is the creature of institutions which must
> be accounted for in terms of historical processes. Nothing could be more false
> historically than the notion that men are naturally free and equal, or even
> that they naturally have a right to freedom. In the light of history as a whole,
> the natural state of man is to live imbedded in a "crust of custom," in which
> most of his activities, thoughts, and feelings are determined by established
> patterns. These are, or were, enforced upon him and also ingrained in his
> being, so that he hardly thought of departure from them and hence had
> little feeling of unfreedom. The existence of man as a free individual is a
> function of free society, which is the product of biological evolution and
> human culture history.[33]

The "Liberal Revolution" that created a specific institutional complex
from the tension between novelty and law as experienced in Western culture
occurred a couple of hundred years ago. Liberalism, therefore, is the emergent
property of certain social and intellectual preconditions that may or may
not be replicated elsewhere.[34] Liberalism was the first institutional form to
build upon the possibilities created by the association of purposive individuals, and is therefore intimately related to democracy. The emergent novelty
that liberalism adds to previous institutional forms is "discussion," creating
a vastly more complex form of social organization—democracy. "The
essence of democracy is the freedom of the people to change the laws at
will, by equal participation, and to have them enforced by agents held
responsible in the same way. . . . The coming of freedom to change, of
course, ended the sanctity of law."[35] For Knight, the "sanctity of law" prior
to the "Liberal Revolution" implied that law was exogenous to human
action: people had lived in a world defined by laws to which they were not
a party.[36] The Liberal Revolution changed that. Liberalism endogenized law
making—it became a part of the human evolutionary process, rather than
something external. Once liberalism emerged, cultural evolution (or, simply,
history) became the process of humans *making*—not only breaking—law.

Knight on Government by Discussion

If the Liberal Revolution was the latest stage of cultural evolution, then the
new layer of complexity that it introduced was the democratic solution of
social problems via social discussion. Knight repeatedly linked democracy to
discussion; indeed, he followed Viscount Bryce's lead in defining democracy

as "government by discussion." Because liberal democracy is the only institutional setting in which the members of a society collectively confront their common problems through discussion, it is the only society in which we might properly speak of "social problems." Liberal democracy "could be defined as the socialization of the problem of law, and it is only democracy which confronts social problems, properly speaking."[37] The links Knight saw between problem solving, freedom, and discussion within a liberal society are clear in the following passage:

> The heart of the modern social-ethical problem is to be found in the premise of freedom in a form distinctive of our culture. This premise, rooted in the elementary notion of freedom of social intercourse or discussion, means the right of individuals to associate voluntarily (and not to associate otherwise) and to form and follow their own ideals as individuals and free groups. However, the conditions of human life on the earth require many groupings accepting common ends, and common activities for their achievement, or formally organized living. Freedom requires that such organizations, based on compulsory unanimity (whether called political or not), be as free as possible and restricted in scope to a right balance with literal individual liberty and strictly voluntary association. Freedom in this conception is the essential meaning of democracy, which, so conceived, is a unique feature of modern Western civilization and gives a unique character to its problems.[38]

Behind the definition of democracy as government by discussion lies the hope that discussion in a free society can rise above the adjudication of conflicting opinions via markets and votes to become the exploration of our society's deepest values. For Frank Knight, finding hope in such discussion was no mean task, because he is well known for his skepticism regarding public opinion and "talk." In a lecture he gave at the University of Chicago on the eve of the 1932 election, Knight had articulated a "sociology of talk," the first law of which was that "Talk is cheap and drives out talk that is less cheap."[39] Such talk about discussion has led Knight's interpreters to call him not only a skeptic but also a pessimist, a cynic, or even just a gadfly.[40] But such interpretations miss the point: Knight's skepticism may dampen his hope, but does not eradicate it. Instead, it ensures that he pays careful attention to the tasks that discussion must fulfill for liberalism to rise above the mere adjudication of interests by rising incomes and majority voting.

Knight identifies five tasks that a liberal democracy can fulfill through social discussion. The first, and most important of these, is agreement on "the kind of civilization it is to create for the future; hence it must agree on the meaning of progress."[41] Whether intentionally or no, social discussion in a democratic society has as its objective "the establishment of agreement upon ethical ideals or values." Such agreement provides society with a means for reconciling the conflicting interests that characterize our social and policy problems. But lest you think Knight sanguine regarding the prospect of reaching agreement on ideals, let me remind you of the maxim Knight proclaimed most vividly in his presidential address to the American Economic Association: for every principle, there is an antiprinciple that is equally true. "The right principle is to respect all the principles, take them fully into account, and then use good judgment as to how far to follow one or another in the case in hand."[42] Reaching agreement on social ideals and their embodiment in social institutions and policies requires us to give up the quest to base society on a small set of basic principles. Instead, our discussion will not only be a pragmatic adjudication of conflicting interests, but will also require resolving the tension between competing principles, within the context of specific problems. We see here the pluralism and complexity of Knight's theory of liberalism: the solution of immediate social problems is simultaneously part of our ethical reflection together of what it means to be human, and ethical reflection is enhanced by debate of particular issues that help us to realize the limitations of our social ideals.[43]

The second requirement is agreement, again through discussion, on the rules for organizing the discussion. Knight generally accepts unanimity as the ideal of discussion within an association of free individuals, but assumes representative democracy using majority voting to be an acceptable proxy.[44] Third, discussion is required regarding the possible options for individuals in society who disagree with its final decision. How tolerant will society be of disagreement, of exit, and of the right to form new groups? Fourth, society has to decide, again via discussion, what can and what cannot be done to make progress toward the ideals that it, at least for the moment, holds as "relatively absolute."[45] Naturally, the latter discussion includes discussion of the limitations of various mechanisms—the market, the state, and other forms of social cooperation—to make progress. Finally, discussion is required of specific proposals for change, within a given definition of the social ideals, the existing rules for organization of discussion, and the chosen mechanisms for social organization. It is in the discussion of real-world situations and problems that we weigh the relevance of competing principles, interests, and claims in order to find solutions. Theory clarifies the principles and their consequences, but cannot dictate ahead of time what choices society will make for particular problems.[46]

If one looks back at the five aspects of discussion Knight identifies, there appears to be a progression from determining our ideals to acting on policy problems. But Knight did not think of these aspects as a five-stage decision-making process, despite the fact that our discussion, at any point in time, may deal with only one or two of the aspects he identified. Instead, he saw these five aspects as layers of discussion—often occurring simultaneously. In fact, he often assumed that the focus of our attention is usually on the pragmatic solution of a policy issue. The problems that arise as we attempt to solve that policy issue allow us, Knight thought, to peel back the layers to address the other layers. At least, intelligent discussion of the issues would move among the layers, redefining our "relatively absolute" absolutes, the rules of the game, and our evaluation of who may be in or out of the group even as we try to find a solution that balances competing interests (and principles) effectively.[47]

Using "Discussion" to Respond to Hayek

For Knight, then, *liberalism is the making of laws through intelligent discussion that embody "relatively absolute" social ideals aimed at solving particular social problems.* While liberal democracy may be "government by law," it is also "government by discussion," because liberalism has endogenized law making through the process of deliberative discussion. Knight's critique of Hayek is built around three arguments that draw upon this pluralistic conception of democracy as discussion.

The first response was aimed at countering Hayek's tendency to think of any government, including democracy, as a form of "government by law." For Knight, as we saw in the previous section, the Liberal Revolution broke the sanctity of law, and vested "the people" with the power to change the law. Hayek, Knight claims, does not understand the importance of the Liberal Revolution.

> Surely the crux of political democracy was and is vesting of sovereign power in "the people," to be exercised through enforcing and making laws by representatives; these are chosen freely—as freely as possible—by majority vote (sometimes plurality) where public opinion (or will) is seriously divided. It is "rule of law" indeed, but where direct force of public attitudes does not suffice, by men authorized to interpret and enforce existing formal law *and moral tradition,* making legislation necessary. The law-makers are chosen through free discussion and voting, and so held "responsible to public opinion," in the only possible way.[48]

Because Hayek is "scornful of politically organized freedom," Knight believes that *The Constitution of Liberty* is "a calumny on democracy." Hayek, we are told, is essentially an anarchist, although Knight suggests that it is "hard to be consistently absurd," and that Hayek ultimately defends policies that "humane liberals, common-sense 'pragmatists' and even popular clamor would have government do"[49]—an obvious reference to Hayek's defense of a basic social safety net and public education.

The second argument Knight makes in his critique of Hayek focuses on the uncertainty regarding institutional design that his conception of government by discussion entails. If discussion is really an exercise in "good judgment" with the goal of resolving simultaneously the overlapping tensions among competing principles and conflicting interests, then the outcome of the discussion cannot be known or determined in advance. No amount of talking about discussion can reveal what social discussion itself will conclude. Although this is, of course, an often-cited defense of Hayek's notion of spontaneous order—no expert planner could know in advance what the outcome of human actions and decisions will be—Knight turns the argument against Hayek himself in regard to his defense of the institutional arrangements of democratic capitalism. Commitment to a free society is commitment to government by discussion; but, Knight claims, commitment to government by discussion cannot guarantee that the outcome of collective action will not be a restriction of individual freedom. Our freely chosen collective decision to solve a social problem may involve the decision to use coercive action.

> The problem is not *laissez faire* versus political planning and control in general, but comparison of the result of market freedom with that of possible action by democratic procedure on specific problems. The citizen must understand the general principles of the two systems but *not* draw practical conclusions from an abstract analysis of either. The basic principles are facts about human nature; and the major difficulty is that this is a tissue of paradox.[50]

Knight concludes his review of Hayek's *Constitution of Liberty* by saying: "The most one can say for freedom is that there is a presumption in its favor unless there is sufficient ground to believe that coercive action will yield a better result in a particular situation.[51]

Knight's last criticism of Hayek focuses on the ethical aspect of government by discussion, and its implications for Hayek's attack on "social justice." While it may be absurd to argue that an entity called "society" has some conception of justice apart from the values accepted by the individuals in the society that will assist with the adjudication of conflicting interests (here Knight concurs with Hayek), Knight still holds out hope that the individuals in society will, through discussion, come to a common conception—at least a "relatively absolute" conception—of what *distributive* justice means for their society, in the context of the particular problems they face at this time. To deny that justice can mean something more than adherence to the law means, for Knight, that one denies the reality of human nature. Knight concludes:

> It seems that all human sense of right and wrong—the latter more real—is also "illusion." Hayek expressly repudiates "social justice." . . . For him, justice is still defined, once and for all, by laws, and those are produced by spontaneous historical growth, not "made" by either men or God.[52]

His brief remarks about Hayek on social justice reflect the tension between pragmatism and idealism present in his pluralistic conception of liberalism. Labelling as "notably absurd" Hayek's views on equality generally, Knight says that "the error is in the extremism," or Hayek's "absolutism." He passes over cursorily the argument Hayek makes regarding the desirability of redistribution as insufficient justification for the use of coercive force, in order to point out that Hayek takes too casually the social requirement for coercion implied by liberalism's adherence to "equality before the law." Does not equality before the law—if not in its maintenance than in its original establishment—require the exercise of coercion as much as redistribution might? And, while power and freedom are separate concepts, Knight argues that it "is absurd for Hayek to ignore the close connection between the two. Freedom, correctly conceived, implies opportunity, unobstructed opportunity, to use power, which must be possessed, to give content to freedom, or make it effective."[53] To Knight, Hayek's failure to acknowledge the relation between power and freedom prevents him from recognizing that "unequal power over things confers power over persons, or that the main general problem of freedom is unequal power, practically covering significant human inequality."[54] Because economic activity in markets creates "unequal power over things," Knight argues that a liberal society must always be thinking about distributive justice as a part of its discussion of social problems.[55] Hayek's limited conception of justice prevented him from realizing that the gradual erosion of economic equality in early twentieth-century America had quite rightly, Knight thought, led to "preventive or offsetting social action on a vast scale,"[56] as social discussion sought a new resolution of the tension between freedom and justice. Thus, for Knight, social justice can be no mirage, even if it is an ideal of which we have only a fleeting glimpse.

Liberalism Reunited: Liberty *and* Justice for All

In conclusion, Knight's response to Hayek's *Constitution of Liberty* is a rejection of Hayek's argument that liberalism had been erroneously divided during the Enlightenment. Rather than affirming "spontaneous order" as the core of true liberalism[57] and rejecting any role for discussion of social ideals and justice in a liberal society, Knight chose to affirm both the order that emerges from a competitive economy *and* the outcomes of social discussions about our ideals, including social justice. Indeed, his argument suggests that the interplay of liberty and justice, carried out in markets and social discussion, is at the core of a liberal democracy. Hayek's refusal to move beyond "government by law" is, for Knight, a rejection of that core, which he believed to be better encapsulated in the notion that democracy is "government by discussion."

Hidden in Knight's affirmation of discussion is an element of hope that is alien to our general understanding of Knight's work. It is the hope for social betterment through discussion, most tantalizingly expressed in his fleeting comments about social justice, that surprises the reader familiar with Knight's more frequent gloomy and skeptical tone. Obvious aspects of his skepticism are present in the response to Hayek—in his talk of conflicting principles and the lack of a universal human nature, for example—but these are mitigated by the hope implicit in his emphatic defense of open discussion. There is no need to defend discussion if the outcome can be known ahead of time, or is simply chaos to be avoided by well-defined and enforced rules for the game. Knight defends discussion because, for him, the future remains open, to both unknown promise and chaos. Despite his fear of chaos, and his belief in human fallibility, Knight holds out hope that intelligent discussion can assist us to create a better world.

What does Hayek fear, what does he believe about human nature, and what does he think the future holds? Ultimately, Knight's challenge to Hayek, and perhaps even to himself, is to provide an account of the future that takes humans as we find them, and still allows something more than the evolution of law—perhaps something like free discussion among humans about their ideals and values—to ensure that the future will provide liberty and justice for all.

Notes

My understanding of both Knight and Hayek has benefited from conversations with David Levy, Jim Buchanan, Warren Samuels, Geoff Brennan, Paul Heyne, Richard Boyd, Bruce Caldwell, Peter Boettke, Sandra Peart, Andrew Farrant, Dan Hammond, and the students in my Constitutional Political Economy senior seminar at James Madison College in Fall 2005. I also wish to thank participants at the earlier presentation of a related paper at the History of Economics Society meeting at Wake Forest University in July 2001 and at the Summer Institute for the Preservation of the History of Economic Thought at the Center for the Study of Public Choice at George Mason University in August 2000 for their comments, as well as Steve Kautz,

Louis Hunt, and Philip Bretton for their questions and comments at the presentation of this paper at the Political Philosophy Colloquium at Michigan State University in September 2006. Permission for the use of materials from the Frank H. Knight Papers has been granted by the University of Chicago Archives. The usual remarks regarding authorial culpability and responsibility apply.

1. James M. Buchanan, *Why I, Too, Am Not A Conservative: The Normative Vision of Classical Liberalism* (Cheltenham, UK: Edward Elgar, 2005), p. 10.
2. F. H. Knight to the General Editor and Committee on Publication, University of Chicago Press, December 10, 1943, Box 40, Folder 17, Frank H. Knight Papers, University of Chicago Archives.
3. See Bruce Caldwell. *Hayek's Challenge: An Intellectual Biography of F. A. Hayek.* (Chicago: University of Chicago Press, 2005), pp. 232–261.
4. Frank H. Knight, "Laissez-Faire: Pro and Con" (1967) in *Selected Essays of Frank H. Knight,* vol. 2, *Laissez-Faire: Pro and Con,* ed. R. B. Emmett (Chicago: University of Chicago Press, 1999), p. 451n. 6.
5. Hayek called social justice a mirage in a book published a few years after Knight's death. See Friedrich A. Hayek, *Law, Legislation and Liberty,* vol. 2, *The Mirage of Social Justice* (Chicago: University of Chicago Press, 1976).
6. Frank H. Knight, "Social Science" (1941), in *On the History and Method of Economics: Selected Essays* (Chicago: University of Chicago Press, 1956), p. 133.
7. The phrase "government by discussion"—frequently repeated in Knight's writing—is borrowed (with acknowledgment) from Viscount James Bryce, who provided us with the other memorable nineteenth-century account of American democracy by a non-American. James Bryce, *The American Commonwealth.* 2 vols. (1888; repr. New York: G. P. Putnam's Sons, 1959).
8. See S. M. Amadae, *Rationalizing Capitalist Democracy: The Cold War Origins of Rational Choice Liberalism* (Chicago: University of Chicago Press, 2003).
9. R. M. Hartwell, *A History of the Mont Pelerin Society* (Indianapolis: Liberty Fund, 1995).
10. Knight offered at best lukewarm support, if not back-room opposition, to an appointment for Hayek in the economics department. Hayek ended up in the Committee on Social Thought (CST), with his salary subsidized by the Volker Fund.
11. See Frank H. Knight, *The Economic Organization* (Chicago: University of Chicago Press, 1933).
12. See Ross B. Emmett, "The Economist and the Entrepreneur: Modernist Impulses in Frank H. Knight's *Risk, Uncertainty and Profit,*" *History of Political Economy* 31 (Spring, 1999): 29–52.
13. See Avi J. Cohen, "The Hayek/Knight Capital Controversy: The Irrelevance of Roundaboutness, or Purging Processes in Time?" *History of Political Economy* 35, no. 3 (2003): 469–490.
14. Peter Boettke and Karen Vaughn, "Knight and the Austrians on Capital, and the Problem of Socialism." *History of Political Economy* 34, no. 1 (2002): 155–176.

15. Friedrich A. Hayek, "On the Relationship between Investment and Output," *Economic Journal* 44 (June 1934): 207–231.

16. F. H. Knight to F. A. Hayek, [December] 1934, Box 60, Folder 10, Frank H. Knight Papers, University of Chicago Archives.

17. Friedrich A. Hayek, "The Intellectuals and Socialism," *University of Chicago Law Review* 16 (Spring 1949): 417–433; and Frank H. Knight, "World Justice, Socialism, and the Intellectuals," *University of Chicago Law Review* 16 (Spring 1949): 433–434.

18. Knight, "Laissez-Faire: Pro and Con."

19. Ibid., p. 451n. 6.

20. Ibid., p. 443.

21. Frank H. Knight and Thornton W. Merriam, *The Economic Order and Religion.* New York: Harper, 1945), pp. 13–126, and Frank H. Knight, "The Sickness of Liberal Society" (1946), in *Selected Essays by Frank H. Knight,* pp. 284–313.

22. Frank H. Knight, "Science, Society, and the Modes of Law" (1956), in *Selected Essays by Frank H. Knight,* pp. 392–410.

23. Frank H. Knight, "Human Nature and World Democracy" (1944), in *Freedom and Reform,* pp. 358–384 at pp. 358–359.

24. Frank H. Knight, "Economics and Human Evolution," Paper presented at Man in Transition—An Anthropological Study, Antioch College Office of Continuing Education, Yellow Springs, Ohio, February 1961. Box 12, Folder 23, Frank H. Knight Papers, University of Chicago Archives.

25. Knight, "Science, Society, and the Modes of Law," p. 401.

26. Knight, "Social Science," pp. 125–126.

27. "Non-Darwinian" is used here to indicate theories of evolution that adopt mechanisms other than chance and natural selection as the primary bases for evolutionary change. No modern theory of evolution denies the role of chance and natural selection; but some deny the primacy they are given in the Darwinian account of evolutionary change.

28. Knight, "Economics and Human Evolution," p. 11.

29. Frank H. Knight, "Philosophy and Social Institutions in the West" (1962), in *Selected Essays by Frank H. Knight,* p. 413.

30. Knight, "Economics and Human Evolution," p. 4.

31. Frank H. Knight, "The Rights of Man and Natural Law" (1944), in *Selected Essays by Frank H. Knight,* pp. 209–242 at p. 233.

32. Frank H. Knight, "Human Nature and World Democracy" (1944), in *Freedom and Reform,* pp. 358–384 at p. 363.

33. Ibid., p. 363.

34. See Knight, "Philosophy and Social Institutions in the West."

35. Knight, "Science, Society, and the Modes of Law," p. 406.

36. Knight quoted favorably the familiar line from William Penn's preface to *The Frame of Government:* "Any government is free to the people under it . . . where the laws rule, and the people are a party to those laws." Knight, "Laissez-Faire: Pro and Con," p. 443.

37. Knight, "Science, Society, and the Modes of Law," p. 394.
38. Knight and Merriam, *The Economic Order and Religion,* pp. 53–54.
39. Frank H. Knight, "The Case for Communism: From the Standpoint of an Ex-Liberal," in *Research in the History of Economic Thought and Methodology, Archival Supplement,* ed. W. J. Samuels (1932; repr., Stamford, CT: JAI Press, 1991), pp. 57–108.
40. See, respectively, Richard A. Gonce, "The Role of Pessimism in Frank H. Knight's Political Economy," Paper presented at History of Economics Society, College of Charleston, South Carolina, 1997; Don Patinkin, "Frank Knight as Teacher," in *Essays on and in the Chicago Tradition* (Durham: Duke University, 1981), pp. 23–51 at p. 48; and Edward A. Purcell, Jr., *The Crisis of Democratic Theory: Scientific Naturalism & the Problem of Value* (Lexington: University Press of Kentucky, 1973), p. 43.
41. Knight, "Science, Society, and the Modes of Law," p. 407.
42. Frank H. Knight, "The Role of Principles in Economics and Politics" (1951), in *Selected Essays by Frank H. Knight,* pp. 361–391 at p. 366.
43. Because this is familiar ground to political theorists, we might pause here to note that Knight makes a parallel move in his discussion of the functions of a market—the other side of the democratic capitalism that he wishes to defend. The first function of an economic system, Knight told us in his earliest "text-book"—*The Economic Organization*—is "the fixing of standards":

> In a world where organizations were absent, where each individual carried on his life activities in isolation and independence of all others, the matter of standards would be simply a matter of individual choice. But when the production of wealth is socialized, there has to be a *social* decision as to the relative importance of different uses of productive power, as to which wants are to be satisfied and which left unsatisfied or to what extent any one is to be satisfied at the expense of any other. In the case of an individual, choice need be made only among his own wants; but in a social system, the wants of different individuals also come into conflict. As far as this is a quantitative question merely, of how far the wants of one are to be gratified at the expense of the wants of another, or left ungratified in favor of another, the problem is one of *distribution,* and will be noticed under another heading (the third function). But to a large and increasing extent, society finds it necessary or advisable further to regulate the individual's regulation of his own want-satisfaction, to enforce a community standard of living. As a matter of fact, these two problems are closely interlaced, the question of *whose* wants and that of *which* wants are to be given preference, and in what measure. It is important to observe that they are largely the same question.
>
> (pp. 6–7)

44. "The ideal meaning of 'government by discussion' . . . would be establishment of unanimous agreement through intellectual process or activity, without any

employment of coercive power. That is, it would be anarchy. But we must assume as admitted that this ideal is impossible." "The Planful Act," p. 402.

45. Knight, "The Rights of Man and Natural Law," pp. 238–240.
46. See Knight, "The Role of Principles in Economics and Politics."
47. See Frank H. Knight, *Intelligence and Democratic Action* (Cambridge: Harvard University Press, 1960).
48. Knight, "Laissez-Faire: Pro and Con," pp. 443.
49. Ibid., pp. 443–444.
50. Ibid., p. 449.
51. Ibid., p. 450.
52. Ibid., p. 448.
53. Ibid., p. 445.
54. Ibid.
55. Knight had arguments for years with Milton Friedman and George Stigler about this issue. See George Stigler, *Memoirs of an Unregulated Economist* (New York: Basic Books, 1988). Against the arguments of Hayek and the Chicago economists, Knight insisted that market exchange and the right of property inheritance necessarily generated greater economic inequality over time.
56. Knight, "Laissez-Faire: Pro and Con," p. 446.
57. See Friedrich A. Hayek, "Individualism: True and False" in (1945), in *Individualism and Economic Order* (Chicago: University of Chicago Press, 1948), pp. 1–32.

CHAPTER 5

F. A. Hayek, Michael Oakeshott, and the Concept of Spontaneous Order

Richard Boyd and James Ashley Morrison

Introduction: The Hayek-Oakeshott Debates

The relationship between F. A. Hayek and Michael Oakeshott presents a puzzle to those interested in classical liberalism and the concept of spontaneous order. Hayek and Oakeshott were arguably two of the most influential postwar critics of state planning and defenders of liberty in the Anglo-American world. They were at least good acquaintances from years in London, exchanging comments on one another's work into the late 1960s.[1] After decades of writing on questions of liberty, the rule of law, and a free society both produced synoptic books in the 1970s—Hayek's *Law, Legislation and Liberty* trilogy, published between 1973 and 1979, and Oakeshott's *On Human Conduct,* published in 1975. These works are not only the culmination of their individual philosophical projects, but they represent a convergence of their ideas after decades of apparent disagreement. For despite their considerable affinities, Hayek and Oakeshott gave every impression of being intellectually at odds with one another throughout their long and distinguished careers.

There was, first, Oakeshott's notorious swipe at Hayek's 1944 book, *The Road to Serfdom.* While acknowledging that "a plan to resist all planning may be better than its opposite," Oakeshott complained that Hayek's libertarianism belonged to the same ideological "style of politics" as the collectivists he was criticizing.[2] For his part, Hayek's appendix to *The Constitution of Liberty* (1960), entitled "Why I Am Not a Conservative," famously juxtaposed his own variant of classical liberalism with a backward-looking and nostalgic conservatism of the sort commonly associated with Oakeshott. According to Hayek, conservatism differs fundamentally from liberalism (in both of its varieties, classical and modern) in terms of its attitude toward social change. Whereas liberals celebrate "evolution and change," conservatives "lack the faith in the spontaneous forces of adjustment which makes the liberal accept changes without apprehension."[3] Despite their common cause in resisting the "collectivist tide," liberals are essentially forward-looking while conservatives cling to a "nostalgic longing for the past or a romantic admiration for what has been."[4] Liberalism's defining characteristic "is that it wants to go elsewhere, not to stand still."[5] Indeed "where spontaneous change has been smothered by government control . . . what is most urgently needed . . . is a thorough sweeping-away of the obstacles to free growth."[6] Hayek even goes so far as to suggest that conservatism's complete lack of "general principles which are always the same" disqualifies it as a political philosophy.[7]

Hayek's dismissal of conservatism as stodgy, authoritarian, and intellectually impoverished stands in vivid contrast to Oakeshott's essay "On Being Conservative," an elegant plea on behalf of the conservative disposition. Like many of the great conservative thinkers before him, Oakeshott indicts wholesale social change as disruptive of the existential sense of familiarity that links us to the past. Oakeshott does not deny that many institutions, moral traditions, and practices are absurd, archaic, and even morally abominable, but his conservatism is rooted in the conviction that every tradition, no matter how flawed, has at least something to recommend it. Conversely, efforts directed toward reform or social improvement—whether initiated from above by would-be planners, or from below by the creative destruction of the free market—are never unalloyed progress. "There is no such thing as an unqualified improvement," and change is by its very nature an "emblem of extinction."[8] The loss of something valuable in a tradition is a certainty, whereas potential gain is only a probability.[9] Although Oakeshott's species of philosophical conservatism is innocent of the imperialistic imposition of one's values on others of which Hayek complained, Oakeshott is guilty as charged in lacking Hayek's "liberal" confidence in the necessary superiority of all future worlds.

The magnitude of these disagreements between two great postwar defenders of liberty calls for explanation, if not reconciliation, and the following chapter will attempt something of both. We will first sketch out the surprising affinities between the two thinkers' social philosophies. Despite their professions to the contrary, Hayek and Oakeshott have remarkably similar understandings of how complex social orders develop spontaneously over time; of the threat that "scientism" and "rationalism," respectively, pose to evolved orders; and of how the spontaneity of a market order is facilitated by what Hayek called "abstract rules of just conduct" or what Oakeshott referred to as the moral rules of "civil association." Having underscored these similarities, we will return to the question of whether there really is a qualitative difference between their variants of "liberalism" and "conservatism." Although these two great "conservative liberal" thinkers may be more intellectually kindred spirits than either was prepared to admit, we conclude that there is indeed a categorical difference between their political theories. While Hayek and Oakeshott found common political cause in resisting the "fatal conceit" of state planning, their philosophical disagreements ultimately stem from Hayek's unwillingness to apply his own epistemological skepticism about human knowledge to the actions of individuals in the market order. Precisely because of this, Hayek's "liberal" optimism about the progressive and cumulative benefits of the competitive market order diverges sharply from Oakeshott's "conservative" skepticism about the ability of human beings—either collectively or individually—to secure an unambiguously superior future.

Hayek and Oakeshott on Spontaneous Orders

A major similarity between Hayek and Oakeshott is their recognition that social orders may be, as Hayek termed it, "the product of human action but not of human design."[10] This notion of "spontaneous order" is already conspicuous in Hayek's *Constitution of Liberty,* but it is developed most fully in volume 1 of *Law, Legislation and Liberty* (1973), where Hayek invents an entirely new conceptual vocabulary to capture the distinction between orders that were deliberately designed and those that evolved spontaneously. The former are known as *taxis,* or "made orders," while *kosmos* describes the latter, "grown" or "spontaneous orders."[11] Hayek's archetypical example of the former was an army or an order of battle—an "organization" that is deliberately planned and where every particular action within the organization is controlled by some superintending entity.[12] Unlike spontaneous orders, which are constituted only by agreement about some basic, underlying rules, these planned orders are determined by "commands" that dictate the actions of all subsidiary parts of the order. In contrast to *taxis,* where there is both a deliberate act of creation and some overarching function or end that this order is intended to fulfill, *kosmos* are the collective product of individuals pursuing their self-chosen ends independent of any superintending purpose or goal. The common rules that bring spontaneous orders into being serve only to minimize uncertainty and maximize predictability and coordination. Examples of spontaneous orders include social institutions such as language, morals, laws (understood as general rules rather than commands), market orders, and other conventions that could have arisen only through an extended order of cooperative interactions.[13]

Spontaneous and planned orders also differ with respect to their complexity. Planned orders do not grow beyond the original designs of their founders, and so it is possible for a given individual to understand both their general structure and internal workings.[14] Spontaneous orders, however, are never planned, and thus their complexity may be infinite.[15] These orders are frequently "adaptation[s] to a large number of particular facts which will not be known in their totality to anyone."[16] Although we can make general predictions about the overall shape these orders will take, "we will never be able to determine more than the general principles on which they operate or to predict the particular changes that any event in the environment will bring about."[17] While this aspect of spontaneous orders might seem intellectually daunting, it is actually one of their main advantages. For if our social cooperation with others were limited only to face-to-face interactions with individuals known personally, something like the "great society" or "extended economic order" in which Hayek invests so much confidence would be impossible.

Because all we can ever know are "the general principles on which they operate," we are "able to influence only the general character and not the detail of the resulting order."[18] Hayek's favorite examples were laboratory-created crystals or iron filings shaped by the fields of force around a magnet. We can apprehend the general pattern of the resulting crystal or the fields of magnetic force revealed by the iron filings, but we can never predict or control the peculiarities of crystals or the location of individual iron filings within the general fields of magnetic force.[19] "In consequence," Hayek infers, "the degree of power of control over the extended and more complex order will be much smaller than that which we could exercise over a made order or *taxis*."[20] This recognition of the limits of our ability to manipulate the outcomes of spontaneous orders becomes the cornerstone of Hayek's political theory. Hayek criticized attempts to "supplement the rules governing a spontaneous order by isolated and subsidiary commands concerning those activities where the actions are guided by the general rules of conduct."[21] While Hayek conceded that it might sometimes be possible "to improve a spontaneous order by revising the general rules on which it rests," this was best avoided.[22]

Like Hayek's spontaneous orders, Oakeshott's customs and traditions are not the product of any individual mind or founder. They are collective achievements of an entire tradition, slowly evolving over many centuries as time-tested institutions and traditions are gradually modified in response to new circumstances. These "practices," "customs," or "traditions" contain a reservoir of practical knowledge that makes them virtually impossible to replicate because of the limitations of human reason. Not only is there a presumptive wisdom embodied in practices and institutions handed down to us from the past, as Edmund Burke and other conservative philosophers argued, but, above and beyond any functional benefit they might confer because of their accumulated wisdom, such practices or customs are also valuable because of their venerable character and existential familiarity.[23]

Oakeshott is also aware of the entrenched assumptions of many that all complex orders must have been created deliberately, and that if they were created, then they can necessarily be recreated or improved. Oakeshott's refutations of these fallacies come very close to Hayek's celebrated formulations. The existing order, in Oakeshott's words, "is an acquired condition, though nobody designed or specifically chose it in preference to all others." This order is nothing more or less than the collective achievement of "human beings impelled by a love of making choices for themselves." Thus its content in the future is as indeterminate and unspecifiable as "the fashion in hats of twenty years' time or the design of motor-cars."[24] Because something as complex as a tradition is the collective accomplishment of an entire civilization, individuals in the present might more easily destroy an inherited tradition than substitute anything of similar resilience and complexity in its place. Traditions are based on the "principle of *continuity*: authority is diffused between past, present, and future; between the old, the new, and what is to come."[25] This is not to say that traditions are monolithic or unvarying. Precisely the contrary: although a given tradition always moves, "it is never wholly in motion; and though it is tranquil, it is never wholly at rest."[26]

Oakeshott, however, went further than Hayek in stressing the aesthetic dimension of evolved orders. Our fondness for doing things in the familiar way stems not so much from any innate superiority or efficiency in this way of arranging one's affairs as from the fact that this is our own way of doing things. Social and political institutions are venerable because of the continuity they provide between our lives and the lives of others who have similarly experienced these orders. This conservative insight is akin to a cultivated taste or sensibility. "Surveying the scene," Oakeshott notes, "some people are provoked by the absence of order and coherence which appears to them to be its dominant feature." They see only its apparent "wastefulness, its frustration, its dissipation of human energy, its lack not merely of a premeditated destination but even of any discernible direction of motion."[27] From this spectacle of apparent disorder it is only one further step to the conclusion that "something . . . ought to be done to convert this so-called chaos into order."[28] But no matter how well intentioned this impulse, it rests on an illusory dream of "human activity co-ordinated and set going in a single direction and of every resource being used to the full." Satisfying this impulse would require this private dream to be imposed upon its subjects against their will.[29]

This leads Oakeshott to be agnostic with respect to the question of whether the future will be better than the past. "Innovating is always an equivocal enterprise," Oakeshott notes, "in which gain and loss (even excluding the loss of familiarity) are so closely interwoven that . . . there is no such thing as an unqualified improvement."[30] Something is lost by *any* change, even if this change is ultimately for the better.[31] Innovation is not improvement so much as the disruption of expectations and familiarity that must be accommodated only with great reluctance and inconvenience. Even the most salutary changes must be "suffered" rather than celebrated.[32] Thus, Oakeshott's skepticism about the relative probability of progress versus regress does not stem from any empirical difference from Hayek's understanding of how spontaneous orders form or evolve. Rather, the difference stems, at least in part, from Oakeshott's philosophical pluralism: the notion that above and beyond standards such as efficiency or utility, there are any number of categorially distinctive moral perspectives—the ethical, aesthetic, religious, or poetic— against which something as amorphous as "progress" can be measured.[33]

Hayek's Critique of Scientism and Oakeshott's Critique of Rationalism

Similarities between Hayek and Oakeshott are not exhausted by their common appreciation of the value of evolved social orders. Both saw spontaneous orders being threatened by a "constructivist rationalism" that had deeply infected modern social and political thought. In a series of influential essays in the 1940s and 1950s, Hayek and Oakeshott criticized the positivistic application of natural science methodologies to social and political orders where they are inappropriate and even dangerous. There are remarkable similarities between what Hayek termed "scientism" and what Oakeshott termed "rationalism," and both saw these pernicious intellectual currents as threatening the idea of social orders as evolved or grown over time.

While Hayek was a lifelong critic of the hubris of state planners who mistakenly claimed to have all the knowledge necessary to order an entire society, his most focused complaints about the fallacy of "scientism" came in a series of essays later collected and published as *The Counter-Revolution of Science* in 1952.[34] There Hayek attacked fashionable attempts to study the social world in the same mode in which the natural sciences study the physical world. As a good liberal, Hayek could not entirely fault the progress of science: "the general spirit of disinterested inquiry" *has* advanced the study of social phenomena.[35] Science has led to the rejection of anthropomorphism, and it has placed greater weight on empirically verifying "concepts formed from ordinary experience on the basis of a systematic testing of the phenomena."[36] Thus Hayek's complaint was not against science but what he called "scientism" and the "scientistic prejudice," "the slavish imitation of the method and language of Science" without taking into account fundamental differences between the physical and the social worlds.[37]

According to Hayek, the social world rests on subjective ideas and perceptions while the physical world comprises objective organisms or elements. "Beliefs" and "attitudes" are "the elements from which we build up the structure of possible relationships between individuals."[38] Thus "social wholes, unlike the biological organisms, are not given to us as natural units, fixed complexes which ordinary experience shows us to belong together, but are recognizable only by a process of mental reconstruction."[39] This means that the social world must be studied differently than the physical universe. Social science must be "subjective" (unlike the "objectivity" of the physical sciences) because "the 'facts' of the social sciences are also opinions," "views held by the people whose actions we study."[40] The "wholes" of the social world are mental constructs that frequently have little or nothing in common from a physical standpoint and which can rarely be expressed in physical terms.[41]

Positivistic social science, however, assumes that the "wholes" of the social world—metaphorical abstractions such as "society," the "economy," or "capitalism"—are "definitely given objects about which we can discover laws by observing their behavior as wholes."[42] This holistic or "collectivist" perspective stands in contrast to the methodological individualism Hayek advocated.[43] The former perspective treats complex social phenomena "not as something of which the human mind is a part and the principles of whose organization we can reconstruct from the familiar parts, but as if they were objects directly perceived by us as wholes."[44] Hayek also attacks the "historicism" of scientism, or the idea that we can look at history and deduce ironclad rules or an inner logic by which historical developments necessarily come to pass. The danger of applying the methodologies of the physical sciences to the social world is not just that positivists get things wrong, but that their holism and determinism lead them to ignore the role of free will, motivations, and subjective ideas in shaping social phenomena.

Scientism further mistakes the character of spontaneous orders. Because they are premised on the subjectivity of individual decisions freely chosen and comprehensible only from the point of view of the individual participants themselves, spontaneous orders are unintelligible in terms of natural, objective units.[45] Collectivists looking at them from the outside as organisms or entities are simply incapable of grasping "how the independent action of many men can produce coherent wholes, persistent structures of relationships which serve important human purposes without having been designed for that end."[46] The constructivist rationalist "belief that nothing which has not been consciously designed can be useful or even essential to the achievement of human purposes" blurs into "the belief that since all 'institutions' have been made by man, we must have complete power to refashion them in any way we desire."[47]

Oakeshott's reputation as the leading postwar conservative philosopher owes much to his celebrated essays collected in *Rationalism in Politics and Other Essays* (originally published in 1962). On the critical side, Oakeshott dissects the modern rationalist impulse that would substitute formal, logical, and rigid principles for the circumstances and contingencies of everyday life. Rather than being informed by a "genuine, concrete knowledge" of existing circumstances, rationalism is the "politics of the felt need," an impulse to reform or reorder a society as "interpreted by reason and satisfied according to the technique of an ideology."[48] This caustic rationalism is inspired by a mistaken confidence that the techniques of the modern natural sciences can be applied with equal success to moral and political orders.[49] Such rational ideas are "political ideologies," "abstract principles" that purport to supply a comprehensive blueprint of how society ought to be ordered and what ends ought properly to be pursued by individual actors. The main task of government in this view is guaranteeing "that the arrangements of society conform to or reflect the chosen abstract idea."[50]

The problem with this kind of rational knowledge is twofold. First, such "false and misleading" ideological visions are at best merely an "abridgment," "caricature," or "distorting mirror" of an infinitely more complex tradition.[51] While they can serve to highlight certain prominent features of the tradition in question, they can never capture all the relevant knowledge demanded by the art of politics. For the same reason that even the tastiest recipe is likely to founder in the hands of an inexperienced cook, such ideological abridgements of practice attempt to substitute scientific, theoretical knowledge in place of concrete, practical knowledge that can never be codified and that can be learnt only by actually doing the activity in question. Second, because these ideological visions are always abstractions from some particular political tradition, there is no Archimedean point of view outside of the tradition itself against which it might be judged or amended. Politics can never be more than the "pursuit of intimations" within the flow of a given tradition of behavior.[52] There is no such thing as a "steady, unchanging, independent guide [such as reason] to which a society might resort."[53]

The very concept of "rationality" rests on a fallacy that there is some transcendental "reason"—or infallible scientific method of designating what is "rational"—that is true in all times and places. According to Oakeshott, the mind is not, as it is often assumed to be, "an independent instrument capable of dealing with experience" but is itself an "offspring of knowledge and activity."[54] Thus it is impossible to speak of something as "rational," independent of the particular exigencies of current circumstances. Even when we are trying to accomplish something as apparently straightforward as baking a cake, our ends can never be premeditated in advance of the broader tradition of cooking of which they are a part.[55] Oakeshott's most famous example was of the Victorian planners who contrived "Bloomers" as the most perfectly "rational" article of women's clothing for riding a bicycle. The so-called "rational" solution at which they arrived is deeply laden with unconsidered assumptions from which these inventors were unable to extricate themselves. Bloomers are not the answer to the question of what clothing is most rational for a woman to wear while propelling a bicycle, but rather to the more conditioned inquiry, "What garment combines within itself the qualities of being well adapted to the activity of propelling a bicycle and of being suitable, all things considered, for a English girl to be seen in when riding a bicycle in 1880?"[56] We must always ask ourselves "rational" according to what? Again, as in the case of progress, the answer cannot be disentangled easily from the assumptions and value judgments that motivate the question itself.

Hayek and Oakeshott on Rules, Order, and Liberty

Yet a third similarity between Hayek and Oakeshott comes clearly into view only in their late, synoptic works: Hayek's *Law, Legislation and Liberty* trilogy and Oakeshott's *On Human Conduct*. Both stress the importance of relatively stable and purposively neutral rules in facilitating the creation of spontaneous orders. For Hayek, these "abstract rules of just conduct" provide underlying agreement about the means individuals may legitimately use in pursuit of their self-chosen ends while leaving the content of those ends unspecified. Likewise, for Oakeshott, the rules of "civil association," like the rules of language, provide "adverbial conditions" that allow individuals to form "enterprise associations" based on shared purposes and to engage in "self-disclosure" and "self-enactment."[57] Both of these works defend purposively neutral legal systems because of the complex orders they make possible. This shift of focus brings to light the "conservative" side of Hayek's writings—namely, his preference for continuity in the rule of law that makes market orders possible—as well as the full extent of Oakeshott's "liberalism"—particularly the value of individual choice in the determination of one's purposes or ends.

For all of Hayek's talk of orders arising "spontaneously," it is important to note that these orders are only possible because of certain "general rules on which [the spontaneous order] rests." *Law, Legislation and Liberty* is concerned with the nature and evolution of "abstract rules of just conduct" the concrete manifestation of which is the rule of law. Law, however, not only provides the framework for spontaneous orders to develop, but under most ordinary circumstances law is itself a kind of spontaneous order. As Hayek notes, "The system of rules as a whole does not owe its structure to the design of either judges or legislators. It is the outcome of a process of evolution in the course of which spontaneous growth of customs and deliberate improvements of the particulars of an existing system have constantly interacted."[58] In the common law system in particular, law develops without any predetermined destination. Ideally the decisions of judges are not guided by "any knowledge of what the whole of society requires at the particular moment, but solely [by] what is demanded by general principles on which the going order of society is based."[59] While Hayek does not rule out the "occasional intervention of a legislator" to "deal with altogether new problems" or to rescue the legal system from certain evolutionary "dead ends," these are exceptions rather than the rule.[60]

Despite his protests against an unthinking conservative reverence for the past and the status quo, Hayek does acknowledge the importance of continuity in the basic structure of society. "Common conventions and traditions," even if informal and unenforceable, "make the behavior of other people predictable" and "enable them to work together smoothly and efficiently."[61] Without some more or less continuous system of justice—property rights, rules of title and transfer, and the enforceability of contracts—the expectations of individuals that are premised on these institutions are likely to be cast into disarray. Nonetheless, even if Hayek does not envision the laws of society to be perfectly static—and he denies that the task of judges is simply to maintain the status quo—the dynamically evolving spontaneous orders he champions are destroyed by radical changes in the underlying legal order of society.[62]

Hayek is also adamant that the law must be purposively neutral.[63] "The aim of the rules of law," Hayek posits, "is merely to prevent as much as possible, by drawing boundaries, the actions of different individuals from interfering with each other; they cannot alone determine, and also therefore cannot be concerned with, what the result for different individuals will be."[64] When the law functions in this way, individuals are able to act freely because the law enhances the "maximal coincidence of expectations" for all parties.[65] These demands include minimizing conflicts and maximizing the satisfaction of legitimate expectations on the part of individuals. Above and beyond this, the rule of law has no predetermined function, end, or goal of its own.

Hayek's description of "abstract rules of just conduct" bears an uncanny resemblance to what Oakeshott calls "general rules of conduct" in "On Being Conservative."[66] Like the moral rules of "civil association" later described in *On Human Conduct,* these general rules of process and procedure are akin to "tools," "instruments," or means "enabling people to pursue the activities of their own choice with the minimum frustration."[67] Although there can of course be some technological change with respect to tools—and new tools may be required in response to new exigencies—without some underlying agreement about these means of proceeding, nothing at all would be accomplished. A plumber would fix few sinks indeed if he had to reinvent the screwdriver or pipe wrench before each and every task. "The chief virtue of these arrangements," Oakeshott notes in language reminiscent of Hayek, "is that they are fixed and familiar" allowing them to "establish and satisfy certain expectations."[68] In the metaphor of language deployed in *On Human Conduct,* without some underlying agreement to subscribe to certain conditions of grammar, syntax, and vocabulary, we would be unable to partake of the goods of conversation or to make utterances that others would find comprehensible.[69]

Interestingly, both Hayek and Oakeshott recur to the analogy of games to account for the relationship between rules, order, and liberty. In an appendix to *The Fatal Conceit* Hayek suggests that too little has been done to explore the idea of freedom in terms of a competitive game, and Oakeshott's defense of the conservative disposition also invokes the metaphor of the game.[70] While enterprising players may devise new tactics in order to best their opponents, it is "supremely inappropriate" to revisit the question of the rules themselves in the midst of the heat of play.[71] Two points deserve emphasis. First, within the horizon of given rules, the outcomes of individual matches and the conduct of individual players will be unpredictable and unspecifiable. Contests between enterprising players may be characterized by fluidity and innovation consistent with the underlying rules. Second, and more importantly, it is inappropriate to tinker with the rules themselves, lest these changes confound the mutual expectations of all the players currently engaged in the activity. "The more eager each side is to win, the more valuable is an inflexible set of rules," Oakeshott notes.[72] While one might want to adjust the rules so as to condition the overall pattern of outcomes, the conservative presumption, for both Hayek and Oakeshott, is that the general framework of the rules of the game ought to be left more or less unchanged.

Oakeshott's defense of purposively neutral rules can be traced to earlier writings, but it reaches its perfection in *On Human Conduct.* Central to this work is the distinction between "civil association" and "enterprise association." Civil association denotes the moral relationship that binds together members of a political community, or *cives* in Oakeshott's parlance. This moral relationship is based on an underlying agreement about the moral rules or "adverbial conditions" to which *cives* must submit their conduct in order for life in civil association to be possible. This arrangement, Oakeshott believes, allows enterprising *cives* the maximum amount of freedom to pursue those purposes they value most highly.

While his theory of civil association has often (and quite properly) been described as a defense of moral individuality, Oakeshott is clear that life in civil association need not be an altogether solitary enterprise. Enterprising *cives* quickly discover that they can more effectively pursue their ends with the cooperation of others. This recognition of the benefits of social cooperation prompts them to enter into another, categorially distinct kind of moral relationship known as "enterprise association." Unlike civil association, which was based on an underlying agreement to submit one's self to "adverbial conditions" pertaining to the means one could use in pursuit of self-chosen ends, enterprise association presupposes agreement about ends and the voluntary choice on the part of *cives* to be associated in the pursuit of them.[73] The forms of enterprise association are multifarious, ranging from religious congregations to bassoon factories. Indeed, the majority of human action takes the form of enterprise association.[74]

The question, then, is how these categories of "civil association" and "enterprise association" relate to the concept of spontaneous order. Most obviously, the moral rules of civil association seem particularly well designed to allow for the formation of a variety of spontaneous orders. By providing (only) a minimum baseline of moral rules, civil association functions in precisely the same way as Hayek's abstract rules of just conduct. The condition of civil association is not like an organization where all the participants share the same goals or purposes and whose actions must be coordinated to achieve them best. Rather, precisely because it has no ends or purposes of its own, civil association is inherently accommodating of an almost unlimited range of goals or purposes that individuals are at liberty to pursue.[75] So while the underlying preconditions of civil association are specifiable—a rule of law that prevents force and fraud and guarantees rules of title, transfer, and freedom of exit—the exact contours of that society can never be specified in advance. Presumably, they are always changing in response to the intelligent (and spontaneous) engagement of enterprising *cives* with the physical and human world. Something like a planned order or an attempt to marshal the resources and participants in civil association toward common projects or goals is anathema to the very nature of civil association. This is an example of what Oakeshott eventually calls "teleocracy," a term whose merits he debated with Hayek in personal correspondence of the late 1960s.[76] In their exchanges, Hayek explicitly connected Oakeshott's treatment of "teleocracy" with his own concept of spontaneous order.[77] In May of 1968, Hayek wrote, "From what you say it appears that our agreement does go even further than I had hoped."[78]

Conclusion: Reconciling Hayek's Liberalism with Oakeshott's Conservatism?

So far we have sketched out three major philosophical affinities between Hayek and Oakeshott. As we have seen, both acknowledge that spontaneous orders require underlying legal orders that establish the rules of the game and circumscribe the means individuals are free to use in pursuit of their self-chosen ends. And with respect to those orders themselves, both are suspicious of central planners, or "teleocrats," who wish to substitute their own ends for those of individual enterprisers. Given these striking similarities, we return to the question with which we began. Namely, why does Hayek so adamantly deny that he is a "conservative," insisting that his political theory is a species of "liberalism," whereas Oakeshott insists on characterizing his own orientation as "conservative"? Is the difference merely semantic—based, as one might suspect, on different connotations of "liberal" and "conservative"? Or is there some essential difference between these two thinkers discernible only upon closer examination? Although we offer several ways of bringing these two thinkers closer together, there are categorical differences between their political theories that stem from their different understandings of the limitations of human knowledge.

Of course, Hayek and Oakeshott's self-identifications as "liberal" and "conservative" may be differences of emphasis rather than qualitative differences. As a consideration of their later works has demonstrated, Hayek's increasing focus on the law reveals the "conservative" underpinnings of his work, while the full magnitude of Oakeshott's "liberalism" emerges only in later works such as *On Human Conduct*.[79] Hayek admits that economic progress requires at least some degree of "conservative" continuity in the underlying legal order, while Oakeshott defends "liberal" tenets such as neutrality, moral individuality, and free choice. To some extent, then, the question of whether one is a liberal, conservative, or some intermediary amalgam boils down to a question of labels. At the minimum Hayek is not as unambiguously "liberal" as he suggests, nor is Oakeshott purely a "conservative" of the variety that Hayek indicts. There are liberal and conservative dimensions to both of their mature political theories.

One reason for this is their focus on different spheres of human experience. While the economist Hayek espouses a "liberal" orientation toward the spontaneous orders of the free market, he also acknowledges that economic orders cannot be formed without some degree of stability in the underlying institutional and legal arrangements of society. With respect to property rights, contracts, currency, and weights and measures, Hayek aims to minimize uncertainty and maximize the legitimate expectations of the various parties. So the irony of Hayek's apparent contempt for tradition and the status quo is his own clear admonition that legal orders should only evolve slowly and intermittently according to changing exigencies. Economic dynamism, change, and creative destruction in the economic order are premised on continuity and predictability in the legal order.

Similarly, Oakeshott concedes that the conservative disposition to enjoy what has been offered "for its own sake" may not be appropriate for spheres of human life such as the marketplace where particular results are sought.[80] He readily admits that the conservative disposition alone is insufficient for someone engaging in instrumental activities for gain, profit, or recompense. One would never content oneself with whatever a particular merchant offered just because it was "present and available regardless of its failure to satisfy any want." At the same time, however, the whole world is not a marketplace, and even the most impersonal economic exchanges can never be reduced to the pure, cold "nexus of supply and demand" abstracted from the "loyalties and attachments that spring from familiarity."[81] While the instrumental mind-set of *homo economicus* is at best an abstraction of the processes of the market, it is grotesquely inappropriate for understanding forms of conduct such as friendship, loyalty, play, poetry, philosophy, and so on, where the engagement is desirable for its own sake, rather than as a means toward some other end. Those who deny this, according to Oakeshott, must have "adjusted their binoculars to exclude a large field of human occasion."[82] Oakeshott's point is that the conservative disposition plays *some* role in everything, even if, as in the market, it is one of several such dispositions at play.

That said, there is an even more basic, qualitative disagreement between Hayek and Oakeshott that stems from the different degrees of their skepticism about the limits of human knowledge. Despite his insistence that no single entity or planner could have the foresight necessary to reorder society, Hayek seems unwilling to apply this same epistemological skepticism to individuals in the competitive economic order.[83] Because no central planner could possibly take into account the infinite complexities of the market, individuals in their own capacity are likely to be in a better position to do so. Not only are particular individuals privy to the best local information or "tacit knowledge" of their own circumstances, but they and they alone are also the moral arbiters of the particular ends they might wish to pursue.[84] Unlike central planners, individuals in a free society are held accountable for their actions because they must internalize the costs of bad decisions. They have a powerful set of incentives to get things right. Because no one knows *better,* Hayek surmises, it is wrong for planners or elites (whether socialist or conservative) to second-guess the choices individuals make for themselves.

These assumptions of human fallibility, however, might just as easily be applied to the decisions of individuals themselves. Why must the unintended consequences of the actions of state planners always be bad and the unintended consequences of the actions of individuals pursuing their own interests always be good? Even assuming that individuals are *relatively* more aware than central planners of the immediate and short-term consequences of their actions, no individual can foresee every long-term ramification. Similarly, individuals possess incentives to get things right from the standpoint of their own interests, but not necessarily from the standpoint of the interests of others. While it is comforting to "presume that all change is, somehow, for the better, and we are easily persuaded that all the consequences of our innovating activity are either themselves improvements or a reasonable price to pay for getting what we want," this optimism is nothing more than "a positive prejudice in favour of the yet untried."[85] The aggregate of individual decisions is just as likely to lead to regress as to progress. Or, at the very least, as Oakeshott demurs, progress in one direction always represents the abandonment of something estimable. Progress is nothing more or less than change, and every so-called improvement will have both merits and demerits.

Ironically, then, Oakeshott seems to take Hayek's knowledge problem more seriously than does Hayek himself. Individuals are rarely aware of all the immediate effects of their actions, let alone the unforeseeable, long-term consequences of social change and technological innovation. When individuals make decisions with an eye toward bettering (or simply changing) their condition, they rarely appreciate all of the gratifying parts of the existing order that these changes, whether on the whole for the better or worse, will extinguish. Nor can they foresee the unsavory parts of the new order to which their decisions might eventually lead. For example, the original decision to forsake horses and buggies in favor of automobiles was undoubtedly a prudent one if the question is a matter of traveling from point A to point B in the least amount of time. But this preference discounts the more pleasurable parts of riding in the open air, the pull of the horses, and one's connection to the landscape. Moreover, the original concerns for efficiency and comfort that led to the widespread adoption of the automobile could never have taken into account the long-run effects of traffic and congestion, pollution, the breakdown of urban centers in favor of suburbs and commuting, and so on. While even a conservative such as Oakeshott might be persuaded that on the whole these changes are for the better, such changes can never be unequivocally described as "progress" or "advance" beyond earlier social orders. Thus, to a skeptic such as Oakeshott, Hayek's "liberal" optimism about the inexorable march of progress seems naively optimistic at best and ideologically motivated at worst.

Notes

1. This correspondence, to which we will refer below, is held in the Hoover Institution's collection of the Hayek papers at Stanford University. We gratefully acknowledge the permission of the Hayek Estate and its executor Bruce Caldwell to publish material from these exchanges.
2. Michael Oakeshott, "Rationalism in Politics," in *Rationalism in Politics and Other Essays.* (Indianapolis: Liberty Press, 1991), p. 26.
3. Friedrich A. Hayek, *The Constitution of Liberty* (Chicago: University of Chicago Press, 1960), p. 400 (hereafter cited as *CL*).
4. Ibid., p. 410.
5. Ibid., p. 399.
6. Ibid.
7. Ibid., p. 411.
8. Michael Oakeshott, "On Being Conservative," in *Rationalism in Politics,* pp. 410–411.
9. Ibid., pp. 411–412.
10. Friedrich A. Hayek, *Law, Legislation, and Liberty,* vol. 1, *Rules and Order.* (Chicago: University of Chicago Press, 1973), p. 20 (hereafter cited as *LLL*). Hayek borrows this formulation from Adam Ferguson, *An Essay on the History of Civil Society,* ed. Fania Oz-Salzberger (Cambridge: Cambridge University Press, 1995), p. 119.
11. Hayek, *LLL,* pp. 36–38.
12. Ibid., p. 37.
13. Ibid., pp. 37, 82; Hayek, *CL,* p. 400.
14. Hayek, *LLL,* pp. 38–41.
15. Ibid., p. 38.
16. Ibid., p. 40.
17. Ibid., p. 63.
18. Ibid., p. 41.
19. Ibid., pp. 39–40.
20. Ibid., p. 42.
21. Ibid., p. 51.
22. Ibid., p. 51.
23. Oakeshott, "On Being Conservative," pp. 408–409.
24. Ibid., p. 425.
25. Michael Oakeshott, "Political Education," in *Rationalism in Politics,* p. 61.
26. Ibid., p. 61.
27. Oakeshott, "On Being Conservative," p. 425.

28. Ibid., p. 426.
29. Ibid., pp. 426–427.
30. Ibid., p. 411.
31. Ibid., p. 409.
32. Ibid., p. 410.
33. Two of the clearest statements of Oakeshott's philosophical pluralism are his early work, *Experience and Its Modes* (Cambridge: Cambridge University Press, 1933) and the essay, "The Voice of Poetry in the Conversation of Mankind," in *Rationalism and Politics*, pp. 488–541. For a thoughtful consideration of the nature and implications of Oakeshott's philosophical pluralism, see Richard Flathman, *Pluralism and Liberal Democracy* (Baltimore: Johns Hopkins University Press, 2005).
34. Friedrich A. Hayek, *The Counter-Revolution of Science: Studies on the Abuse of Reason* (Glencoe, IL: Free Press, 1952) (hereafter cited as *CRS*).
35. Ibid., pp. 14–15.
36. Ibid., pp. 18–25.
37. Ibid., pp. 14–15.
38. Ibid., p. 39.
39. Ibid., p. 82.
40. Ibid., pp. 28–30.
41. Ibid., p. 46.
42. Ibid., p. 53.
43. An especially clear statement by Hayek on the nature of methodological individualism and how it differs from holistic theories is "Individualism: True and False," in *Individualism and Economic Order* (Chicago: University of Chicago Press, 1948), esp. pp. 6–7.
44. Hayek, *CRS*, p. 53. Cf. *CRS*, p. 91.
45. Ibid., p. 40.
46. Ibid., p. 80.
47. Ibid., p. 83.
48. Oakeshott, "Rationalism in Politics," p. 27.
49. Ibid., pp. 34–35.
50. Oakeshott, "Political Education," pp. 48–49.
51. Ibid., p. 58.
52. Ibid., pp. 57–59.
53. Ibid., p. 59.
54. Michael Oakeshott, "Rational Conduct," in *Rationalism in Politics*, pp. 106, 109.
55. Ibid., p. 119.
56. Ibid., pp. 115–116.
57. Michael Oakeshott, *On Human Conduct* (Oxford: Clarendon Press, 1991), especially pp. 57–60, 63, 70–78, 112–122 (hereafter cited as *OHC*).
58. Hayek, *LLL*, p. 100.
59. Ibid., p. 87.
60. Ibid., pp. 88–89, 100.

61. Hayek, "Individualism: True and False," pp. 22–23, where Hayek cites approvingly the "true individualism" of so-called "conservative" thinkers such as Edmund Burke, Alexis de Tocqueville, and Lord Acton.

62. Hayek, *LLL,* p. 120.

63. Ibid., pp. 38–39, 50, 141–143.

64. Ibid., p. 108.

65. Ibid., pp. 101–107.

66. Oakeshott, "On Being Conservative," p. 421.

67. Ibid., pp. 421, 424.

68. Ibid., p. 421.

69. Oakeshott, *OHC,* p. 113.

70. Friedrich A. Hayek, *The Fatal Conceit: The Errors of Socialism,* ed. W. W. Bartley III (Chicago: University of Chicago Press, 1988), p. 154.

71. Oakeshott, "On Being Conservative," p. 422.

72. Ibid.

73. Oakeshott, *OHC,* pp. 114–119, 157–158. For a full account of this distinction between civil association and enterprise association, see Richard Boyd, "Michael Oakeshott on Civility, Civil Society, and Civil Association," *Political Studies* 52 (October 2004): 603–622.

74. Oakeshott, *OHC,* pp. 114, 117.

75. Ibid., pp. 314–316.

76. For Oakeshott's characterization of the modern European state as a "teleocracy," see especially *OHC,* pp. 284–313. On their exchanges over the term "teleocracy," see the Hayek-Oakeshott correspondence, Letters of January 5, 1965, January 19, 1968, and January 29, 1968. In Oakeshott's letter of January 19, 1968, he accedes to Hayek's advice to replace "telocracy" with "teleocracy."

77. "As I now deal with the problem, the contrast between nomocracy and teleocracy takes a somewhat secondary place after what is to me the primary distinction between a spontaneous order and cosmos and an organization or taxis." Hayek continued, "But to bring out certain attributes of these two forms of order I still find your terms very useful." Hayek-Oakeshott correspondence, January 29, 1968.

78. Hayek-Oakeshott correspondence, Hayek to Oakeshott (May 7, 1968).

79. While many continue to characterize Oakeshott as a "conservative," there is a growing recognition among political theorists that Oakeshott is better understood as a conservative liberal pluralist. Oakeshott's commitment to liberal neutrality, moral individuality, and classical liberal freedoms have been emphasized by Lee Auspitz, "Individuality, Civility, and Theory: The Philosophical Imagination of Michael Oakeshott," *Political Theory* 4 (August 1976): 261–294; Terry Nardin, *The Philosophy of Michael Oakeshott* (University Park: Penn State University Press, 2001); and Richard Flathman, *Reflections of a Would-be Anarchist: Ideals and Institutions of Liberalism* (Minneapolis: University of Minnesota Press, 1998).

80. Oakeshott, "On Being Conservative," p. 416.

81. Ibid., pp. 415–416.
82. Ibid., p. 418.
83. Hayek's classic statement of this "knowledge problem" is "The Use of Knowledge in Society," in Hayek, *Individualism and Economic Order* (Chicago: University of Chicago Press, 1948), pp. 1–32.
84. Both Hayek and Oakeshott acknowledge the influence of Michael Polanyi and his pathbreaking work on personal or tacit knowledge. See especially, Michael Polanyi, *The Logic of Liberty: Reflections and Rejoinders* (Chicago: University of Chicago Press, 1951) and *The Tacit Dimension* (Garden City, NY: Doubleday, 1966).
85. Oakeshott, "On Being Conservative," p. 414.

CHAPTER 6

Spontaneous Order and the Problem of Religious Revolution

Scott Yenor

Hayek uses spontaneous order to explain how free markets operate and how they arise. Explaining how markets operate, Hayek argues that economic efficiency on a global scale arises as the consequence of many discrete, individual, dispersed actions. Individuals possess pieces of knowledge necessary to pursue interests, and the price system of the free market acts as an uncontrolled and uncontrollable mechanism sending signals to people as they pursue their interests. The positive results of this free market system are twofold and mutually reinforcing: producers and consumers cooperate in exchanging goods and the economy as a whole achieves high levels of productivity in goods produced. Following Smith's famous thesis about the "invisible hand," Hayek holds that no single mind is capacious or competent enough to move the pieces of the free market chessboard as efficiently as the free market itself. This led Hayek to believe in the spontaneous ascension of the spontaneous order itself. The Great Society arose as the product of cultural evolution whereby "institutions and morals, language and law have evolved by a process of cumulative growth and that it is only with and within this framework that human reason has grown and can successfully operate."[1] This evolution also is Darwinian because homegrown traditions survive when they, unlike competing traditions, successfully meet needs.[2]

At the intersection of these two contentions is the most controversial contention of Hayek's thought. Hayek argues that homegrown traditions sustain the informal mores on which the modern commercial republic or Great Society rests. Hayek finds inspiration for his explanation from the thinkers of the Scottish Enlightenment, who showed, in Hayek's judgment, "that an evident order which was not the product of a designing human intelligence need not therefore be ascribed to the design of a higher, supernatural intelligence, but that there was a third possibility—the emergence of order as the result of adaptive evolution."[3] Must, and can, a free society remain, in Hayek's phrase, a "tradition-bound society"?[4] The Great Society that Hayek envisions depends on a mixture of a traditional morality cultivating trust, promise keeping, and unifying habits on the one hand and dynamic, progressive individualism on the other. Tradition-bound societies are based on reverential or deferential attitudes to the past, while the Great Society cultivates a spirit of innovation, progress, confidence, audacity, and dynamism. In the long term, deferential embraces of tradition will not exist with the spirit of progressive audacity liberated in the Great Society. Persistent deference to the "burden of tradition"[5] in a dynamic society is the dubious assumption on which Hayek's thought depends. Hayek is a scientist charting the "survival of the successful,"[6] not a philosopher engaging moral questions about happiness or about the conditions for human thriving. It is at this juncture that Hayek is furthest from the more and less skeptical Scots; he is both more conservative and more dynamic than the Scots.

In this chapter I argue that Hayek mis-calibrates the extent to which reason can direct and grasp the world around us. This argument has three stages. First, relying on Hume's *History of England,* I argue that Hayek's view of cultural evolution underestimates the role played by intentional design and statesmanship in bringing about the Great Society. Many have observed this problem in Hayek's thought (and attribute it to his suspicion of ideologies in the twentieth century), but few have considered this problem in all of its implications. It is not a mere technical error; it is a window to shortcomings in Hayek's understanding of reason and philosophy. Second, again relying on Hume, I argue that the theory of spontaneous order is inconsistent with religion as it is traditionally understood. In fact, Hayek's account of religion, as it has been defanged in the modern world, is based on two errors. Because of the success of the dynamic order, religion is no longer strong enough to guard tradition in the manner Hayek contends; and religion was once a near-mortal enemy of the commercial system Hayek favors. Third, I allude to an alternative defense of the commercial republic based in Hume's thought. Hume endorses elements of Hayek's thought, but he adds them up differently so as to defend the commercial republic as a reasonable response to our mixed condition. Hume endorses the modern commercial republic not because it organizes our ignorance in productive ways, but because it reflects the proper moral response to our ignorance and conduces to happiness.

Spontaneous Order and Tradition in History

Historians who live in democratic times . . . not only deny to a few citizens the power to act on the destiny of a people, they also take away from peoples themselves the ability to modify their own fate, and they subject them either to an inflexible providence or to a sort of blind fatality.

Alexis de Tocqueville[7]

Let me first turn to the question of design in history. Hayek's theory of how the spontaneous order arose reflects an understanding of how and whether human reason guides history. At one end of a continuum sit the "constructive rationalists," who embody a view of historical change and economics that awards a paramount role to intentional human reason. Reason, in this account, appears (to use Hume's formulation) "to be in possession of the throne, prescribing laws, and imposing maxims, with an absolute sway and authority" (*A Treatise of Human Nature [T]* 186).[8] Exposing the pride of this view unites Hume with Hayek as both of them diagnosed the temper of their age tending toward "constructive rational-ism" (Hayek) or "speculative system[s] of principles" (*Essays, Moral, Political, and Literary [E]* 465). At the other end of the continuum appears to be a stance of resignation, quietism, and, perhaps, despair at our inabil-ity to shape our destiny through the use of our most angelic (and devilish) faculty. The political upshot of this stance is a comprehensive policy of laissez-faire.

It is by no means easy to know where human beings fall on this continuum. Perhaps no thinker can be located *at* one of these poles, though the tone of Hayek's presentation often reflects an either-or analysis. If there is no purity on the issue, we must ask: In what ways can reason guide or correct action? What are the obstacles to guidance by reason? Hume and Hayek answer these questions differently, with Hayek being more skeptical than Hume of reason's capacity to guide action.

This difference manifests itself despite their shared aim of showing the limits of reason's ability to plan and guide human action. Hume often dep-recates prudence and foresight and elevates the role of accident and sponta-neous change in his political writings because the main challenge to sound political practice in his day came from the rationalism of Whig speculators. In the last words he wrote in his *History of England,* Hume announces his hope to educate people "in the great mixture of accident, which commonly concurs with a small ingredient of wisdom and foresight, in erecting the complicated fabric of the most perfect government" (II.525). Moreover, Hume's account of human conduct emphasizes the central role played by habit and custom (see, e.g., II.86; V.159). Like Hayek, Hume's account of society emphasizes the way in which modern political economy does away with the need for the revolutionary reshaping of society and acts to hedge in the exertions of statesmanship.[9] Against shallow rationalists, Hume emphasizes (perhaps overemphasizes) the fragility of the humane English Constitution: what chance gives, it can rip away. Hume also sometimes emphasizes (perhaps overemphasizes) the un-importance of policy in bringing forth the English Constitution. Hayek and advocates of spontaneous order theories seize on this side of Hume in tracing the theory to the Scots.

This reading, true as far as it goes, is neither exhaustive nor sensitive to Hume's rhetorical situation. Hume's teaching is always double-edged. The chapters in Hume's *History of England* are named for monarchs because Hume has unvarnished praise for statesmanship and therewith for intentional design.

> Of all men, that distinguish themselves by memorable achievements, the first place of honour seems due to LEGISLATORS and founders of states, who transmit a system of laws and institutions to secure peace, happiness, and liberty of future generations.
>
> (*E* 54)

Nor is this statesmanship, for Hume, merely a negative phenomenon—wherein statesmen tear down economic and religious obstacles to the full flowering of spontaneous order. The establishment of a legal system depends on repeated actions of design, just as the introduction of free markets relies, in part, on designs of statesmen. Though the English Constitution is considered an example of governance by custom and spontaneity, Hume shows how intentional construction and destruction interact with unintended consequences and natural mechanisms to give rise to England's unique polity.

Alfred the Great introduced England's legal system (I.172) and is praised more effusively than any other statesman in the *History of England* (I.74). Aside from designing a system of county courts wherein citizen juries heard appeals, he guided those charged with administering justice when he "framed a body of laws; which . . . is generally deemed the origin of what is denominated the COMMON LAW" (I.78). Alfred gazed over the landscape, saw the need for a system of courts, saw the seedlings for a court system, and then designed a system by executive actions. Even the common law, in appearance a most spontaneous of creatures, has its origins partly in design. Hume's praise for Edward I—an "English Justinian"—is almost as strong. Edward's accomplishment lay not only in his "correction, extension, amendment, and establishment of laws," but in his desire to make those laws effective through his vigorous administration against the tyrannical barons. Edward stripped power from the chief justice and introduced different and independent courts of law, which competed with one another to become the most just courts in England (II.141–142). More profound were Henry VII's laws allowing the nobles and gentry to break up ancient entails and alienate their estates. As Tocqueville observed, such laws dissipate the property of the great and lead to more fluid economic arrangements. Hume believes Henry VII "foresaw and intended" this consequence, because his policy consisted in "depressing the great" and exalting the "men of new families" (III.77).

The mixture of foresight on the one hand and evolutionary change on the other is seen in the fall of the feudal order. The religious aspect of feudalism's fall shows the extent to which Hume thinks intentional conduct affects human destiny. First I describe how the natural mechanism of human nature and progress works and then I discuss how superstition acted as a governor on the engine of progress and how England kicked the belief in superstition.

For Hume, the most important feature leading to the commercial republic is the rule of law. The natural mechanism of progress implicates a series of human goods. Law gives rise to expectations, among which are expectations that lead one to feel secure in one's person and property, to begin the discovery process, and to act on one's localized knowledge. The beginnings of this process are "altogether necessary," but later steps are "more accidental" (*E* 118). This natural mechanism culminates in an ethic of "*industry, knowledge,* and *humanity*" that "are linked together by an indissoluble chain" (*E* 271). This natural mechanism can be suppressed when laws are unstable, knowledge is not valued, curiosity is discouraged, industry is curbed, or virtues are inhumane. When viewed in historical perspective people have not often lived in humane commercial republics; this suggests that this mechanism does not run of itself. Superstition is in a perpetual battle with humanity for supremacy, and humanity first emerged victorious in England. How did England's superstitious edifice crumble? At stake in this question is the ability of the spontaneous order theory to give an account of religion. Do religions rise and fall spontaneously? What accounts for differences among religions?

Let us begin at the depths of feudalism when the church's power was at its height and the pope lifted "his head openly above all the princes of Europe" (I.151; also I.265). After the Norman conquest, "devoted attachment to Rome continually encreased in England; and being favoured by the sentiments of the conquerors, as well as the monastic establishments . . . it soon reached the same height, at which it had, during some time, stood in France and Italy" (I.207). Monkish historians praised policies that augmented the church's power in temporal affairs. From humble beginnings and without relying on arms, the church established a "universal and almost absolute monarchy in Europe." The church's instrument was not brilliant policy, in Hume's judgment, so much as it was "the ignorance and superstition of the people," which is "so gross an engine, of such universal prevalence, and so little liable to accident and disorder, that it may be successful even in the most unskilful hands" (I.264; also I.237). When kings such as William Rufus or Henry I asserted power over the investiture of prelates or control of revenues, the church won (see I.422). People were more attached to the church than to their relatively powerless kings; more attached to monkish virtues than to the virtues of humanity; and more taken with piety than with self-interest.

Amid these realities, the natural mechanism of progress was stifled. As John W. Danford catalogues,[10] the feudal system, where serfs occupied land in exchange for promised military service, gave way to an arrangement where serfs held land by annual contracts, then for life, then finally as part of an inheritance. "The idea of something like property" stole on minds (I.458), abetted, perhaps, by the recovery of the Pandects of Justinian (AD 1130). But these ideas were not effective immediately. Ideas of property and law percolated for three hundred years before Hume notes the engine of progress revving up. A hundred years after the Pandects gained attention, "regular administration was [still] not any where known"; commerce was "in a wretched condition"; and "bad police" rendered "all communication dangerous, and all property precarious" (II.20, 69).[11] Even during Edward I's forceful reign (1272–1307), the "feeble execution of the laws had given license to all orders of men" (II.99, 95). Throughout volume II, Hume shows that trade and manufacturing was "at a very low ebb" (II.178 and 279) and that the kingdom "abounded . . . little in commodities" (II.275). Ruffians, thieves, robbers, and murderers roamed the country as late as Henry V's reign (1413–1422) and, despite Edward's efforts, "no law could be executed against those criminals" (II.279). The economic factors noted by Danford and others were key, but secondary factors in bringing forth the modern English Constitution.[12]

More significant in bringing about the English system of liberty is the waning of superstition, which had encouraged submission to civil and ecclesiastical authorities. It encouraged belief in and fear of "invisible and unknown" powers that must be appeased by "equally unaccountable . . . ceremonies, observances, mortifications, sacrifices, presents, or in any practice, however absurd or frivolous, which either folly or knavery recommends to a blind and terrified credulity" (E 74). While superstitious attachment to Rome persisted, political authority remained tenuous, the administration of law unsteady, property insecure, and progress in arts and sciences unrealized. In sum, the feudal regime did not have effective laws necessary for property, personal security, and liberty.[13]

Volume II traces the waning of superstition. Papal supremacy tempted religious authorities into abuses.[14] Rome's rapacity became "palpable to the blindness of superstition itself" and was "the ground of general complaint" (II.23–24). During Henry III's reign, "papal power was at its summit, and was even beginning insensibly to decline, by reason of immeasurable avarice and extortions of the court of Rome, which disgusted the clergy as well as laity, in every kingdom of Europe. England itself, though sunk in the deepest abyss of ignorance and superstition, had seriously entertained thoughts of shaking off the papal yoke" (II.70). Edward I seized church property and announced that Catholic priests would not be afforded protection of the laws; he encouraged people "to throw off that respect for the sacred order, by which they had so long been overawed and governed" (II.116; also II.278). Exertions of papal power diminished it (II.124) because priestly rapacity offended sensibilities favorable to justice and national feeling; the church's grip on the popular imagination, which is weak, as Hume thinks, in the nature of things, loosened insensibly.

This "insensible" decay soon became "a sensible decay of ecclesiastical authority." The country was "very much weaned . . . from superstition" due to the "numerous usurpations both of the court of Rome, and of their own clergy" (II.325). Two instances reveal this change: John Ball's insurrection (1381) in the name of equality and liberty (II.289–292) and John Wickliffe's (d. 1385) more popular attempt to reform the church. Hume concludes that the age "seemed strongly disposed to receive" Wickliffe's doctrines, but "affairs were not yet fully ripe for this great revolution; and the finishing blow to ecclesiastical power was reserved to a period of more curiosity, literature, and inclination for novelties" (II.329). Likewise the Lollards (II.357). Such movements were unthinkable only 50 years before; they were not yet pervasive enough to be successful as the Tudors ascended the throne. Remnants of this movement would shake the English Constitution to its core a century later.

Henry VIII's reign is the key to how this revolution unfolded. Henry's desire for a divorce and remarriage united him with growing discontent against the church. The issue, for Henry as for the English, was the effect of papal authority on royal power and the rule of law (III.189, 201). The church inhibited the "execution of justice" by exempting clergy from criminal and civil penalties and by offering sanctuary and forgiveness to criminals (III.324). Further, the church maintained monasteries, where "many of the lowest vulgar were taken from the useful arts, and maintained in those receptacles of sloth and ignorance." The church also regulated culture as a means of maintaining unity and hegemony: "All liberty of thought ran a manifest risqué of being extinguished; and violent persecutions, or what was worse, a stupid and abject credulity took place every where" (III.136). Henry established the regular administration of justice by restraining the taxing impositions of the clergy (III.186–187), closing monasteries,[15] ending religious practices such as pilgrimages and the cult of the saints, ending church holidays, and seizing church property.[16] Suppressing the monasteries was an important and violent change in England's Constitution. Monasteries were "the radical inconvenience of the catholic religion": "Papal usurpations, the tyranny of the inquisition, the multiplicity of holidays; all these fetters on liberty and industry were ultimately derived from the authority and insinuation of monks." Hume notes the extraordinary nature of Henry's statesmanship: "The violence of changing so suddenly the whole system of government, and making it treason to deny what, during many ages, it had been heresy to assert, is an event which may appear somewhat extraordinary." Henry introduced "violent innovations in religion," proceeded at a stroke in his "great work" to abolish utterly "the monastic order," succeeded in "one of the most perilous enterprises, which any sovereign can attempt," and introduced a "great innovation" (III.220, 227, 229, 244, 252).

Hume's praise of Henry's actions serves to highlight the issue of intentional design and spontaneous order.

> A way was also prepared for checking the exorbitancies of superstition, and breaking those shackles, by which human reason, policy, and industry had so long been encumbered. The prince, it may be supposed, being the head of the religion, as well as of the temporal jurisdiction of the kingdom, though he might sometimes employ the former as an engine of government, had no interest, like the Roman pontiff, in nourishing its excessive growth; and except when blinded by his own ignorance or bigotry, would be sure to retain it within tolerable limits and prevent its abuses. And on the whole, there followed from this revolution many beneficial consequences; though perhaps neither foreseen nor intended by the persons who had a chief hand in conducting it.
>
> (III.206–207)

There was a gap between Henry's intention to maintain absolute rule while diminishing Rome's power and the outcome of his reforms. However, this gap neither implies that Henry could not have wished the destruction of his own monarchy nor that he was unsuccessful in achieving some of (or most of) his goals. His religious revolution accelerated and consolidated changes afoot in England. In Hume's idea of religious revolution and political development, statesmen establish the rule of law and destroy political and religious forces inimical to progress. This kind of revolution does not begin spontaneously or bloodlessly, though many of its untold benefits accord with the unintended consequences portion of the spontaneous order theory. Henry VIII intended to destroy the church, and this statesmanship created significant unintended consequences that were, at best, only dimly part of his intentions. The sine qua non of England's system of liberty was undressing superstitious authority—and this proceeded neither spontaneously nor unintentionally.

Let me place developments into a broader context. Progress and spontaneous order are impossible under a comprehensive, superstitious, religious establishment. The Tudors ruled during and brought about the destruction of the Catholic consensus. "The minds of men, somewhat awakened from a profound sleep of so many centuries, were prepared for every novelty, and scrupled less to tread in any unusual path, which was opened them" (III.140). That which suppressed and distorted the natural mechanism eroded throughout Europe, and absolute monarchies were agents of this erosion. Beating back lawless barons and unproductive superstitions, the Tudors established law, security, orthodoxy, and commerce. No longer would the church impede the administration of justice, nor would it prevent the novelties and innovations from being introduced into all spheres of human life, nor would science be superstition's handmaiden. The Tudors oversaw creeping democratic changes to English culture, while they tried to keep a governor on the democratization of political power.

From Hume's perspective, Hayek's theory of spontaneous order miscalibrates the extent to which foresight and statesmanship shape and maintain the spontaneous order. Forceful and even violent executive decisions remove obstacles to the commercial republic, while statesmen also act to establish a legal framework wherein spontaneous order will develop. When faced with the menace of Catholic monasteries, Henry VIII could have taken a range of actions—including allowing them to wither on the vine spontaneously, supporting them with state monies to bribe their indolence, and uprooting them entirely. His decision to destroy the monasteries was unpopular to many in England (as is seen by insurrections that broke out, III.244–245, 280). Henry pushed the envelope as far as he could; that is, he violently introduced innovations at the edge of what public opinion allowed. His severity abetted the creation of the modern English Constitution. Hayek's principled, either-or answer to the question of whether reason guides history prevents him from seeing such deliverances of prudence.

Religious Devotion, Spontaneous Order, and the Necessity of Revolution

This problem of calibrating how much intentional statesmanship can guide human history is related to problems in Hayek's treatment of religion. With occasional exceptions, Hayek underestimates the threat posed to the emergence of the Great Society by superstitious religious devotion. Hayek's account of history is too seamless; his depiction of how the Great Society emerges relies on a sanitized reading of Christianity that serves Hayek's purpose in preserving traditional elements he thinks may be needed in the future. Hume's account of how Christianity crippled the English Constitution reflects a better reading of history, a more sophisticated (or at least a different) psychology of religion, and an appreciation for the distinctiveness of religious devotion.

For Hayek, religion guards and transmits traditions, and the Judeo-Christian religion has been especially effective in this regard.

> We owe it partly to mystical and religious beliefs, and, I believe, particularly to the main monotheistic ones, that beneficial traditions have been preserved and transmitted at least long enough to enable those groups following them to grow, and to have the opportunity to spread by natural or cultural selection. This means that . . . we owe the persistence of certain practices, and the civilisation that resulted from them, in part to support from beliefs which are not true. . . . Even now the loss of these beliefs, whether true or false, creates great difficulties.[17]

Religions that do not support private property or the family have declined, while *"the only religions that have survived are those which support property and the family."* Hayek reasons thus. The rational justification for property rights is too difficult for most people to understand and, even if they could see that rationale, many are tempted to violate property rights when it suits their immediate interests. Much the same is true of monogamous relationships. People often see the immediate benefits of giving into temptation if it will not hurt them personally. Society would be harmed if individuals indulged their immediate desires over their collective interests in such cases. Strong taboos provided by religion—and, perhaps, in sublimated religion found in traditional morality—counteract these knavish impulses.

Hayek believes that the Judeo-Christian tradition supported (and may continue to support) the Great Society, but the relationship is more accidental than essential. "The undoubted *historical* connection between religion and the values that have shaped and furthered our civilization, such as the family and several property, does not of course mean that there is any *intrinsic* connection between religion and such values."[18] There are two nexuses of this argument. First, religion supports the family and property; and second, the family and property support the Great Society. The first is historical, while the second is more or less intrinsic (though there is some ambiguity on this).[19] Such an analysis is subject to two objections. First, religion may not be an indispensable, or even a convenient, means to a necessary cultural institution. For instance, perhaps property rights may be as secure in the absence of religious belief as they are in its presence. Second, assuming that religion is an indispensable means to sustaining such values, religion may serve an end that is not a fundamental commitment of civilization. Religion, for instance, may be superfluous or hostile to civilization because the end it serves (e.g., the family) is superfluous or hostile to an adaptive, healthy civilization. In the absence of convincing evidence, Hayek thinks a country will be best served adhering to tested traditions on these social matters.

Consider the first nexus. The historical relationship between Christianity and the "values that have shaped and furthered our civilization" misreads the Christian tradition. Here Hume's account of how superstitious feudal order stifled the mechanism of progress is indispensable. Hume is much less taken with the Christian tradition than Hayek because it harbors values inconsistent with the emergence of a commercial republic. For Hume, tradition is almost a dirty word. The result of Hume's analysis is an account of the Judeo-Christian tradition at once more serious and more hostile to it than Hayek's.

In what manner can Christianity be said to support the idea of private property and commerce on which the Great Society is founded? We have already seen how, in Hume's view, monasteries in particular and Catholic superstitions in general were hostile to the emergence of liberty. Again, as a matter of history, the English Constitution and the dedication to commercial values did not emerge until religious devotion itself had sufficiently waned. Hayek mentions only the prohibition on usury as a means of showing how the Christian tradition was hostile to an ethic of innovative commerce. The institutional, perhaps even inherent hostility between superstition and commerce is deeper than Hayek lets on.[20] Consider, again, the issue of primogeniture and entail dismantled by Henry VII. The church had a stake in the continuation of primogeniture. Under conditions where the eldest son mattered most to the father, the effectively disinherited sons and daughters turned to monasteries and convents. These laws populated what Hume called the "receptacles of sloth and ignorance." Most, if not all, of the obstacles to the emergence of the spontaneous order were grounded in superstition.

This points to a deeper issue. A survey of history reveals that the Great Society is a late occurrence. Societies based on religious fanaticism, superstition, classical patriotism, and enthusiasm have been more prominent and often more lasting than the Great Society itself has thus far been. Why have deviant, relatively weak, moral systems been the norm in human history, while the Great Society has been the exception? How can we explain the persistence of deviant systems and the amazingly quick expansion of free systems in terms of evolution?

Hume provides a discussion of where these deviant systems of morality come from because he thinks there is an intractable incompatibility between the virtues of superstition and those of humanity.[21] This view shapes Hume's moral philosophy, which pits the "monkish virtues" (*Enquiry Concerning the Principles of Morals [EPM]* 270) against the natural morality characteristic of commercial republics.[22] It leads him to view religion as inconsistent with humane moral instruction as well.

Whence the attachment to monkish virtues and why is the commitment to those monkish virtues strong? Religious belief springs "not from an original instinct or primary impression of nature, such as gives rise to self-love . . . since every instinct of this kind has been found absolutely universal in all nations and ages." Religious "principles must be secondary," Hume continues, since they "may easily be perverted by various accidents and causes" and their operation "may, by an extraordinary concurrences of circumstances, be altogether prevented" (*The Natural History of Religion [NHR]* 21). As the *History of England* shows, after Catholicism dissolved, people must have the same desires, hopes, and fears and they must be willing to listen to the same religious authorities for there to be consensus.

Hume's philosophy of religion involves connecting the social institutions and original psychological characteristics with religious beliefs. The "first ideas of religion arose . . . from a concern with regard to the events of life, and from the incessant hopes and fears, which actuate the human mind."[23] Blind to "the true springs and causes of every event" and hanging between "life and death, health and sickness, and plenty and want," people impute power to "*unknown causes*" that become "the constant objects of our hope and fear; and while the passions are kept in perpetual alarm by an anxious expectation of the events, the imagination is equally employed in forming ideas of those powers, on which we have so entire a dependance" (*NHR* 27–29). Religious passions, for Hume, express fundamental fears, human ignorance, desperation, psychological disorder, and powerlessness, not merely, as for Hayek, a divine endorsement for sound morality.

Here the distorting codependence between the vulgar and the prophet—and the inequality of premodern times—is important. Disorders impress upon ignorant people "the strongest sentiments of religion" and those vulgar sorts obey those who seem to be impressed with God's stamp. Misery and melancholy force people to embrace a clergy because people are ignorant of how the world operates (*NHR* 75), and the fear of death adds urgency to devotion (*E* 580, 588). People are haunted with terror, and zealots exploit them (*NHR* 73). Allaying such fears requires, Hume's priests teach, direct and "immediate service of the supreme Being." Such services bear as little relationship to the ordinary duties of life as possible because no one wants to risk mixing selfish motives with pure motives. Fasting or subjecting oneself to a "sound whipping" are revealed as having "direct reference . . . to the service of God" because they are of no use. Strict regimens suggest to the devout superiority over infidels and allow them to participate in priestly superiority (*NHR* 70–71). Devotion, persecution, and, generally, the propagation of monkish virtues follow from this aspiration to orthodoxy fostered by priestly ambition.

That monkish moral systems are maintained by hierarchical, intentional, rigorous moral teachings cannot be gainsaid. Neither can the fact that such systems have earned hegemony throughout history. The persistence of superstition and the prevalence of systems defined by monkish virtues speak to the success of intentional designers.[24] To be more precise, the inequality manifest in premodern times and natural human concerns converge to create conditions for priestly scheming. Monasteries were a problem, for Hume, precisely because priests were good at creating and shaping public opinion toward a moral system emphasizing "celibacy, fasting, penance, mortification, self-denial, humility, silence, [and] solitude" (*EPM* 270); these divines sowed a "dismal dress" with the fabric of "useless austerities and rigours, suffering and self-denial" (*EPM* 279). Catholicism was a problem because people believed in its supernatural, otherworldly views. The success of the spontaneous order required the decline of religious authority and the psychological dynamic that gives rise to it. Modern commercial society displaces religious beliefs and redirects devotion from heavenly to earthly activities.

Hume's writings derive from a period in which England was beginning to enjoy the fruits of having destroyed the feudal constitution more completely than (almost) any nation in Europe. For this reason, Hume and his Scottish colleagues saw less need for state action to destroy the institutional and moral power of religion. This placed Hume in opposition to the French rationalists who would, after Hume's death, reduce the *ancient regime* to rubble. But his hostility to traditional religion also shows Hume's deep spiritual kinship with the French *philosophes* Hayek despised (and contrasted to the supposedly more sober Scots).[25] Hume could recommend soft, moderate policies of commerce because obstacles to the Great Society were removed earlier in Great Britain. This means that, for Hume, the customs and habits that he saw supporting the English Constitution already reflected a nation sunk "into the greatest remissness and coolness in sacred matters" (*E* 77). This was, for Hume, the object of the modern commercial republic. Modern commercial arrangements weaken the hold of irrational customs, practices, and traditions; modern commerce expands at the expense of traditional religion as commerce reflects a democratic view of the world while traditional religion is a vestige of aristocratic ages.

Hume cuts the argument for tradition out from under Hayek's feet because, unlike Hayek, Hume thinks that there is a reasonable standard by which to judge traditions and that Christian religion failed to meet it. To borrow a phrase from James Otteson (though not his thinking), there is little room for traditional religion in the "marketplace of life."

Spontaneous Order and the Challenge of Moral Philosophy

Ages of Refinement are both the happiest and most virtuous.

David Hume[26]

There is in fact no reason to expect that the selection by evolution of habitual practices should produce happiness. The focus on happiness was introduced by rationalist philosophers who supposed that a conscious reason had to be discovered for the choice of men's morals, and that that reason might prove to be the deliberate pursuit of happiness.

Friedrich Hayek[27]

Hayek's emphasis on how tradition sustains the Great Society is part of his attempt to explain the success of the English tradition of ordered liberty. Many have accused Hayek of committing the naturalistic fallacy in his defense of the Great Society. While I am sympathetic to this charge, it is true only in a strange, but revealing way. The naturalistic fallacy would manifest itself in his contention that successful social practices emerge from the evolutionary process because they are the best according to some standard of goodness (i.e., most efficient or most conducive to happiness). Hayek is at pains to show that this is not the case. "Only eventual results can show whether the ideals which guide a group are beneficial or destructive" in the survival of the group.[28] Furthermore, new societies may be based on greater knowledge, but that does not guarantee that "the new state [of affairs] will give us more satisfaction than the old."[29] As Bruce Caldwell shows, Hayek's "evolutionary thought had no teleology attached to it."[30] The central feature of Hayek's political teaching involves discovering the cultural variables that allow social orders to thrive in the competition among social orders. The evolutionary process is predictable enough and evolutionary changes slow enough for scientists to be able to make sound judgments about the need for cultural institutions.

Hayek distances himself from the naturalistic fallacy by avoiding moral judgments altogether and by dismissing the language of happiness, virtue, and human thriving as vestiges of rationalistic philosophy. Never abandoning nature, he abandons moral philosophy and thereby abandons nature as a normative standard. Hayek's worry that government might elevate human values such as equality or the "race" over all others and enforce that value through its coercive powers led him to what he deemed as the safer position of a value-free, evolutionary account of the Great Society. Governments that abolish property or propagate atheism are, in his judgment, unlikely to survive, but they are not vicious or immoral. This perspective is at once serious, understandable, and regrettable.

Hume's philosophic perspective provides an alternative. The section's epigraphs provide a useful starting place for the contrast between Hayek's and Hume's defense of the Great Society. Hume is concerned to defend modern commercial arrangements in explicitly moral terms. This follows directly from our conclusions in the previous two sections. Because Hume thinks that statesmen can guide action to a degree, because he is situated to notice real conflict between moral systems, and because he believes he has the ability to condemn superstitious moral systems as deviants, Hume must think of himself as able to make reasonable judgments about the naturalness of the modern system of morals. Moreover, it seems irresponsible to end a chapter on the nature of modernity without defending modernity (to an extent). Hayek is one of the great defenders of modern commercial republics in this past century. His insights do not provide sufficient defense because he underestimates the tendency of the market to colonize all facets of life (and thereby to undercut the traditions on which he believes the market to rest) and because he underestimates the powers of reason to direct action and to comprehend moral judgments. Such a defense, found in Hume, allows us to embrace parts of Hayek's thesis while placing it on more reliable philosophical foundations.

Hume's defense of the modern commercial republic derives from his account of the human condition. Hume's is a five-step argument.[31] First, ours is a mixed condition. Second, scientific modesty is the proper reaction to that condition. Third, the virtues of humanity are scientific modesty refracted into social life. Fourth, the modern commercial republic is the place where humane virtues are most at home. Fifth, humane virtues make human beings happy by reflecting the proper reaction to their condition. Please allow me to sketch this argument.

First, ours is a fundamentally mixed and in-between condition. Faculties lead us above ignorance, but below knowledge; faculties that lead us to know also lead us astray. These observations led Hume to reflect on the human condition:

> Man is a reasonable being; and as such, receives from science his proper food and nourishment: But so narrow are the bounds of human understanding, that little satisfaction can be hoped for in this particular, either from the

extent of security or his acquisitions. Man is a sociable, no less than a reasonable being: But neither can he always enjoy company agreeable and amusing, or preserve the proper relish for them. Man is also an active being; and from that disposition, as well as from the various necessities of human life, must submit to business and occupation: But the mind requires some relaxation, and cannot always support its bent to care and industry. It seems, then, that nature has pointed out a mixed kind of life as most suitable to the human race, and secretly admonished them to allow none of these biasses to draw too much, so as to incapacitate them for their occupations and entertainments.

(*Enquiry Concerning the Principles of Human Understanding [EHU]* 8–9)

Philosophy's task is to articulate the mixed blessings as a means of promoting moderation and describing our condition.

It belongs, therefore, to a philosopher alone, who is of neither party, to put all the circumstances in the scale, and assign to each of them its proper poise and influence. Such a one will readily, at first, acknowledge that all political questions are infinitely complicated, and that there scarcely ever occurs, in any deliberation, a choice, which is either purely good, or purely evil. Consequences, mixed and varied, may be foreseen to flow from every measure: And many consequences, unforeseen, do always, in fact, result from every one. Hesitation, and reserve, and suspence, are, therefore, the only sentiments he brings to this essay or trial. Or if he indulges any passion, it is that of derision against the ignorant multitude, who are always clamorous and dogmatical, even in the nicest questions, of which, from want of temper, perhaps still more than of understanding, they are altogether unfit judges.

(*E* 507; also 130–131; *NHR* 74)

Hayek's task and temper are quite different from Hume's. Hume's strategy for dealing with the ills of an excessively theoretical politics is accommodationist and gray, unlike Hayek's strident, black-and-white description of political disputes. Hume seeks to show that there are not matters of principle separating various parties in politics, but rather only more or less reasonable differences of degree.[32]

Second, a disposition of modesty—somewhere between assertiveness and resignation—is the proper scientific reaction to our mixed condition (*EHU* 161–162). Third, gentle and humane mores reflect the proper social reaction to our "mixed kind of life," in that they are self-effacing, corrosive of excessive pride, reasonable, productive of action, and friendly (*EPM* 263–265). Humane virtues provide a context for deciding conflict by civilized debate, instead of calls to arms; for peaceful assertions of personal ambition (i.e., commerce), instead of violence and fraud; and for modest Enlightenment, not superstition and enthusiasm. The virtues of humanity provide the basis for criticizing an excessively theoretical politics. For Hume, excessive theorizing may work (this places him somewhat in contrast to Hayek), but in order for it to work, it must often undermine the humane, gentle institutions characteristic of the modern commercial republic.

Fourth, modern commercial society hems in exertions of force while emphasizing easy sociability, human industriousness, vigorous intellectual activity, uncoerced cooperation, and the waning of class, religious, and racial prejudice (*E* 269–274). This leads to the most decisive, fifth point. Hume considers the "ages of refinement" to be the "happiest and most virtuous" of all ages (*E* 269; *EPM* 256–257). His defense is grounded on an appeal to the nature of human happiness. Human happiness "seems to consist in three ingredients; action, pleasure, and indolence" (*E* 269). Happiness is experienced when people properly mix activity and indolence. A happy human life exists somewhere in the middle of a continuum between the extremes of activity and leisure. Most find happiness by finding pleasure in action. However, a life of pure action is self-defeating. "That quick march of the spirit, which takes men from himself, and chiefly gives satisfaction, does in the end exhaust the mind, and requires some intervals of repose." Rest is "agreeable for a moment," but "if prolonged, beget[s] a langour and lethargy, that destroys all enjoyment." Activity centered on the arts and industry is crucial to invigorating the human spirit. "Banish those arts from society, you deprive men both of action and of pleasure; and leaving nothing but indolence in their place, you even destroy the relish of indolence, which is never agreeable, but when it succeeds to labour, and recruits the spirits, exhausted by too much application and fatigue" (*E* 270). Where the division of labor advances and opportunities for advancement abound, men are spurred to action. Lives involved with arts and industry foster happiness by encouraging people to improve themselves. "The spirit of the age affects all the arts; and the minds of men, being once roused from their lethargy, and put into a fermentation, turn themselves on all sides, and carry improvements into every art and science. . . . Men enjoy the privilege of rational creatures, to think as well as to eat, to cultivate the pleasures of the mind as well as those of the body." Hume concludes that "*industry, knowledge,* and *humanity,* are linked together by an indissoluble chain, and are found, from experience as well as reason, to be peculiar to . . . the more luxurious ages" (*E* 271).[33]

Hume's defense of modern commercial arrangements speaks to his belief that human nature reveals standards for herself whether or not the system is successful in practice. Hume nevertheless would expect a large degree of overlap between successful systems and those that comport with human nature; success derives from reflecting and satisfying nature—not the other way around. This account of the elements of human happiness allows Hume to place limits on spontaneous order. Just as Hume's defense of modern commerce is more open to moral judgment than Hayek's so also is his account of the human condition more open to revealed religion than Hayek's. This is paradoxical since Hayek has the reputation of being friendly to religious traditions, while Hume is rightly considered a great infidel. Nevertheless, because Hume grounds his entire philosophic project on an account of the human condition, his thought begs the question, "Why is human nature the way it is?" Once *that* is the question, religion and poetry have a place at the table. Hayek's science condescends to religion by sanitizing it; his unwillingness to ground his defense of the Great Society in an account of the human condition forecloses all attempts to take religion seriously as religion.

Notes

1. Friedrich A. Hayek, *The Constitution of Liberty* (Chicago: University of Chicago Press, 1960), p. 57.
2. Friedrich A. Hayek, *The Fatal Conceit: The Errors of Socialism* (Chicago: University of Chicago Press, 1988), p. 23.
3. Hayek, *Constitution of Liberty*, p. 59. Hayek calls Hume his "constant companion and sage guide" (p. 420) throughout the *Constitution of Liberty*.
4. Hayek, *Constitution of Liberty*, p. 61, where Hayek concedes that this is a paradoxical argument.
5. Hayek, *Fatal Conceit*, p. 63, where Hayek contends that an unwillingness to "shoulder the burden of tradition" will lead to a world characterized by "poverty and famine." His alternative to the tradition-based dynamic society appears to be barbarism.
6. Hayek, *Constitution of Liberty*, p. 57.
7. Alexis de Tocqueville, "On Some Tendencies Particular to Historians in Democratic Centuries," in *Democracy in America*, trans. Harvey C. Mansfield and Delba Winthrop (Chicago and London: University of Chicago Press, 2000).
8. Hume's works will be cited as follows: *Treatise of Human Nature*, ed. L. A. Selby-Bigge, 2nd ed., with text revised and variant readings by P. H. Nidditch (Oxford: Clarendon Press, 1978 (hereafter cited as *T*); *History of England*. 6 vols (Indianapolis: Liberty Fund, 1983) (cited with volume number and page number); *Enquiry Concerning the Principles of Human Understanding*, ed. L. A. Selby-Bigge. 3rd ed. rev. P. H. Nidditch (Oxford: Clarendon, 1975) (hereafter cited as *EHU*); *Enquiry Concerning the Principles of Morals*, ed. L. A. Selby-Bigge, 3rd ed. rev. P. H. Nidditch (Oxford: Clarendon, 1975) (hereafter cited as *EPM*); *The Natural History of Religion*, ed. H. E. Root (Stanford: Stanford University

Press, 1957) (hereafter cited as *NHR*), and *Essays, Moral, Political, and Literary,* ed. Eugene F. Miller (Indianapolis: Liberty Fund, 1985) (hereafter cited as *E*).

9. See Hume's "Of Civil Liberty" (*E* 93–94) for an account of how princes are tamed in the modern commercial republic. See also Peter McNamara, *Political Economy and Statesmanship: Smith, Hamilton, and the Foundation of the Commercial Republic* (De Kalb: Northern Illinois University Press, 1998), pp. 82–83.

10. John W. Danford, *David Hume and the Problem of Reason: Recovering the Human Sciences* (New Haven: Yale University Press, 1990), pp. 126–132.

11. These descriptions are taken from Hume's account of Henry III (1216–1272). Robberies were common and "these crimes escaped with impunity, because the ministers of justice themselves were in a confederacy with the robbers" (II.70).

12. Scholars attempting to account for the rise of civilization tend to emphasize economics and the institution of the rule of law at the expense of the withering of superstition. The topic of religion normally arises only as these scholars explain the decline of absolute monarchy. Consider Danford, *Hume and the Problem of Reason,* pp. 109–135; Craig Walton, "Hume's *History of England* as a Natural History of Morals" in *Liberty in Hume's History of England,* eds. Nicholas Capaldi and Donald Livingston (Amsterdam: Kluwer, 1990), p. 42; Eugene F. Miller, "Hume on Liberty in the English Constitutions," in *Liberty in Hume's History of England,* ed. Nicholas Capaldi and Donald Livingston (Amsterdam: Kluwer, 1990), pp. 80–81; and Nicholas Capaldi, "The Preservation of Liberty," in *Liberty in Hume's History of England,* p. 211.

13. Miller, "Hume on Liberty in the English Constitutions," p. 75.

14. Hume mentions the following abuses: the pope obtained one-tenth of all revenues; ecclesiastical pardons and office were openly sold; favors and repentance could be obtained only by bribery; the church demanded that sovereigns contribute soldiers and treasure for crusade after crusade; church officials lived extravagantly; threats of excommunication and interdiction peeved princes; and the pope insisted on filling most offices with foreigners (as he hoped to extend his influence).

15. Follow Henry's efforts to suppress the monasteries with III.161, 186, 227, and 251.

16. Eamon Duffy's *Stripping of the Altars: Traditional Religion in England 1400–1580* (New Haven: Yale University Press, 1992), chapters 11–13 provide a full catalogue of Henry's concerted and intentional "attack on traditional religion."

17. Hayek, *The Fatal Conceit,* pp. 136–137.

18. Ibid., p. 137.

19. See the controversial comment in *The Fatal Conceit,* p. 51, "New factual knowledge has in some measure deprived traditional rules of sexual morality of some of their foundation" and "it seems likely that in this area substantial changes are bound to occur."

20. Consider Jerry Z. Muller, *The Mind and the Market: Capitalism in Modern European Thought* (New York: Knopf, 2002), chapter 1.

21. Consider the last paragraph of Hume's *Natural History of Religion,* p. 76 for a discussion of how superstition and philosophy must have an antagonistic relationship with one another.

22. Consider also Hume, *EPM,* 279–280.

23. "No passions . . . can be supposed to work upon such barbarians, but the ordinary affections of human life; the anxious concern for happiness, the dread of future misery, the terror of death, the thirst for revenge, the appetite for food, and other necessaries" (*NHR* 28).

24. Similarly, ancient cities depended on "violent" statesmanship, whereby statesmen and founders converted the city into "a kind of fortified camp" and infused in each person "a passion for the public good" (*E* 262).

25. Hayek, *The Constitution of Liberty,* chapter 4.

26. David Hume, "Of Refinement in the Arts," in *Essays, Moral, Political, and Literary,* ed. Eugene F. Miller (Indianapolis: Liberty Fund, 1985).

27. Friedrich Hayek, *The Fatal Conceit: The Errors of Socialism,* ed. W.W. Bartley III (Chicago: University of Chicago Press).

28. Ibid., p. 67. See also Hayek, *Law, Legislation and Liberty,* vol. 1, pp. 24 and 88; and *The Fatal Conceit,* p. 20.

29. Hayek, *The Constitution of Liberty,* p. 41.

30. Bruce Caldwell, *Hayek's Challenge: An Intellectual Biography of F. A. Hayek* (Chicago: University of Chicago Press, 2004), pp. 356–357.

31. I have developed this argument in "Between Rationalism and Postmodernism: David Hume's Political Science of 'Our Mixed Condition,'" *Political Research Quarterly* 55, no. 2 (June 2002).

32. For an example of how Hume accomplishes this goal, consider his argument in favor of what had come to be called parliamentary corruption in "Of the Independency of Parliament" (*E* 42–46).

33. Consider also Hume's praise of the "middling rank of men" (*E* 277–278) and his essay "Of the Middle Station of Life," in *Essays, Moral, Political, and Literary.*

CHAPTER 7

Friedrich Hayek's Darwinian Conservatism

Larry Arnhart

Conservatives need Charles Darwin. They need him because a Darwinian science of human nature supports the conservative commitment to liberty as rooted in nature, custom, and reason. The intellectual vitality of conservatism in the twenty-first century will depend upon the success of conservatives in appealing to advances in the biology of human nature as confirming conservative social thought.

Conservatism and Darwinism are both rooted in the idea of spontaneous order. This becomes clear in the work of Friedrich Hayek, a conservative political philosopher who defended the importance of spontaneous order and Darwinian evolution in explaining human society. The idea of spontaneous order is part of a comprehensive view of the world that runs through Darwinian conservatism—a tragic vision of human nature as imperfect, in contrast to the utopian vision of human nature as perfectible.

In his defense of spontaneous order, Hayek stresses the primacy of habit or custom as distinct both from natural instinct and from rational design. And yet, he implies that a full account of social order requires a nested hierarchy of three kinds of order—natural order, customary order, and rational order—so that custom is constrained by nature, and reason is constrained both by custom and by nature. Darwinian conservatism at its best recognizes all three sources of order.

Consequently, Darwinian conservatives explain the conditions for ordered liberty as arising from the spontaneous orders of human nature and human custom and from the deliberate order of human reason. Those conditions for ordered liberty include private property, family life, and limited government.[1]

Spontaneous Order

A spontaneous order is an unintended order. It is a complex order that arises not as the intended outcome of the intelligent design of any one mind or a group of minds, but as the unintended outcome of many individual actions to satisfy short-term needs. Spontaneous order is design without a designer.

Language, for example, is a spontaneous order. Language is a highly complex instrument for verbal communication that has emerged from the verbal activity of millions of people over thousands of years without anyone having intended the outcome by deliberate design.

So, for instance, those of us who speak English have inherited our language as a customary legacy of a long history of linguistic practices, and each of us contributes to the evolution of the English language by every utterance we make, without being able to predict or to intend the outcome. Our language has been enriched by a few great minds such as William Shakespeare and the translators of the King James Bible and by the many small minds of ordinary people in ordinary speech.

Some people might think that our English would be better if we had a committee of English linguists who could reform our language from the top down. But the proponents of spontaneous order doubt that that is either possible or desirable. People who compile dictionaries, people who write textbooks of English grammar, and people such as William Safire who criticize contemporary English usage can have some influence on the future of English. But their influence will be only a small part of a complex cultural evolution in which every speaker of the language contributes something.

In 1951, Michael Polanyi originated the term "spontaneous order" as applied to an unintended but complex order that arises from the mutual adjustment of individual things or people. Hayek began to employ Polanyi's term in 1960.[2] But the idea of a spontaneous order was first elaborated by the eighteenth-century Scottish philosophers—particularly, Adam Ferguson, Adam Smith, and David Hume.[3] Edmund Burke adopted this idea in arguing that social order arises best from the gradual evolution of customs over many generations rather than from the rational design of some social reformer.

Spontaneous order is the fundamental insight in the conservative view of liberty. It is often assumed that any complex order in human society requires centralized planning and direction in which some people give orders and others obey. But conservatives maintain that an order consistent with liberty arises from the mutual adjustment of individuals and groups acting for their own interests and free from the specific commands of a central authority. Although libertarian conservatives and traditionalist conservatives disagree on some issues, they agree in affirming the importance of spontaneous order. Libertarians follow Adam Smith in stressing the spontaneous order of free markets. Traditionalists follow Edmund Burke in stressing the spontaneous order of customary practices. Both sides see spontaneous order as the only way in which social order can be achieved in a manner that is compatible with individual liberty. Hayek's thought shows the fusion of libertarianism and traditionalism through the notion of spontaneous order.

Darwin employed this idea of spontaneously evolving order to explain the evolution of complex order in living things through random heritable variation with selective retention by natural selection. Hayek repeatedly drew attention to Darwin's debt to the eighteenth-century understanding of spontaneous order. Thinkers such as Adam Smith and Edmund Burke were "Darwinians before Darwin," who showed the "evolutionary approach" to social science.[4] Hayek employed Darwinian reasoning in explaining the evolution of liberty. In a study of Hayek's thought, Alan Ebenstein notes that Hayek's father and his paternal grandfather were biologists, and that Hayek's thinking was influenced by Darwinian science throughout his life. Ebenstein concludes that "his work was in large part an attempt to apply the truths of natural physical evolution to society."[5] More clearly than any other conservative thinker, Hayek prepared the way for Darwinian conservatism.

In calling Hayek a "conservative," I go against his own preference for calling himself a "liberal" in the classical, nineteenth-century sense. But even in denying that he was a conservative, Hayek praised conservative thinkers for "their loving and reverential study of the value of grown institutions." He also showed his tie to the intellectual founder of conservatism—Edmund Burke—by saying that he would prefer to call himself "an unrepentant Old Whig," while identifying Burke as one who "remained an Old Whig to the end."[6]

Hayek thought that "the most objectionable feature of the conservative attitude" was its "obscurantism" in resisting modern science, and particularly Darwinian science. "I have little patience with those who oppose, for instance, the theory of evolution or what are called 'mechanistic' explanations of the phenomena of life simply because of certain moral consequences which at first seem to follow from these theories, and still less with those who regard it as irreverent or impious to ask certain questions at all. By refusing to face the facts, the conservative only weakens his own position."[7] Clearly, Hayek would have no patience with those conservatives today who look to "intelligent design theory" as an alternative to Darwinian science. Indeed, the fundamental premise of the "intelligent design" argument is that complex order in the living world must be the deliberately contrived work of an intelligent designer, which denies Hayek's notion of spontaneous order.[8]

The Tragic Vision of Human Nature

Hayek's Darwinian conservatism belongs to one of two competing visions of the human condition that have dominated political thought over the past two centuries. Elaborating a distinction made by Hayek, Thomas Sowell distinguishes the "constrained vision" from the "unconstrained vision."[9] Steven Pinker uses more vivid terms in distinguishing the "tragic vision" and the "utopian vision."[10] In the tragic vision, which can be traced back to Adam Smith and Edmund Burke, human beings are naturally limited in their knowledge and virtue, and social life must accommodate these limitations of human nature. In the utopian vision, which can be traced back to Jean-Jacques Rousseau and William Godwin, human beings are shaped by their social conditions, and therefore we can achieve social perfection by rationally constructing a perfect social order to create perfect human beings. The tragic vision was manifested in the American Revolution and in the framing and ratification of the American Constitution. The utopian vision was manifested in the French Revolution, and later in the Russian Revolution and the Chinese Revolution.

Typically, the tragic vision belongs to the political Right, while the utopian vision belongs to the political Left. Manifesting the utopian vision, the liberal followers of Robert F. Kennedy in the 1960s were inspired by his declaration, "Some people see things as they are and ask 'Why?'; I dream things that never were and ask 'Why not?'" This quotation comes originally from socialist George Bernard Shaw, who also believed, "There is nothing that can be changed more completely than human nature when the job is taken in hand early enough."[11] By contrast, Ludwig von Mises expressed the tragic vision in criticizing the socialist tendency "to discover in social institutions the origin of unalterable facts of nature, and to endeavour, by reforming these institutions, to reform nature." On the contrary, Mises insisted, "we have no reason to assume that human nature will be any different under socialism from what it is now."[12]

The utopian vision is driven by what Hayek called "constructivist rationalism." This assumes that complex social orders can be rationally constructed from the top down to serve some deliberately designed end. To achieve this, the inherited social order of habit and custom might have to be totally swept away. The tragic vision rejects this because utopian reconstructionism unwisely presumes that human beings have enough knowledge of all the numerous and ever-changing factors influencing a social order so that they can plan out its future to attain a prescribed goal without unintended consequences. Conservatives such as Hayek deny that any human being has such knowledge. They also deny that any human being could be trusted to exercise the power to command such a centrally planned order without using that power for self-serving, despotic ends. Allowing social order to arise spontaneously through the mutual adjustment of individuals and groups seeking their particular ends, without anyone being permitted to arbitrarily coerce anyone else, is compatible with our given human nature as beings with limited knowledge and limited virtue.

The utopian vision commonly assumes that the communal sharing that is possible within a single family can be extended to encompass an entire society. The socialist attempts to abolish private property and private families to secure such a communal spirit. But the tragic vision assumes that human nature is such that people care more for their own kin than for non-kin, and that the bond within a family cannot be extended to embrace an entire society. The love of one's own is a natural disposition.

On all of these points, the Darwinian science of human nature confirms the tragic vision of the political Right and refutes the utopian vision of the political Left. This is clear in some of the recent surveys of the political implications of Darwinian science.[13] The best of these is Paul Rubin's book *Darwinian Politics: The Evolutionary Origins of Freedom.*[14]

Even when Peter Singer tries to defend the idea of a "Darwinian Left," he actually reveals how implausible such a position would be. Singer acknowledges that the Left has traditionally believed that human nature is so malleable that it can be shaped in almost any direction, and therefore social problems can be solved through utopian programs that would make human nature conform to rationally planned arrangements for social harmony. Although Karl Marx and Friedrich Engels accepted Darwinism in explaining the animal world, they thought that human history manifested the uniquely human freedom to transcend nature. Marxist biologists such as Richard Lewontin and Stephen Jay Gould have continued this tradition by insisting on human freedom from the constraints of biological nature. Singer seems to reject this utopian tradition. He suggests that a "Darwinian Left" would accept "that there is such a thing as human nature, and seek to find out more about it, so that policies can be grounded on the best available evidence of what human beings are like." Such a Left would realize that natural tendencies (such as social ranking, male dominance, private property, sex roles, and attachment to one's kin) cannot simply be abolished by decree. And yet the strain in his argument is clear when he confesses that "in some ways, this is a sharply deflated vision of the left, its utopian ideas replaced by a coolly realistic view of what can be achieved." So "deflated" is his version of leftist thought, that much of it would seem quite acceptable to conservatives, who have long assumed that conformity to human nature is a fundamental standard for good public policy. Singer even agrees with Adam Smith about the benefits of a market economy in channeling the selfish motivations of human nature in ways that serve public good.[15] Singer's tortuous attempt to establish a "Darwinian Left" only strengthens the case for a "Darwinian Right."

Nature, Custom, and Reason

Darwinian conservatism explains social order as the product of three kinds of order: natural order, customary (or habitual) order, and rational (or deliberate) order. This analysis of order as natural, customary, and rational was first stated by Aristotle and later adopted by philosophers such as Cicero and Thomas Aquinas. It is also implicit in Darwin's account of the human moral sense. Hayek employs the same analysis, but his stress on customary order obscures the hierarchical relationship between these three kinds of order. Hayek also fails to see how a Darwinian account of morality and social order includes these three sources of order.

As originally suggested by Aristotle, we can explain both the social order of a community and the moral order of an individual life as the product of nature (*physis*), custom or habit (*ethos*), and reason or deliberation (*logos*).[16] Instead of seeing an antithetical dichotomy of nature versus convention, we should see a three-level hierarchy in which custom presupposes nature, and reason presupposes both nature and custom. The fully developed order in a community or an individual arises as the joint product of natural propensities, the development of those propensities through habit or custom, and the rational deliberation about those propensities, habits, and customs.

This same trichotomy of order is implicit in Darwin's biological account of the human moral sense. As naturally social animals, human beings are endowed with social instincts, so that they feel a concern for others and are affected by social praise and blame. As animals capable of learning by habit and imitation, human beings will develop habits and customs that reflect the social norms of their community. And as intellectual animals, human beings can rationally deliberate about their social instincts and social customs to formulate abstract rules of conduct that satisfy their natural desires as social animals. This allows for moral progress through history, which eventually leads to the formulation of moral principles such as the Golden Rule.[17] Darwin concluded: "Ultimately a highly complex sentiment, having its first origin in the social instincts, largely guided by the approbation of our fellow-men, ruled by reason, self-interest, and in later times by deep religious feelings, confirmed by instruction and habit, all combined, constitute our moral sense or conscience."[18]

The fundamental weakness in the tradition of "social Darwinism" was in speaking about "evolution" in such a vague way that the evolution of instincts and the evolution of culture were confused. Early critics of "social Darwinism" such as David Ritchie recognized that this was not Darwin's confusion, because Darwin saw the differences between organic evolution and cultural evolution, while he also saw that the former made the latter possible.[19] Similarly, Hayek stressed the distinction between the natural selection of innate traits and the cultural selection of inherited traditions, although "the basic conception of evolution is still the same in both fields."[20]

A Darwinian account of social and moral order must see such order as the joint product of genetic evolution, cultural evolution, and deliberate choice. As products of evolution by natural selection, human beings are genetically inclined to adapt themselves to their physical and social environment through cultural learning and rational deliberation. Seeing the importance of culture and reason for human social and moral order should not obscure the importance of genetic instincts. If human beings were "blank slates" at birth, they could not acquire culture, and they could not develop into mature adults capable of deliberating about their circumstances. Rather, human beings are born with the natural instincts of cultural and rational animals. A Darwinian explanation of ethics and politics requires a theory of the coevolution of genes and culture in shaping the moral sentiments that guide moral and political judgment.[21]

Although Hayek came close to recognizing the fruitfulness of this Aristotelian and Darwinian account of the three kinds of order, he never quite got it right. In the third volume of *Law, Legislation and Liberty,* Hayek added an Epilogue—"The Three Sources of Human Values"—that, he said, expressed most directly his "general view of moral and political evolution."[22] This Epilogue was originally delivered as the Hobhouse Lecture at the London School of Economics in 1978.

The fundamental problem in the Hobhouse Lecture is suggested by the contrast between the title of the lecture and the text of the lecture. The title indicates that "human values" have "three sources," and as the lecture indicates, these three sources would be natural instincts, cultural traditions, and rational deliberation. That's a reasonable position, and it would be consistent with Darwin's account of the moral sense as a joint product of nature, custom, and reason. But in the text of the lecture, Hayek contradicted this thought by arguing that cultural tradition alone, in opposition to nature and reason, is the true source of value—or, at least, the true basis for the goods that arise in "the open society of free men."

Hayek insisted that "what has made men good is neither nature nor reason but tradition." He explains: "That neither what is instinctively recognized as right, nor what is rationally recognized as serving specific purposes, but inherited traditional rules, or that what is neither instinct nor reason but tradition should often be most beneficial to the functioning of society, is a truth which the dominant constructivistic outlook of our times refuses to accept."[23] Hayek was right to reject the simple dichotomy between nature and reason as the two sources of social and moral order, because this ignores the place of custom or habit as that which comes "between instinct and reason."[24] But I cannot see why he then had to so elevate customary tradition over nature and reason that tradition became the only source of morality and social order for human beings.

It would be more sensible to say that moral and social order arises as a joint product of natural propensities, cultural traditions, and rational deliberation. We could then say that it would be a mistake to try to reduce morality or social order to one of these three without the others, because each is necessary but not sufficient. Human moral order requires certain natural propensities of the human species as shaped by natural selection in evolutionary history. But then these natural propensities must be developed through individual habituation and social customs as shaped by the history of cultural evolution. And, finally, we assume that mature adults can deliberately reflect on their individual habits and social customs so that they might reform some of those habits and customs, but without expecting a radical reconstruction that would sweep away all that has gone before. If it is not to be an exercise in utopian fantasy, deliberate choice will always be constrained by human nature and human culture.

Hayek's insistence that cultural tradition is the only source of moral and social order created at least three problems. First, it committed him to a Freudian view of civilization as the repression of all natural instincts. Cultural evolution creates civilization by suppressing the innate desires of human beings.[25] By contrast, Hayek believed, socialism represents a "revival of primordial instincts" through restoring the rules of communal living that governed primitive human beings in hunting-gathering groups.[26] But if this is so, then why would human beings want to live in Hayek's "Great Society," if that means repressing all of their natural instincts? If such a life is purely painful, why would anyone desire it? Occasionally, Hayek said that civilization required repressing only "some" of the innate rules.[27] Then we wonder whether Hayek's "Great Society" does satisfy at least some natural instincts. He said that the cultural evolution of civilization

does bring to ever-increasing numbers what they have been mainly striving for. We often do not like it because the new possibilities always also bring a new discipline. Man has been civilized very much against his wishes. It was the price he had to pay for being able to raise a larger number of children.[28]

But is it really true that "a larger number of children" is what human beings mainly strive for? This seems to be the thought in Hayek's often-repeated observation that the "great society" has made possible an unprecedented growth in population.[29] And yet even the Darwinian biologist would not say that all human striving can be reduced to the desire to produce more children. Although natural selection ultimately favors those traits that enhance survival and reproduction, the actual psychological motivations of human beings will be quite diverse, and the conscious desire to produce children will be only one of many desires.

At one point, in speaking about morality, Hayek said that "all that is innate is the fear of the frown and other signs of disapproval of our fellows."[30] So it seems that morality is rooted in the natural instinct for receiving social approbation and avoiding social disapprobation, which is part of Darwin's account of the natural moral sense. Hayek said that "all morals rest on the different esteem in which different persons are held by their fellows according to their conforming to accepted moral standards."[31] But if this is so, then cultural tradition is not the only source of morality, because it depends on the natural social instincts of the human animal.

A second problem in Hayek's elevation of cultural tradition over natural instinct and rational design is that it suggests a cultural relativism that subverts Hayek's whole position. All of Hayek's writing promoted the "open society of free men." And he spoke of the "progress" that has led us toward such a society.[32] But to speak of "progress" and of one kind of society as better than others implies some standard of better and worse. And yet if morality is rooted only in cultural tradition, and if there are competing traditions, it is hard to see how we can properly judge one moral tradition as better than another. Hayek wrote:

> What makes an individual a member of society and gives him claims is that he obeys its rules. Wholly contradictory views may give him rights in other societies but not in ours. For the science of anthropology all cultures or morals may be equally good, but we maintain our society by treating others as less so.[33]

As far as I can see, the only escape from such cultural relativism is to argue that there is a universal human nature of natural instincts and desires, and that we can judge some societies—such as the "open society of free men"— as satisfying those natural desires more fully than other societies. To make such an argument, Hayek should have conceded that cultural traditions are not the only source of morality, because the natural instincts of human beings provide a natural ground for the moral sense, just as Darwin argued.

A third problem in Hayek's stress on cultural tradition as the only source of social order is that it ignores the role of deliberate choice. Hayek made powerful arguments for why "rational constructivism"—the idea that we can rationally design social order from the top down—is mistaken. But it does not follow that there is no room at all for any exercise of deliberate choice in social order. Here I agree with Jerry Gaus that Hayek failed to give enough weight to deliberate choice in the moral criticism of social traditions.[34]

Of course, Hayek did acknowledge that deliberate choices are often important in the history of a society. For example, while he praises the "grown law" of the English common law as a crucial form of spontaneous order that was not intentionally designed by any legislator, he concedes that there have been times when the judge-made common law had to be corrected by deliberate legislation.[35] Even so, this does not go far enough, because he seems to assume that the common law itself was a purely customary tradition without any conscious design. In fact, the history of the common law shows that at crucial points, decisions from the English king and his council shaped the direction of common law. The common law was originally a law for an agrarian society, and so the development of the commercial legal instruments necessary for the sort of commercial society that Hayek favored had to be consciously designed by judges who understood the need for commercial law.[36]

By recognizing all three sources of order, we can clarify, if not resolve, much of the debate in the philosophy of law as to the fundamental character of law. The proponents of natural law are correct insofar as law is rooted in natural human propensities. The proponents of customary law are correct insofar as natural human propensities are expressed through customary traditions of law. And the proponents of legal positivism are correct insofar as legislators have the power of positing stipulated legal rules, although this stipulation is constrained by both nature and custom. To fully explain legal order, we need all three—natural law, customary law, and positive law.[37]

While cultural tradition is one important source of moral and social order, it is only one of three sources. This trichotomy of order provides the fundamental framework for a Darwinian conservatism.

Darwinian Morality as a Spontaneous and Deliberate Order

Darwinian conservatism explains morality as both a spontaneous order and a deliberate order. Morality arises from two kinds of spontaneous order—human nature and human custom. Morality also arises from the deliberate order of human reason. Mistakes are made when people think that one of these three kinds of order is sufficient.

Human nature is a spontaneous order because it has arisen as a product of genetic evolution by natural selection in which complex order arises without a designer. As Hayek indicates, Darwin borrowed the idea of spontaneous order from Adam Smith and David Hume in developing his idea of the origin of species through natural selection working on random heritable traits.[38] In fact, both Smith and Hume came close to formulating Darwin's idea of natural selection to explain the order in organic nature.[39]

Human culture is a spontaneous order because the customs of social life develop over history through an evolutionary process of random variation and selective retention to create a complex cultural order that has not been intentionally designed. While the natural selection of genetically inherited traits is usually very slow, the social selection of culturally transmitted traits can be much faster. Human reason can be a source of deliberate order because the human capacity for deliberating about present actions in the light of past experience and future expectations allows human beings to intentionally choose courses of action designed to satisfy their desires.

Biology broadly conceived encompasses all three sources of human order—human nature, human culture, and human reason. Here I disagree with Hayek when he says that "what is not transmitted by genes is not a biological phenomenon," and therefore cultural evolution is not biological.[40] Biology is more than genetics. Developmental biology, behavioral biology, and biological psychology, for example, study the biological mechanisms of behavior that are constrained by genes but not simply determined by them. Biologists who study animal behavior have seen remarkably complex patterns of cultural evolution in many animals.[41] For instance, different chimpanzee communities in Africa have unique behavioral repertoires that have arisen by cultural evolution.[42] In fact, Hayek recognized that animal societies manifested cultural traditions that included rules of property and social ranking. He thought that human beings were unique only because their capacities for speech and reason allowed them to formally articulate and deliberate about the rules implicit in cultural traditions.[43]

Biologists who study the brain have uncovered the neural basis for rational choice.[44] Now, in the newly emerging field of neuroeconomics, economists working with neuroscientists are studying the brain mechanisms underlying human decision making.[45] Hayek himself showed his interest in biological psychology in his book *The Sensory Order*.[46]

These advances in the biological study of human nature, and of human culture and human reason as expressions of human nature, open up the possibility of fulfilling the original vision of Smith and Hume for a comprehensive science of human nature. Such a science must include a scientific account of how morality arises from moral sentiments and moral reasoning. Darwin was striving for such a science as early as the 1830s, when he began reading Smith, Hume, and the other Scottish philosophers, because he wanted to develop a biological science of the moral sense. In 1871, he finally published his biological explanation of morality as rooted in a natural moral sense instilled in human nature by natural selection and expressed in human culture and human reasoning. Recently, sociobiology and evolutionary psychology have extended and confirmed Darwin's reasoning. Darwinian conservatism would appropriate this Darwinian science of the moral sense to support a conservative view of moral and social order.[47]

To show what this Darwinian conservatism would look like, I will first offer a very general sketch, and then I will turn to some concrete examples. The general sketch moves through three steps. The first step is to see that there is a universal human nature shaped by natural selection that supports the natural desires that drive moral judgment. The good is the desirable, and there are at least 20 natural desires that are universal to all human societies because they are rooted in human biology, that provide a universal basis for moral experience. Human beings generally desire a complete life, parental care, sexual identity, sexual mating, familial bonding, friendship, social ranking, justice as reciprocity, political rule, war, health, beauty, wealth, speech, practical habituation, practical reasoning, practical arts, aesthetic pleasure, religious understanding, and intellectual understanding.[48]

The second step is to see that while human cultures throughout history have manifested great diversity in their behavioral patterns, there are hundreds of human cultural universals that appear in some form in all societies.[49] These universals cluster around the 20 natural desires. For example, there are many universals associated with parental care, sexual mating, social ranking, and so on. This reinforces my earlier thought about how human cultural evolution is constrained by human nature. Moreover, it also supports my earlier claim that we can judge cultural traditions as good or bad depending on how well they satisfy universal human desires.

The third step is to see how human reason is constrained and guided by both human nature and human culture in making particular decisions. Deciding what to do in particular cases requires prudential judgment about what is best for particular individuals and particular societies in particular circumstances. There can never be precision or certainty in such decisions. But, as Hayek suggested, we can still make "pattern predictions" based on reasonable expectations as grounded in our experience of human nature and human culture. "The theory of evolution proper provides no more than an account of a process the outcome of which will depend on a very large number of particular facts, far too numerous for us to know in their entirety, and therefore does not lead to predictions about the future. We are in consequence confined to 'explanations of the principle' or to predictions merely of the abstract pattern the process will follow."[50] So, for instance, while we could not have predicted the collapse of the Soviet Union's system in 1989, we could have predicted that socialist systems in general will eventually fail because they are contrary to human nature.

For some concrete illustrations of how the reasoning for Darwinian conservatism would work, consider what many conservatives would agree to be the most important conditions for liberty: private property, family life, and limited government. Each of these can be explained through a Darwinian science of human nature.

Private Property

Hayek expresses a fundamental principle of conservative thought when he says that recognizing private property is an essential condition for protecting individual liberty as a private sphere of action free from coercion. This must be so because "we are rarely in a position to carry out a coherent plan of action unless we are certain of our exclusive control of some material objects; and where we do not control them, it is necessary that we know who does if we are to collaborate with others."[51]

The anthropological evidence indicates that every human society has had some notion of the right to property or ownership. There is always some concept of property by which people distinguish between what belongs to some individual or group of individuals and what belongs to others.[52] Edward Westermarck surveyed the anthropological evidence showing that this universality of property is rooted in a natural desire to appropriate and keep what one has appropriated, a desire shared with some nonhuman animals, and a desire that was shaped in human evolutionary history.[53] Similarly, the conservative historian Richard Pipes argues in his book *Property and Freedom* that property is a natural instinct.[54]

This natural sense of ownership supports the natural tendency to trade what one owns for something else owned by another. Adam Smith saw the division of labor as a spontaneous order that arose from "a certain propensity in human nature . . . the propensity to truck, barter, and exchange one thing for another." Smith wondered "whether this propensity be one of those original principles in human nature, of which no further account can be given; or whether, as seems more probable, it be the necessary consequence of the faculties of reason and speech."[55] The evidence for extensive trading networks among ancient human ancestors suggests that the propensity to trade one thing for another might have been a crucial factor in the genetic evolution of Homo sapiens and not just a by-product of other evolved human traits.[56] In any case, property and trade are rooted in human biological nature.

The social recognition of particular property claims depends on custom. The right of ownership by occupation and the right of an owner to transfer this property to another are common customary rules in many societies.[57] The importance of customary law is clear, for example, in the development of medieval commercial law, the "Law Merchant." In the tenth and eleventh centuries, professional merchants developed a body of international commercial law to facilitate international trade. This law arose voluntarily as people recognized the mutual benefits from a system of fairness as reciprocity in economic transactions. Merchants set up their own courts to settle disputes, and the decisions of these courts were enforced by the threat of ostracism. This body of international commercial law emerged as a spontaneous order of custom, and it continues today to provide the foundation for modern commercial law.[58]

Although legislators are constrained both by the natural desire for property and the customary rules of property, they can deliberately stipulate rules of property when this is necessary to settle disagreements or to foster economic development. Hernando de Soto has noted how the history of property law shows that human beings will naturally appropriate property informally even when they have no formal legal claim. Their property rights are recognized by informal social custom. But then in order to use this property as capital investment, they need formal legal recognition. In the underdeveloped world, poor people actually have huge accumulations of property in the informal or illegal economy, but they cannot use this property as capital assets without formal legal titles.[59]

Richard Pipes has compared the examples of England and Russia to show how a country such as England that has promoted property rights fosters freedom, while a country such as Russia that has restricted property rights fosters tyranny. Freedom requires social protection for the natural propensity of human beings to own property and to freely trade property with others.[60]

The Darwinian conservative sees property and trade as a primary means for securing social cooperation through reciprocal exchange in which people enjoy the mutual gains from trade. This expresses the natural desires for wealth and fairness as reciprocity that support customary laws of property and commerce, which are subject to deliberate stipulation by legislation.

Family Life

Private property is an important source of moral rules sustaining liberty. But family life is equally important. Hayek identified private property and the family as representing the "two crucial groups of rules of conduct" underlying civilization. The rationalist reformers who attack property also attack the family, because both arise from cultural tradition rather than pure reason.[61] Hayek rejected the "false individualism" that saw the deliberately organized state and the individual as the only social realities. Rather, he defended the "true individualism" that saw the importance of intermediate associations between the state and the individual, and he thought the family was essential for sustaining those intermediate associations that would arise from customary social traditions.[62]

Family life is rooted in the natural human desires for sexual mating, parental care, and familial bonding, which were shaped by natural selection in human evolutionary history.[63] The specific rules of marriage and family life are determined by customary traditions. While these traditions are variable across societies, the natural desires constrain those traditions to follow certain universal patterns. As with other mammals, human offspring cannot survive without extensive and prolonged parental care. Typically, mothers provide more care than others. But generally fathers also contribute something to the rearing of their children.

The marital bond shows a universal pattern. Monogamy is the preferred marital arrangement for most human beings. Polygyny—one man with multiple wives—is common. Polyandry—one woman with multiple husbands—is extremely rare. Polygyny can work, but it produces conflict because of the jealousy between the co-wives, because of the husband's power of exploitation, and because it allows a few rich and powerful men to have many wives, leaving many other men without mates. Because of this concentration of power, polygyny tends to support violence and despotism. The despotic character of Islamic societies is to a large degree a product of a polygynous marital system. This is why Ludwig von Mises condemned polygamy as a marital system based on the principle of violence, with the husband exploiting his wives. By contrast, he saw modern monogamous marriage as based on the principle of contract, with husband and wife bound by mutual fidelity.[64]

Although the laws of marriage and the family are thus constrained by human nature and human custom, legislators and judges still have some room for resolving disputes or uncertainty in this area by deliberate stipulations. Consider, for example, the laws governing incest and homosexuality. All societies have an incest taboo. And although there is variation in the customary rules of what counts as incest, there is a natural tendency for human beings to feel a sexual aversion toward those with whom they have been raised, a natural tendency shaped by natural selection to avoid the deleterious effects of inbreeding.[65] Consequently, all societies prohibit marriage between brother and sister and between parent and child. But beyond the nuclear family, there is variation in positive law. For example, cousin marriage is legal throughout Europe; but in the United States, some states permit cousin marriage, while others prohibit it.[66]

Similarly, by cultural tradition, homosexuals are prohibited from marrying. But as sexual mating, parental care, and familial bonding have increasingly been put under the principle of contractual agreement between adults, it has become harder to reject the claim of some homosexuals that they should have the right to marry. Nature and custom structure this debate, but the final outcome will be a deliberate choice by legislators, judges, and citizens.

Darwinian conservatives will support marriage and family life as founded in natural human desires shaped in evolutionary history. But on some issues—such as the question of homosexual marriage—libertarian conservatives will be inclined to favor the right of homosexuals to marry, while traditionalist conservatives will be inclined to reject this putative right as subversive of traditional marriage.

Limited Government

For Hayek and other conservatives, there is no necessary opposition between government and liberty. Arbitrary, absolute government threatens liberty. But limited government under the rule of law enables liberty.[67] Governmental coercion that works through general rules of law rather than particular decrees of rulers secures the general framework of public conduct within which the spontaneous orders of liberty can flourish. Freedom in economic exchange and family life requires general laws that enforce standards for property rights, contracts, marriage, and familial rights, as well as a system of criminal law to protect individuals against unjustified violence. The anarchist dream of spontaneous cooperation without any governmental coercion is a utopian vision rejected by both traditionalist and libertarian conservatives. Those who embrace libertarian anarchism have joined the utopian Left.

Human beings have a natural desire for political rule or government.[68] Human beings are by nature political animals, because they naturally live in social systems that require (at least occasionally) central coordination.[69] In some primitive human communities, such as hunter-gatherer bands, this centralized coordination of society is informal and episodic. In larger and more complex communities, such as bureaucratic states, this centralized coordination is formal and enduring. Political life cannot be completely autocratic, because no single human being can rule absolutely without some support from others. Nor can it be completely democratic, because all members of a community cannot rule as equals in every decision. Consequently, every political community is some form of oligarchy.

Human politics is also a sphere for male dominance. No political community has ever been matriarchal.[70] Although women often exercise great power in other areas of life, and although many women often enter the political sphere, the public arenas of political life are generally dominated by men.

Darwinian social theorists explain the evolved human nature supporting government in a manner that sustains the conservative conclusion that limited government under the rule of law is the best government. More particularly, Darwinian theorists confirm the conservative belief that the kind of constitutional government established in the United States by American founders such as James Madison is the best regime for securing liberty.[71]

Human beings evolved during the Pleistocene period, from about 1.6 million to about 10 thousand years ago, when all human ancestors lived as hunter-gatherers. Darwinian psychologists argue that human beings still show the evolved desires formed for that hunting-gathering environment—the "environment of evolutionary adaptedness" (EEA). The social problem for people in the EEA was how to secure the benefits of mutual cooperation while protecting against free riding by cheaters. A cooperative social order arose from the bonds of kinship and reciprocity, and the cheaters who violated the norms of cooperation were punished. Although this hunting-gathering society was roughly egalitarian, there were some differences in status and power. Human beings in the EEA showed both a desire for dominance and a desire not to be dominated. While some people could become dominant, their dominance was checked by the resistance of subordinates who refused to be exploited.

The development of complex, agricultural societies allowed human beings to move from small foraging groups to large farming groups. With the emergence of large, bureaucratically centralized states over the past ten thousand years, most human beings have been exploited, to varying degrees, by dominant ruling classes, and thus the freedom that people had in hunting-gathering society was lost. Only in the last few centuries have human beings developed the modern principles of free markets, civil liberty, and limited democratic government that restore the freedom that our ancestors enjoyed in the evolutionary past.

Consequently, Darwinian social theorists can conclude that modern constitutional republics under the rule of law satisfy the evolved desires of human beings better than any other social order. A capitalist economy based on private property allows human beings to divide their labor—so that people can specialize in doing what they do best—and then exchange the products of their labor. This satisfies the evolved desires for survival, status, and wealth. A free society allows human beings to form nuclear families and diverse social groups. This satisfies the evolved desires for sexual mating, familial bonding, parental care, and friendship. A representative government with limited powers allows those with political ambition to seek public office, while preventing them from becoming an oppressive elite. This satisfies the evolved desire of the ruling few to dominate while also satisfying the evolved desire of the subordinate many to be free from exploitative dominance.

The founding of the American constitutional regime illustrates how limited government under the rule of law arises as the joint product of human nature, human custom, and human reason. The framers of the American Constitution thought that it conformed to human nature. As James Madison argued in *The Federalist*, government is "the greatest of all reflections on human nature." And so, for example, since human beings with political power will be naturally inclined to abuse their power for selfish ends, protecting liberty requires a system of checks and balances.[72] The American Constitution is also rooted in the customary traditions of Anglo-American law and government—for example, the British common law, the experience of the American colonies, and the American state constitutions.[73] But while those who framed and ratified the Constitution were constrained by both human nature and human custom, they also had the freedom to deliberately adopt some novel practices and institutions. For example, although the American presidency incorporated elements from the British monarchic tradition and from the experience with American state governors, the presidency as designed in Article II of the Constitution was a deliberately new institution.[74] Moreover, the framers of the Constitution provided for constitutional amendments so that future generations could exercise deliberate choice in changing the Constitution.

We can judge political regimes as good or bad, depending on how well they satisfy the evolved desires of human nature. And we can judge that the American regime is the best regime because it satisfies those evolved desires more fully than any other.

Private property, family life, and limited government sustain regimes of ordered liberty in ways that illustrate the hierarchy of social order that arises from human nature, human custom, and human deliberation. Hayek's evolutionary approach to social order helps us to see how the order of human society emerges as the joint product of genetic evolution, cultural evolution, and deliberate choice. This evolutionary science of social order conforms to the imperfection of human beings as limited in their knowledge and their virtue. Such an evolutionary science is the foundation of Darwinian conservatism.

Notes

1. For elaboration of my reasoning, see Larry Arnhart, *Darwinian Conservatism* (Exeter, UK: Imprint Academic, 2005). For criticisms of my reasoning, see Carson Holloway, *The Right Darwin?* (Dallas: Spence Publishing, 2006); and John G. West, *Darwin's Conservatives: The Misguided Quest* (Seattle: Discovery Institute Press, 2006).

2. Michael Polanyi, *The Logic of Liberty: Reflections and Rejoinders* (Chicago: University of Chicago Press, 1951), pp. 154–178; Friedrich A. Hayek, *The Constitution of Liberty* (Chicago: University of Chicago Press, 1960), pp. 159–161.

3. Ronald Hamowy, *The Scottish Enlightenment and the Theory of Spontaneous Order* (Carbondale: Southern Illinois University Press, 1987).

4. Friedrich A. Hayek, *Law, Legislation and Liberty*, vol. 1, *Rules and Order* (Chicago: University of Chicago Press, 1973), pp. 22–23.

5. Alan Ebenstein, *Hayek's Journey: The Mind of Friedrich Hayek* (New York: Palgrave Macmillan, 2003), p. 6.

6. Hayek, *Constitution,* pp. 399–401, 409.

7. Ibid., pp. 404–405.

8. I have defended Darwinian evolution in debates with Michael Behe, William Dembski, and other conservative proponents of "intelligent design." See Larry Arnhart, "Conservatives, Darwin, and Design," *First Things,* 107 (November 2000): 23–31; "Evolution and the New Creationism," *Skeptic* 8, no. 4 (2001): 46–52; and "Assault on Evolution," *Salon.com,* February 28, 2001, www.salon.com/books/feature/2001/02/28/idt/print.html.

9. Hayek, *Constitution,* pp. 54–70; Thomas Sowell, *A Conflict of Visions: Ideological Origins of Political Struggles* (New York: Basic Books, 2002).

10. Steven Pinker, *The Blank Slate: The Modern Denial of Human Nature* (New York: Viking, 2002), pp. 283–305.

11. Quoted in Pinker, *Blank Slate,* pp. 287–288.

12. Ludwig von Mises, *Socialism: An Economic and Sociological Analysis,* trans. J. Kahane (Indianapolis: Liberty Classics, 1981), pp. 87, 157.

13. See Pinker, *Blank Slate,* pp. 151–173, 283–305, 393.

14. Paul Rubin, *Darwinian Politics: The Evolutionary Origins of Freedom* (New Brunswick, NJ: Rutgers University Press, 2002).

15. Peter Singer, *A Darwinian Left: Politics, Evolution and Cooperation* (New Haven, CT: Yale University Press, 1999).

16. James Bernard Murphy provides the best account of this trichotomy of order in his book *The Moral Economy of Labor: Aristotelian Themes in Economic Theory* (New Haven, CT: Yale University Press, 1993) and in "Nature, Custom, and Reason as the Explanatory and Practical Principles of Aristotelian Political Science," *The Review of Politics* 64 (2002): 469–495. See also Larry Arnhart, *Aristotle on Political Reasoning: A Commentary on the "Rhetoric"* (DeKalb: Northern Illinois University, 1981), pp. 102–105; *Political Questions: Political Philosophy from Plato to Rawls,* 3rd ed. (Prospect Heights, IL: Waveland Press, 2003), pp. 97–98.

17. Charles Darwin, *The Descent of Man, and Selection in Relation to Sex,* 2 vols. (London: J. Murray, 1871), 1: 70–106, 158–167; 2: 390–394.

18. Darwin, *Descent,* 1: 165–166.

19. David Ritchie, *Darwinism and Politics* (New York: Charles Scribner's Sons, 1901), pp. 6–7, 42–49.

20. Hayek, *Rules and Order,* p. 23.

21. For examples of coevolutionary theory, see Edward O. Wilson, *Consilience: The Unity of Knowledge* (New York: Knopf, 1998); and Peter J. Richerson and Robert Boyd, *Not by Genes Alone: How Culture Transformed Human Evolution* (Chicago: University of Chicago Press, 2005).

22. Friedrich A. Hayek, *Law, Legislation and Liberty,* vol. 3, *The Political Order of a Free People* (Chicago: University of Chicago Press, 1979), pp. xi, 153–176.

23. Ibid., pp. 160, 162.

24. This rejection of instinct versus reason as a false dichotomy that ignores the place of custom is a persistent theme in Hayek's writing. See, for example, Hayek, *Rules and Order,* 20–21; and *The Fatal Conceit: The Errors of Socialism* (Chicago: University of Chicago Press, 1988), pp. 6–28, 143–147.

25. Hayek, *Political Order,* pp. 155–156, 160–161, 163–165, 167–169.

26. Ibid., pp. 169–170.

27. Ibid., pp. 160–161.

28. Ibid., p. 168.

29. See, for example, Hayek, *Fatal Conceit,* pp. 120–134.

30. Hayek, *Political Order,* p. 167.

31. Ibid., p. 171.

32. Ibid., pp. 167–169.

33. Ibid., p. 172.

34. See Gerald F. Gaus, "Social Complexity and Evolved Moral Rules," chap. 8 below.

35. Hayek, *Rules and Order,* pp. 88–89.

36. See Ronald Hamowy, "F. A. Hayek and the Common Law," *The Cato Journal,* 23 (Fall 2003): 241–264.

37. For elaboration of this point, see James Bernard Murphy, "Nature, Custom, and Stipulation in Law and Jurisprudence," *Review of Metaphysics* 43 (June 1990): 751–790.

38. See Hayek, *Constitution,* pp. 58–59; *Rules and Order,* pp. 22–24; and *Studies in Philosophy, Politics, and Economics* (Chicago: University of Chicago Press, 1967), pp. 111, 119.

39. See Adam Smith, *The Theory of Moral Sentiments* (Indianapolis: Liberty Classics, 1982), pp. 77, 87, 142; and David Hume, "Dialogues Concerning Natural Religion," in *Writings on Religion,* ed. Antony Flew (La Salle, IL: Open Court, 1992), pp. 228–229, 240–242, 246–247.

40. Hayek, *Fatal Conceit,* p. 25.

41. See Larry Arnhart, *Darwinian Natural Right: The Biological Ethics of Human Nature* (Albany: State University of New York Press, 1998), pp. 36–44, 56–58;

John T. Bonner, *The Evolution of Culture in Animals* (Princeton: Princeton University Press, 1980); and Frans de Waal, *The Apes and the Sushi Master* (New York: Basic Books, 2001).

42. See A. Whiten et al., "Cultures in Chimpanzees," *Nature* 399 (1999): 682–685; William C. McGrew, *The Cultured Chimpanzee: Reflections on Cultural Primatology* (Cambridge: Cambridge University Press, 2004).

43. Hayek, *Rules and Order,* pp. 74–75.

44. See, for example, Antonio Damasio, *Descartes's Error: Emotion, Reason, and the Human Brain* (New York: G. P. Putnam's Sons, 1994); and Michael S. Gazzaniga, Richard B. Ivry, and George R. Mangun, *Cognitive Neuroscience: The Biology of the Mind,* 2nd ed. (New York: Norton, 2002), pp. 445–576.

45. See Paul Glimcher, *Decisions, Uncertainty, and the Brain: The Science of Neuroeconomics* (Cambridge: MIT Press, 2003).

46. Friedrich A. Hayek, *The Sensory Order* (Chicago: University of Chicago, 1952).

47. What I say here is only a summary of points I have elaborated in my book *Darwinian Natural Right* and in a paper, "Thomistic Natural Law as Darwinian Natural Right," in Ellen Frankel Paul, Fred D. Miller, and Jeffrey Paul, eds., *Natural Law and Modern Moral Philosophy* (New York: Cambridge University Press, 2001), pp. 1–33.

48. For a sketch of these 20 natural desires, see Arnhart, *Darwinian Conservatism,* pp. 26–34.

49. See Donald Brown, *Human Universals* (Philadelphia: Temple University Press, 1991); and Pinker, *Blank Slate,* pp. 435–439.

50. Hayek, *Rules and Order,* pp. 23–24.

51. Hayek, *Constitution,* pp. 140–141.

52. See Edward Westermarck, *The Origin and Development of the Moral Ideas,* 2 vols. (London: Macmillan, 1908), 2: 1–71; and Brown, *Human Universals,* pp. 139–140.

53. Westermarck, *Moral Ideas,* 2: 51–53.

54. Richard Pipes, *Property and Freedom* (New York: Alfred A. Knopf, 1999), pp. 65–88.

55. Adam Smith, *An Inquiry into the Nature and Causes of the Wealth of Nations,* 2 vols., eds. R. H. Campbell and A. S. Skinner (Indianapolis: Liberty Fund, 1981), 1: 25.

56. See Haim Ofek, *Second Nature: Economic Origins of Human Evolution* (Cambridge: Cambridge University Press, 2001).

57. Westermarck, *Moral Ideas,* 2: 35–43.

58. See Bruce L. Benson, *The Enterprise of Law: Justice without the State* (San Francisco, CA: Pacific Research Institute for Public Policy, 1990), pp. 11–36; and "Customary Law as a Social Contract: International Commercial Law," *Constitutional Political Economy* 3 (1992): 1–27.

59. See Hernando de Soto, *The Mystery of Capital: Why Capitalism Triumphs in the West and Fails Everywhere Else* (New York: Basic Books, 2000).

60. See Pipes, *Property and Freedom.*

61. Friedrich Hayek, "Origins and Effects of Our Morals," in *The Essence of Hayek,* eds. Chiaki Nishiyama and Kurt R. Leube, (Stanford, CA: Hoover Institution Press, 1984), pp. 318–330.

62. Hayek, *Individualism and Economic Order* (Chicago: University of Chicago Press, 1948), pp. 22–23.

63. On the human nature of sexual and familial bonding, see Arnhart, *Darwinian Natural Right,* 89–160; and "Thomistic Natural Law as Darwinian Natural Right."

64. von Mises, *Socialism,* pp. 80–87.

65. See Arnhart, "Thomistic Natural Law as Darwinian Natural Right"; and "The Incest Taboo as Darwinian Natural Right," in *Incest, Inbreeding, and the Westermarck Effect,* ed. Arthur Wolf and William Durham, (Stanford, CA: Stanford University Press, 2004), pp. 190–218.

66. See Martin Ottenheimer, *Forbidden Relatives: The American Myth of Cousin Marriage* (Urbana: University of Illinois Press, 1996).

67. See Hayek, *Constitution,* pp. 162–175, 220–222.

68. This paragraph is taken—with some slight alterations—from Arnhart, *Darwinian Natural Right,* pp. 33–34.

69. See Gary Johnson, "The Evolutionary Origins of Government and Politics," in *Human Nature and Politics,* ed. Joseph Losco and Albert Somit (Greenwich, CT: JAI Press, 1995), pp. 243–305.

70. See Steven Goldberg, *Why Men Rule: A Theory of Male Dominance* (LaSalle, IL: Open Court, 1993); and Arnold Ludwig, *King of the Mountain: The Nature of Political Leadership* (Lexington: University Press of Kentucky, 2002).

71. See, for example, Pinker, *Blank Slate,* 283–305; Mark F. Grady and Michael T. McGuire, "The Nature of Constitutions," *Journal of Bioeconomics* 1 (1999): 227–240; and Paul H. Rubin, *Darwinian Politics: The Evolutionary Origin of Freedom* (New Brunswick, NJ: Rutgers University Press, 2002).

72. Alexander Hamilton, James Madison, and John Jay, *The Federalist Papers,* No. 51 (New York: Random House, Modern Library, 1937), 337–339.

73. See George Anastaplo, *The Constitution of 1787: A Commentary* (Baltimore, MD: Johns Hopkins University Press, 1989), 1–12; and Donald S. Lutz, *The Origins of American Constitutionalism* (Baton Rouge: Louisiana State University Press, 1988).

74. See Charles Thach, *The Creation of the Presidency, 1775–1789* (Baltimore, MD: Johns Hopkins University Press, 1969).

CHAPTER 8

Social Complexity and Evolved Moral Principles[1]

Gerald F. Gaus

Introduction

A central theme in F. A. Hayek's work is the contrast between principles and expediency, and the insistence that governments follow abstract general principles rather than pursue apparently expedient social and economic policies that seek to make us better off.[2] This is a radical and striking thesis, especially from an economist: governments should abjure the pursuit of social and economic policies that aim to improve welfare and, instead, adhere to moral principles. In this chapter I defend this radical claim. I begin by explicating and defending Hayek's argument against the pursuit of expediency based on his analysis of economic and social complexity. I then turn to a rather more critical examination of his evolutionary account of moral principles.

The Characteristics of Complex Phenomena

Hayek is famous (in some quarters, infamous) for his idea of a spontaneous order. A spontaneous order is a "grown order":

> Its degree of complexity is not limited to what a human mind can muster. Its existence need not manifest itself to our senses but may be based on purely *abstract* relations which we can only mentally reconstruct. And not having been made it *cannot* legitimately be said to *have a particular purpose,* although our awareness of its existence may be extremely important for the successful pursuit of a great variety of different purposes.[3]

Although spontaneous orders also may be complex, they need not be.[4] Crucial to Hayek's analysis of economic and social orders is that they are not only spontaneous, but also complex. Indeed, although most readings of Hayek stress the idea of a spontaneous order, I believe Hayek's great contribution to social and political theory is the notion of an organized complexity, and it is this idea that poses the biggest challenge for expediency as the aim of social policy. Hayek's analysis of social complexity, especially the complexity of economic systems, points to eight elements, which remain part of current analyses of complexity.[5]

(i) Complex phenomena, according to Hayek, display abstract patterns composed of a large number of variables.[6] Although the sheer number of elements may figure into an analysis of complexity (see emergent properties under the next point), nonlinearity and path dependency are more fundamental, as Hayek's own work suggests.[7]

(ii) Organized complexity occurs "when the character of the structures showing it depends not only on the properties of the individual elements of which they are composed, and the relative frequency with which they occur, but also on the manner in which the individual elements are connected with each other."[8] Hayek thus recognizes the crucial notion of an emergent property:

> The "emergence" of "new" patterns as a result in the number of elements between which simple relations exist means that this larger structure as a whole will possess certain general or abstract features which will recur independently of the particular values of the individual data, so long as the general structure (as described, e.g., by an algebraic equation) is preserved. Such "wholes," defined in terms of certain general properties of their structure, will constitute distinctive objects of explanation for a theory, *even though such a theory may be merely a particular way of fitting together statements about the relation between individual elements.*[9]

The basic idea, then, is that a large number of variables may interact in complex ways to give rise to patterns that constitute "wholes"—distinctive complex phenomena that cannot be reduced to the particular properties of each element.[10] Contemporary complexity theorists thus, for example, see liquidity as an emergent property of a huge number of related water molecules; although liquidity is a property that causally arises out of the interaction of billions of individual molecules, the precise properties of waves and ripples cannot be predicted from what we know about molecular chemistry.[11]

(iii) Complex systems can be tightly coupled.[12] As Hayek notes, in a complex system the state of the system at any one time depends on a number of factors, and if even one is varied, there may be profound changes throughout the system.[13] The behavior of tightly coupled systems is difficult to predict as they are characterized by error inflation: a small error in predicting one variable can lead to drastic errors in predicting the overall system's state.[14] The combination of complexity and tight coupling is especially troublesome to successful manipulation of the system: "Complexity makes it impossible for anyone to understand how the system might act; tight coupling spreads problems once they begin."[15]

(iv) Closely related to this is the sensitivity of the system to the initial conditions; slight differences in the initial conditions of the elements can result in very different system states.[16] Hayek is clear that at any time t_i, the state of a spontaneous order is dependent on the "initial position" of its elements at t_0.[17]

(v) Complex systems often display micro unpredictability with some range of macro predictability (this is closely tied to emergent properties, point [ii]).[18] This is crucial in understanding Hayek's conception of social complexity. It was no part of Hayek's intention to argue that economies or societies are too complex to predict, or that we could not possess a predictive social science. His claim, rather, was that in complex systems the only successful predictions will be "pattern predictions," not predictions of specific states of the system at particular times.[19] That is, we can predict a certain "range of possibilities" for the system or, we might say, parameters within which the system will settle. Thus Hayek insisted that theories of complex phenomena were testable as they predict a range of possible system states.[20] However, because of the nonlinearity of the relations in the system, there is no unique solution; only predictions of ranges of possibilities are possible.[21]

(vi) In many complex systems we cannot measure how close the system is to equilibrium, though we have good grounds to suppose it is never in equilibrium. The most our theories can do is tell how the system moves toward equilibrium.[22] Thus our theories of equilibrium (say, price theory) will not allow us to reliably predict actual prices.[23]

(vii) Complex systems such as the economy are characterized by constant *novelty*.[24] We need to remember that Hayek, like the Austrian school of economics in general, insisted on the importance of dynamic and unknown factors in economic life. "The solution of the economic problem of society . . . is always a voyage of exploration into the unknown, an attempt to discover new ways of doing things better than they have been done before."[25] Although mainstream economics generally has been critical of this emphasis on the novelty of entrepreneurship in Austrian economics, understanding the differing effects of predictable and unpredictable developments has been the core of rational expectations theory.[26] One of the main reasons the economic system is characterized by novelty is that economic agents make, and change, their own predictions of the future behavior of others; the economy is a system of mutually adjusting expectations. Hence, it appears that "the equations of economic models will not remain invariant to policy; in other words, economic models will change as different policies are implemented."[27] Because an economic agent adjusts to economic models predicting his behavior, mere knowledge of a model changes behavior.

(viii) Because of the complexity of the system, there is "no global controller that can exploit all opportunities or interactions."[28] This brings us to the very heart of Hayek's economics: global planners cannot secure and employ sufficient information to direct individuals to employ their capital and labor in a way that will tend to a social optimum.[29] This was the crux of Hayek's position in the socialist calculation debate: "The 'data' from which the economic calculus starts are never for the whole society 'given' to a single mind which could work out the implications and can never be so given."[30]

Politico-Economic Complexity and the Perils of Expediency: No Fine-Grained Predictions, No Sound Basis for Expedient Policies

In Hayek's eyes the economy and, more generally, the social order, is a complex system. As we can see from point (iv) above, understanding the economy as a complex system is consistent with a science of economics that generates testable propositions. But these propositions will concern a range of possible states of the system or, rather, "a range of values" of key variables in the model.[31] However, as Hayek himself stressed—and some contemporary proponents of economic complexity have agreed—complexity renders economic models less empirically testable than does a naive understanding of classical economic models.[32] (However, it is important to stress that it is only in relation to a "naive" view of classical economics that the contrast is striking: there is remarkably little empirical testing of economic models.)[33]

In any event, Hayek's conclusion is that our best economic models will not provide the fine-grained predictions we would need for effective, expedient economic policy. And it is widely agreed that "[e]conomists need to be able to predict . . . because predictions are necessary if they are to fulfill the role of providing policy advice."[34] We need to be careful here: Hayek suggests two types of arguments against detailed economic predictions.

In the first argument, based on the ideas of path-dependency (element [i]), tight-coupling (element [iii]), sensitivity to initial conditions (element [iv]), and novelty (element [viii]), Hayek presents a general case for inherent and steep barriers to useful predictions in both micro- and macroeconomics. Call this the *General Skeptical Analysis*. Although the General Skeptical Analysis does not preclude the possibility of sound economic predictions, it greatly circumscribes them. For example, given sensitivity to initial conditions, similar systems can go off on very different trajectories; thus we would need extremely fine-grained knowledge of the current system state to predict what path it will take.[35] Given the property of nonlinearity, even given detailed knowledge, sound predictions will not identify a unique future system state (a range of values can satisfy the relevant equations). Although defenders of Hayek wish to stress that he is not simply skeptical about economic knowledge, this is but half true; while he is not totally skeptical, the theory of complex phenomena indicates that predictions are hard to come by.

The second part of Hayek's analysis indicates that the sound predictions we might generate will not concern the specific future states of the micro elements (e.g., economic agents) in an economic system. Call this the *No Fine-Grained Predictions Thesis*. The analysis of complexity seems to allow for two general types of predictions: (a) the prediction of broad patterns of micro behaviors (people will consume less as price increases), and (b) the prediction of some macro (emergent) properties even though predicting the states of the micro elements on which they rely may be quite beyond us (elements [ii] and [v]). (Interestingly, then, Hayek, and any theorist who takes emergent properties seriously, would seem to endorse just what most economists reject: a macro economics without strong micro foundations.)

From the perspective of the theory of complexity, the problem with expediency qua, say, utilitarianism, is that it requires extensive predictions of the future states of the micro elements. Remember, the pursuit of utilitarian expediency is not simply committed to *some* prediction: it must predict the aggregative well-being of the micro agents (individual persons) under any given policy. To see the importance of micro predictions for expediency, assume that we can predict that policy P_1 would produce a growth rate of x percent, but we can only say that this will yield an aggregate welfare w_y, where $w_x < w_y < w_z$, and where $w_x - w_z$ is some large interval, and cannot predict where in that interval w_y will be. But suppose that we are also considering policy P_2, which can be predicted to lead to growth of x-n percent, and all we can say is that the resulting welfare also will be between w_x and w_z (say because P_2 will produce less growth but also less congestion). If so, our ability to make accurate system-level predictions is of no avail when seeking expedient (qua aggregative, individual welfare-enhancing) policies.[36]

From Theory to Empirics

Complexity, Tight-Coupling, and Policy: Some Examples of Complexity and the Perils of Prediction

As it has been developed in the past decades, complexity theory is mathematical and computational, involving systems of nonlinear equations. Hayek's own account was neither, but it too was often abstract like the complexity theory. It might help to bring our discussion down to more specific policy problems. Edward Tanner, in his popular book *Why Things Bite Back,* points out several complicating effects of complexity and tight-coupling for predicting the consequences of changes. *Revenge effects* are the unintended and unexpected consequences of our actions and policies that tend to nullify them. For example, in the early 1970s, utility companies constructed giant smokestacks (some 1,000 feet high) to meet new local clean air standards; the effect was to push pollution into the upper atmosphere, contributing to acid rain.[37] Similarly, a policy that increases the "efficiency" of hospitals by ensuring that all beds are occupied may increase cross-infections among patients.[38] *Rearranging effects* occur when actions unexpectedly transfer the target problem to a new area (erosion control on beaches often erodes beaches further along the coast).[39] *Repeating effects* take place when a successful innovation may encourage people to increase an activity, ultimately producing unexpected harm. Improvements in medical care and coverage, for example, encourage people to undergo more procedures, but all hospital stays have a nonnegligible risk of harm through error. One study concludes that one patient in a hundred is negligently injured; as people enter hospitals for increasingly minor procedures, the number of those "unnecessarily" injured will increase. According to another estimate, avoidable injuries in hospitals cause twice as many deaths each year as highway accidents.[40] *Recomplicating effects* occur as innovative policies and procedures begin to interact, creating new problems. The growth of government and its policy aims have led to huge recomplicating effects as, for example, policies aiming at growth, environmental protection, and urban renewal, all affect each other, and make it increasingly likely that the intended benefits in one area will be offset by policies in another. And, of course, often our actions have side effects that we could never have foreseen, which render them inexpedient. The agreement of the northern states at the constitutional convention to accept, as the price of union (and the regulation of navigation), the importation of slaves for 20 years, though seen as an expedient compromise at the time, was most unwise in retrospect. Tanner concludes his account of predicting progress and policies by observing "[w]hat is almost a constant, though, is that the real benefits usually are not the ones we expected, and the real perils are not the ones we feared."[41]

Does Economics Accurately Predict?

It is not my ambition to demonstrate that Hayek is correct on these matters; rather, I aim to stress that his theory of complex phenomena is sophisticated, and provides a strong theoretical reason to reject expediency as a basis for policy. Still, many readers tend to think Hayek's account of complexity *must* be wrong since it is obvious that economics does yield useful policy predictions all the time.

Does it? This is a matter of dispute within economics and the philosophy of economics. Philosophers such as Alex Rosenberg and economists such as Diedre McCloskey insist that economics has been a failure as a predictive science.[42] The empirical evidence as to whether economics accurately predicts is mixed, though even supporters of the progress of economics as an empirical science admit that it has not lived up to earlier expectations.[43] Research does indicate that economists tend to converge on many microeconomic prescriptions, as well as on some important ones in macroeconomics. Richard M. Alston, J. R. Kearl, and Michael B. Vaughan found some consensus on 40 propositions, many of which were concerned with microeconomic policy, with high consensus on some claims such as "tariffs and import quotas usually reduce general economic welfare."[44] Of course consensus among economists does not demonstrate correctness. Alston, Kearl, and Vaughan discovered that the decade in which an economist was trained affects his or her views, suggesting that socialization during graduate school may have an important influence on economists' views throughout their career.[45] At the same time, they found that on half the propositions studied in a 1976 study, the economic consensus had changed in 1992. More disturbing for those who claim that, as a matter of fact, the economics profession displays great consensus on basic lawlike propositions is the phenomena of emerging contrary results. Robert S. Goldfarb's study of the empirical literature in economics reveals a pattern according to which "first, evidence accumulates to support an empirical result. As time passes, however, contrary results emerge that challenge that result," leading to a regular overturning of apparently established empirical findings.[46] Although better data and more advanced mathematical techniques are a factor in over half the changes, Goldfarb concludes that the instability of empirical economic findings represents "a serious problem for the conscientious economist trying to make warranted inferences from empirical literature in economics. If seemingly established results often provoke the emergence of contradictory findings, the dependability of inferences based on existing literature is weakened."[47]

Most striking of all is the recent work of Philip E. Tetlock, who has studied the predictions of experts across a range of political and economic issues. For over a decade Tetlock studied the ability of political and economic experts to predict, among other things, economic performance (growth rates in GDP, inflation, unemployment rates) as well as political developments.[48] Tetlock asked experts in history, political science, and economics to predict future events and the movement of key variables. Would key variables go up (in both the short term and the long term), go down, or stay the same? The good news is political and economic experts do better than undergraduates at predicting future events in their field of expertise. Unfortunately, that is about all the good news. Experts do not do significantly better that what Tetlock calls "dilettantes"—people who regularly read the *Economist* or the *New York Times*. Tetlock distinguished two criteria of a good prediction: discrimination (how precise the prediction is) and calibration (how accurate the prediction is). Someone who always makes very general predictions (for example, "a 33% chance of a downward movement in an index") would make a number of accurate predictions (by chance they would be correct one-third of the time), but she would score low on discrimination; someone who predicts "a 80% chance the variable will fall" aims at a precise prediction, but of course she may sacrifice accuracy: she is more apt to go wrong since she is trying to give a precise prediction. On the discrimination measure—how precise the predictions are—the experts and dilettantes would beat a chimpanzee that made predictions by throwing a dart at a board on which the dart can land on "variable will go up," "variable will go down," or "variable will stay the same." Unfortunately the chimpanzee beats the dilettantes and experts on the accuracy score.

All this is about comparative performance. What about absolute performance? Experts are better, I have said, on the discrimination dimension—they make more precise, if less accurate, predictions than does the chimpanzee. How good are they? The better half of the expert group predicts a meager 18 percent of the variance, the less good group about 14 percent. An average of about 16 percent of the variance is accounted for by expert prediction.[49] On the basis of these findings, Tetlock is forced to concede the crux of the skeptical hypothesis (which he relates to complexity theory): expert prediction and guesswork are essentially the same.[50]

The Complex Complexity of Politico-Economic Systems

We now come to an obvious, major, objection: although economics is complex, so are many natural sciences, including biology. But, it is said, natural science has dealt well with complexity, and its increasingly complex models have not detracted from our ability to predict—quite the opposite, they have enhanced it.[51] Look (the objection continues) at medicine: we have mastered interventions in a complex system, the human body, to obtain our predicted results. Even if we accept that economics is to be understood in terms of complexity, we should not accept that complexity blocks a predictive economic science that can be employed to guide policy.

Donald Saari, a mathematician, argues, though, that it is simply false to suppose that the complexity in the natural sciences approaches that of economics:

> [W]hat we do know indicates that even the simple models from introductory courses in economics can exhibit dynamical behavior far more complex than anything found in classical physics or biology. In fact, all kinds of complicated dynamics (e.g., involving topological entropy, strange attractors, and even conditions yet to be found) already arise in elementary models that only describe how people exchange goods (a pure exchange model).
>
> Instead of being an anomaly, the mathematical source of this complexity is so common to the social sciences that I suspect it highlights a general problem plaguing these areas. If true, this assertion explains why it is so difficult to achieve progress in the social sciences while underscoring the need for new mathematical tools.[52]

To cut to the chase (i.e., to omit the mathematics), Sarri shows that the hidden complexity of social science derives from aggregation out of the unlimited variety of preferences, "preferences that define a sufficiently large dimensional domain that, when aggregated, can generate all imaginable forms of pathological behavior."[53] It should be noted that Sarri shows that this should lead to some doubts about the efficacy of Smith's invisible hand (not that it is especially clear just what Smith meant by the idea).[54]

Insofar as our concern is *expedient public policy*, the economist's policy advice is given to politicians. However, the political system itself, especially one chosen through elections, is itself chaotic, characterized by similar sources of complexity. As Sarri says of electoral politics: "*Beware!* Beware of aggregation procedures because, in an unexpected manner, they allow unanticipated outcomes."[55] We thus have a recipe for tremendous unpredictability: a coupling of two highly complex systems, the economic and political. The coupling of complex systems induces recomplicating effects, leading us further into complexity.[56]

In Hayekian-level complex systems, novelty and unpredictable innovations are the norm. The level of complexity is thus akin to evolutionary theory, not, say, to physiology. This was a point upon which Hayek himself insisted: "Probably the best illustration of a theory of complex phenomena which is of great value, although it describes merely a general pattern whose detail we can never fill in, is the Darwinian theory of evolution by natural selection."[57] Evolutionary biologists cannot predict the course of evolution, though they can predict that some developments will not occur, "e.g., that horses suddenly should begin to give birth to young with wings."[58] What evolutionary and economic science can do is uncover the general principles regulating the system, not predict anything that approximates future developments of the systems.

Why Devaluing the Pursuit of Expediency Is Not Sufficient

The Principle of Insufficient Reason

Hayek insists that we should *never* give in to expediency: "A successful defense of freedom . . . must be dogmatic and make no concessions to expediency, even where it is not possible to show that, besides the known beneficial effects, some particular harmful result would also follow from its infringement."[59] The crux of complexity theory is that our predictions about what will occur are likely to be wrong. There is, then, a very strong case that our interventions are not apt to be expedient because we have radically incomplete knowledge. It is not obvious, though, that a blanket prohibition on the pursuit of expediency is warranted. Is it irrational to act on radically partial knowledge?

To appreciate the problem, suppose we are evaluating two proposed policies that aim at expedient outcomes, P_1 and P_2. Suppose that we have good reason to assume that the predictable consequences of P_1 will be more expedient than the predictable consequences of P_2. Hayek argues that in such situations we will ignore all the unpredictable effects and focus on the known benefits, and so will act in ignorance of most of the costs of our choice.[60] But it is not at all clear that this is irrational. If we suppose that in some instance great values are at stake and the power of our predictive theories is such that we have a good grasp of how to achieve those values within some specified range, and we are confident that these values are so great that unforeseen consequences are to be put aside, then perhaps expedient policy can be advocated. After all, in *The Constitution of Liberty* Hayek himself made concessions to expediency, allowing for, among other policies, state funding of education (including some higher education), public assistance to the very poor, compulsory provision for one's old age, and so on.[61]

Even when great values are not at stake, it is uncertain that acting on only the known costs and benefits is irrational. In such cases are we to say that our expected utility calculations are really indeterminate, and so we should ignore utility considerations? Or are we to say that our calculations, uncertain as they are, still yield guidance? Just what it means to say that expected utility calculations are indeterminate, and what is the best response to such indeterminacy, are difficult matters.[62] But consider a simple case. Suppose, as far as we can tell, that the expected net utility of P_1 is 1,000 while our best estimate of the expected net value of P_2 is 500; suppose further we know that this is a small fraction of the total costs and benefits of our choice, but these other utilities are entirely unpredictable. Call the latter the *unknown, large residue*. So our calculations include some known, small costs and benefits and the unknown, large residue. There are two interesting possibilities: the unknown, large residue of P_1 is either (i) greater than P_2 or (ii) less than P_2. Now at this point some might appeal to the (controversial) principle of insufficient reason that explicitly directs us to treat (i) and (ii) as equally probable; they are mutually exclusive events, and we have no reason to assign different probabilities to them.[63] But if we treat (i) and (ii) as equally probable, then the expected utility of the unknown, large residue of P_1 and P_2 is a wash: it provides no grounds for deciding between them. So then it appears as if the only grounds for deciding between them are the known, even if fairly insignificant, local effects: P_1 beats P_2 on this score (1,000 to 500), so we finally have a ground for choice. However, it now looks as if the Hayekian analyses of complexity and the barriers to prediction make no real difference regarding what we should do: we should do our best with what we know, and what is beyond our knowledge should be ignored.

The Relevance of Rules

So long as our only reasons to choose are reasons of expediency—aiming to bring about good results—there is a plausible case for choosing P_1 even though we are well aware it is only a small improvement on a random choice. This is important: if our only reasons to choose are reasons that aim at producing good results, then even if P_1 has only a miniscule advantage in expediency, we have reason to choose it, though we have firm grounds to doubt that choosing it is likely to turn out better than opting for P_2. The key to avoiding this is to allow another sort of reasoning: rule- or principle-based reasoning of the sort that is not outcome oriented.[64] We might say that the total set of reasons (R_t) to opt for P_1 depend on both the strength of one's reasons of expediency (R_e) and the strength one's rule- or principle-based reasons (R_r).[65] So, we can say $R_t = (w_i)R_e + (w_{1-i})R_r$, where w_i is a weight between 0 and 1 attached to reasons of expediency.[66]

Now we can see that if rule-based reasons do not enter into the choice, (the weight for $R_e = 1$), then it is plausible that even the weakest reasons of expediency still determine R_t. However, if, as Hayek argues, our reasons of expediency are mightily weak (they will approach, but not equal, zero), and if there are relevant principle- or rule-based reasons, then even rules that are weighted modestly will almost certainly determine R_t. This is interesting: Hayek need not really show that rule-based reasons are terribly strong (i.e., that they always have a greater weight attached to them), since his analysis of complexity implies that, at least when it comes to government policy, the value of R_e will be so low that even a high weight (say, where $R_e = 9$) will not greatly affect R_t.

However, Hayek has to show that we have good reasons to abide by rules or principles, so that we can rationally give them some positive weighting in decisions. Consequently, he devotes a good deal of his work to providing the case that we have excellent grounds for following the moral rules and, in general, the traditional norms of our society.[67] The key here is his account of social evolution, to which I now turn.

The Strong Appeal to Cultural Evolution

A Sketch of Hayek's Account

Hayek famously employs an evolutionary account of rules. His theory of social evolution is complex and, as I have argued elsewhere, widely misunderstood; I cannot do justice to it here.[68] A rough sketch will have to suffice.

Hayek's is an account of social, not biological, evolution. That which he sets out to explain is the rise of what he calls "the social order of actions"—the orderly cooperation of different individuals—which he sees as an emergent property of a system of rules.

> It is the resulting overall order of actions but not the regularity of the actions of the separate individuals as such which is important for the preservation of the group; and a certain kind of overall order may in the same manner contribute to the survival of the members of the group whatever the particular rules of individual conduct that bring it about.[69]

Hayek's fundamental insight is that the success of a society in terms of growth, prosperity, immigration, and the copying of its institutions by others depends on the emergent property of orderly cooperation of different individuals that has a complex relation to the rules of conduct individuals follow. As Hayek says, "The selection process will operate on the order as a whole."[70] This is the "Great Society": an overall spontaneous order of adaptations that allows for coordinated action. Hayek, then, sets out to provide an evolutionary account whereby the rules and institutions that give rise to this order (i.e., this emergent property) are selected via a competition ("in the widest sense")[71] among social orders. The emergent property arises out of a system of rules; therefore the competition among these social orders is determined by their constituent rules and institutions as they operate in specific environments. "Society can thus exist only if by a process of selection rules have evolved which lead individuals to behave in a manner which makes social life possible."[72]

Evolutionary accounts are enormously attractive to complexity theorists. We have seen that complex systems—such as the order of actions—are too unpredictable for us to design rules that are expedient. Rules arise in an undersigned, spontaneous manner. But what gives us any confidence that these spontaneous rules are worthy of being followed? Hayek's answer is that they have arisen in a competitive environment and the success of our current order depends on them.

> To understand our civilisation one must appreciate that the extended order resulted not from human design or intention but spontaneously: it arose from the unintentional conforming to certain traditional and largely *moral* practices, many of which men tend to dislike, whose significance they usually fail to understand, whose validity they cannot prove, and which have nonetheless fairly rapidly spread by means of an evolutionary selection—the comparative increase of population and wealth—of those groups that happened to follow them.[73]

An evolutionary account can claim that, without planning or design, the rules we have are superior (in a sense that we have yet to consider) to at least a certain class of past rules, so it would seem that in some sense the rules we have are *good rules,* having survived a competition with other candidates.[74] And that would show we should take account of the rules in our decisions: they are good moral rules.[75] Moreover, just as the future of complex systems is, except concerning broad patterns, unpredictable, so too is the course of evolution; thus, we seem to have a method of explanation that perfectly suits the development of spontaneous orders.[76]

The Rejection of the Sufficiency Claim

Can some such evolutionary account provide a justification for following the moral rules and principles constituent of our complex order of actions? The most radical view, which I think is ultimately unacceptable, is that if a moral rule has evolved as part of our complex order of actions, then we have good reason to follow it. Having evolved as part of the complex order would be sufficient to give us good reason to follow the rule or principle. Indeed, it looks as if sometimes Hayek almost wants to claim that being the product of social evolution is a sufficient *and* necessary condition for having good reasons to follow a principle. This, though, would be far too strong, since Hayek does allow for incremental moral reform. Let us focus on the evolutionist's Sufficiency Claim.

To see our way to an evaluation of this claim, let us begin by granting the following:

(a) Given some selection mechanism M, our current system of moral principles has been selected (in a competition with other orders of actions over the course of history).

A selection mechanism is supposed by an evolutionary account that, like Hayek's, conceives of evolution as the outcome of a competition between some units (e.g., genes, individuals, rules, cultures) in an environment. There must be some selection mechanism that determines the outcome of the competition, and so the evolutionary winner at any given time. For present purposes we can leave M unspecified, though we must not forget that Hayek insisted that the selection mechanism for cultural evolution is not the same as in Darwin's account of biological evolution.[77]

Claim (a) itself does not provide us with reason to follow a moral principle. Suppose we accept that M has selected an order of actions that includes some rule r. It certainly seems that we can now step back and reflect whether r is mere superstition, or whatever.[78] That a whole set of evolved norms might be very bad is the moral of H. G. Wells's *Time Machine*. In Wells's novel, postapocalyptic humanity has split into two groups: the Morlock and Eoli. The Morlocks feed, clothe, and then eat the Eoli. These norms—certainly accepted by the Morlocks and to some extent by the Eoli too—had indeed developed during a long process of cultural evolution lasting many centuries, but we (and Wells's time traveler) can see that their entire moral code is deeply objectionable. But perhaps this is too quick a conclusion. Someone may object that, though of course the Morlock and Eloi norms are immoral *to us (and the time traveler), given our evolved norms,* we cannot say that they are objectionable, full stop, or from some neutral, objective, point of view. *We* reject the norms of the Morlock and Eloi in light of *our own* morality, but (says the objector) this is to simply draw on our own evolution. What we cannot do is to reject *our own* evolved morality in toto, though we can reject some of our moral rules because, say, they conflict with parts of our evolved morality.

Hayek seems attracted to what I have called the "objector's" position: we can only consider the adequacy of some moral principles in the light of the "giveness" of the others, and that only an ill-advised rationalism would radically question the overall outcome of social evolution.[79] He writes:

> It is the submission to undesigned rules and conventions whose significance and importance we largely do not understand, this reverence for the traditional,

that the rationalistic type of mind finds so uncongenial, though it is indispensable for the working of a free society. It has its foundation in the insight which David Hume stressed and which is of decisive importance for the antirationalist, evolutionary, tradition—namely, that the "rules of morality are not the conclusions of our reason." Like all other values, *our morals are not a product but a presupposition of reason, part of the ends which the instrument of our intellect has been developed to serve.* At any one stage of our evolution the system of values into which we are born supplies the ends which our reason must serve.[80]

Hayek advances a radical proposal: morality did not arise out of reason and, indeed, since our reason is itself the product of social evolution, it does not give us an Archimedean point to stand outside of cultural evolution and evaluate its norms.[81] However, even if morality and reason are the product of some process M, it does not follow that reason, having developed, cannot evaluate M. As Anthony O'Hear rightly points out, once our capacities have evolved via M, they may develop and be exercised in ways that M would never select.[82] Even if, say, our intelligence was selected as a way to obtain better food in competition with other primates, our intelligence could now lead us to go on a hunger strike against the mistreatment of other primates at the local zoo.

What would have to be true for us to accept our evolved moral rules as necessarily worthy of our allegiance? Consider:

(b) M selects what we reflectively think to be the best principles/rules.

Claim (b), however, undermines any justificatory force of the evolutionist account, since it is our reflective capacity that allows us to identify the best principles. That they are produced by M would certainly be of interest, but M would not seem to be doing the justificatory work: our reflective reason would tell us what the best rules are. A robust evolutionary justification of morality could, in contrast, be grounded on:

(c) M-selected rules are the most worthy principles/rules, though we cannot know this by inspecting each principle/rule.

This would certainly show that rules selected by M warrant our acceptance. But (c) articulates precisely the Panglossian view that advocates of cultural evolution, including Hayek, have been careful to avoid: cultural evolution does not imply that we possess the best of all possible moral rules. For (c) to be justified, an evolutionist would have to show:

(d) Cultural evolution has proceeded for an infinite amount of time, such that every possible set of cultural rules (or cultures) has competed with every other one, with M finally selecting our rules;

(e) The endogenous and exogenous states of the complex system are stable. The environment is unchanging.[83]

Unless (d) is true, we cannot say that our rules are the best, as M is still in the process of selecting rules; and unless (e) is true, there is no reason to suppose what M has selected in past will be selected in the future, as selection occurs in the context of a given environment. What M selects in a preindustrial economy need not be selected by M in a postindustrial one.

These assumptions are, of course, so strong that (c), the claim that our rules are the best possible set of rules (though we have no direct reflective access to this), must be set aside. In its place, it would seem that the best we can do is:

(f) At each point in the past t, M selected principles at t that were more worthy than the available competing principles, though we cannot know this by inspecting each principle.

It is important that we cannot say either that our present principles are better than all the other principles that have been eliminated or even that our present principles are better than our own past ones. Evolution, as Hayek realized, is path dependent.[84] Suppose that at time t_1 (in environment E_1) M selects A over B; at time t_2 (in environment E_2), M selects C over A. When we get to t_3 (in environment E_3), where M selects D over C, we cannot say that our now-evolved D rule is better than either A or B. Even if we suppose that the environment is stable, if evolution is path dependent in the sense that once a rule is defeated by another it is deleted from the option set, the evolutionary outcome may be inferior to some previously defeated option.[85]

Of course, just because path dependence is possible, and so may lead to outcomes inferior to eliminated options, it does not follow that it is common.[86] It is, though, certainly a bar to inferring that later is better than earlier. Moreover, if we suppose that the rate of social change is rapid, we have good grounds for doubting that our current rules are especially good in the current environment. *Ex hypothesi*, they were selected by M as more worthy than some competitors at t, but if $t + n$ is very different, there is not much of a presumption that the rules are more worthy now, unless we suppose that M operates very quickly. The upshot is this: *even if we make the strong assumption that the selection mechanism inherently selects rules we consider worthy, if social change is rapid we cannot conclude our current rules are worthy unless social evolution occurs rapidly.* All we can say is that at some point in the past the rules were more worthy than a set of competitors.

Even (f) is too strong. Although we might accept that, as a whole, the set of current rules tend to track our reflective conceptions of right and value, it is doubtful that this is true of every rule. Even biological evolution produces traits that have no current survival value, and are actually maladaptive (e.g., our appendix), and no doubt cultural evolution does too.[87] If so, then some of our rules may not tend in any way to track our notion of worthy rules. *Pace* Hayek, even on an evolutionary account some rules might correctly be described as "superstitious" and without any merit whatsoever.

A Modest Defense of Evolutionary Morality

Qualified Rational Deferral to the Outcome of Evolution

We must, I think, reject any claim that just because a rule or principle is the product of social evolution we have good grounds to follow it. What Hayek needs is a justification for an attitude of *qualified rational deferral to current moral rules.* Overall, a successful Hayekian evolutionary defense of principled moral action must show the following:

(a) A system of rules is necessary.
(b) We cannot rationally construct such a system.
(c) Social evolution can explain the rise of such a system.
(d) Rational reflection indicates that we often ought to follow these evolved rules (partly) because they are the evolved rules of our society.

Let us see how these four claims might be endorsed within a broadly Hayekian framework. Note at this point our discussion is "Hayekean," rather than Hayek's. I will try to show that important themes in Hayek's philosophy support these claims, even though it leads to a more modest evolutionary account of ethics than he proposed.

Claim (a): Complex Systems as Rule Governed

One of Hayek's core claims is that spontaneous complex orders—unplanned complex systems—depend on their elements following certain rules. A spontaneous order is partially characterized by the rules that govern the behavior of its elements, and any such system must be rule-governed.[88] Spontaneous orders, then, arise among humans because we are rule-followers, and so can develop systems of cooperation in which we can form reasonable micro expectations about the behavior of others. Such rules need not be conscious; indeed, many are not.[89] Hayek also insists that the system of rules must be abstract, and not aim at "known particular results . . . but is preserved as a means for assisting in the pursuit of a great variety of individual purposes."[90] Given the analysis of complex systems it is clear why the rules cannot aim at "known particular results"—the particular results of the system cannot be known. And given the unpredictability of the system, the rules will have to be applicable to new situations; thus it is plausible that the fundamental ones defining the system will be abstract. So "principle" may be a better term than "rule," as many of these rules are abstract and only implicitly understood.[91]

The point here is that complex systems are inherently principle following; the social order of actions is structured by the principle-guided action of its members. The order of actions cannot persist if each acts solely to maximize his own utility: uncertainty about what is the best course of action, transaction costs, lack of predictability, all conspire to make human societies necessarily rule-governed. The distance between Hayek and neo-Humean game theorists such as Ken Binmore is not nearly as great as we might think: both believe that inherent to the structure of complex human action is settling on shared rules or norms to guide behavior.[92]

Claim (b): Hayek's Anti-Constructivism

Principles are necessary to the functioning of complex systems, but such a system of rules cannot be rationally constructed. We cannot rationally construct the best system of principles because we do not have a good grasp of the consequences and interaction effects of the principles that compose the system. Remember that Hayek insists that the order of actions is an emergent property of the system of principles: if so, the basis for social cooperation emerges in a complex way from the entire order of rules and principles. Consequently, the project of designing a new system would require a depth of knowledge that far exceeds what is available to us. This is the real crux of Hayek's anticonstructivism, and it is solidly grounded in his theory of complexity.

So far, so good. But while Hayek has an overwhelming case against total social reconstruction of the sort envisaged by revolutionary regimes of the twentieth century, it is not at all clear that this account gives us reason to defer to any specific rule or principle because it is the product of social evolution. True, we cannot redesign the entire system of principles, but there seems no reason why we must pay heed to any specific one. One justification for strict rule conformity to every principle can be derived from what we might call the *Burkean Fragility Thesis.* Implicit in much of Hayek's evolutionary argument is a Burkean "reverence for tradition." Since we cannot know the purposes of our principles, a reformist attitude is apt to alter so many of them that the system will not be able to adapt. If the complex system has limited capacities for adaptation and self-maintenance then, prima facie, it would seem wise not to tinker with it, since almost any significant change might upset its fragile equilibrium, and we have no confidence that it will adapt and move to a new equilibrium. This would indeed instill what Hayek describes as a "reverence for the traditional," for the traditional embodies a difficult-to-achieve social stability.[93]

The worry, though, is that if Hayek really embraces the idea that somehow complex systems are fragile, he will, despite his disclaimers, be led from classical liberalism to conservatism. A commitment to fragility leads to precisely what Hayek finds so objectionable about conservatism—a suspicion of, and resistance to, change as such, for all change is a threat to a fragile social order. In contrast, says Hayek, "the liberal position is based on courage and confidence, on a preparedness to let change run its course, even if we cannot predict where it will lead."[94] Indeed, Hayek stresses that complex systems are usually self-maintaining.[95] By this Hayek means that complex systems have a tendency to persist and to respond to a range of exogenous and endogenous changes.[96] Alternatively, we can say that complex systems are adaptive: "the agents in these systems in some sense learn to better deal with their environments. They are continually organizing and reorganizing their building blocks according to the payoffs they receive from the activities."[97] If, though, *this* is the nature of complex systems, then it is hard to see why it does not apply to moral innovation as well: the self-adaptive characteristic of the social and economic order will respond, in unpredictable ways to be sure, to moral change as it does do to the host of other disturbances to which it is subjected.

Hayek's use of the Burkean case for current moral rules, then, drives him into a dilemma. If the social order really is fragile, so that change and innovation raises the specter of social disintegration, there is a reasonable argument for reverence for current moral rules. But then Hayek's liberalism is itself called into question, for it is premised on the insistence that society can adjust to widespread innovative behavior.[98] We still are searching for the grounds of *qualified* rational deferral to current moral principles.

Claims (c) and (d): Why We Should Pay Attention to the Results of Social Evolution

If morality is to perform the function of providing rule-based expectations for social interactions, allowing coordination, and so on, it must be publicly known and shared. Philosophers are apt to conceive morality *simply* as something that is justified, or correct, or true, as if one person could have the only correct view of morality, just as one person might have the only correct view of the type of life on some distant planet. Morality, though, is first and foremost, a practical matter of shared principles that structure complex interactions: principles that are true or the best, but are not shared, simply cannot perform the task of morality in a complex system.

For morality to serve its purposes, then, we must coordinate on the same morality. The relevant moral principles on which we act must be a matter of common knowledge: I must know that you are following the common principles and you know that I am, and know that I know that you are.

In this sense morality must be public: if moral principles are to perform their task in a complex order, they must be publicly acknowledged. Moral duty is not, in the first instance, a matter of getting things epistemically correct; it is, first and foremost, a practical guarantee about legitimate expectations.

The problem, however, is that it is largely indeterminate which of the many different systems of rules and principles we shall coordinate. Traditional social contract theory is objectionably constructivist because it seeks to identify a unique set of political principles, or principles of justice, on which rational people must agree. But there are many different possible sets of principles or rules on which we might coordinate. We can think of the problem in terms of an impure coordination game along the lines of figure 1. Suppose that X and Y are alternative moral principles regulating some practice. The numbers in the matrix refer to ordinal utility, with high numbers indicating highly ranked options; in each cell, Alf's utility is in the lower left, Betty's in the upper right. The uncoordinated outcomes indicate no moral principles at all on this matter (each acts as he or she wishes). Looked at ex ante, Betty has reason to endorse practice X; Alf to endorse Y. Ex ante, Betty does not have reason to endorse Y as legitimate over X, nor does Alf have a reason to endorse X rather than Y. They do, however, have reason to coordinate on either the X or the Y principle.

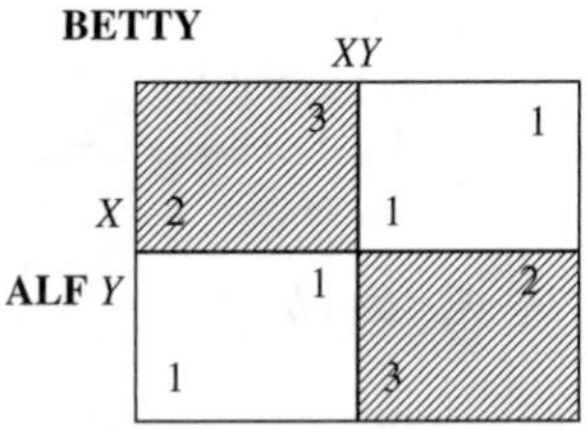

Figure 1 A simple coordination game

Should Alf and Betty find themselves at X,X, neither would have reason to change his or her action. Given each of their preferences, they have the most reason to act on practice X. Should they instead find themselves at Y,Y, each will then have most reason to act on practice Y.

A one-shot two-person game can give us an insight, but it is clearly an inadequate way to model the evolution of a morality. The social coordination problem is not a single- play game, but an iterated game with numerous players. We have a number of encounters with others, and each can be understood as a play in a series of impure coordination games. In large, N-person coordination games with multiple equilibria, a bandwagon effect easily takes over. As Hume observed, the convention grows through "a slow progression, and by our repeated experience of the inconveniences of transgressing it."[99] The key here is the increasing returns to playing the same rule (say, Y): the more people play Y, the more it makes sense for others to play Y, even those who strongly prefer X. The same reasoning that shows why I am now using the qwerty keyboard and Microsoft Windows (the increasing returns of shared keyboards and operating systems) shows how we can all come to accept the same moral principles despite beginning with diverse evaluations. What is fascinating is that increasing returns are often a feature of complex systems—and so the system can go off in very different directions depending on small chance events.[100] For example, if X players tend to be more visible, people may come to think that X is a popular principle, and the more popular people think it is, the more people will be attracted to it, and so X may gain currency and dominate; in slightly different circumstances Y could have dominated. Thus we see how the evolution of coordination itself exhibits complex features.

This does not mean that we must embrace the whole of our morality: we certainly can stand back and evaluate moral principles and refuse to abide by those parts of our social morality that are unjust, inhumane, or unfair. In terms of the coordination game modeling, only if the current coordination is better than no coordination at all should rational individuals continue to embrace it. Thus we can see how it is both rational to embrace the outcome of social evolution (we accept principle Y because it is the evolved rule, even though in our hearts we might think X is better), but we still can have a critical attitude toward current morality.[101] If coordinating on a moral rule is worse than going it alone (coordination is not a Nash equilibrium), individuals will defect and the rule will be weakened, and perhaps, eventually abandoned. We thus have arrived at a justification for what Hayek needs: a qualified rational deference to current moral rules.

Conclusion

I have tried to show here how Hayek's original and insightful analyses of complexity and the evolution of moral principles provide compelling grounds for his striking claim that we ought to follow abstract general principles or rules rather than pursue apparently expedient social and economic policies that aim to make us better off. It is not that the aim of making us better off is not admirable, but in large-scale decisions such as those undertaken by government, we do not have the information to do it. Given how little guidance expediency gives us, we are driven to rely on evolved moral principles. I have argued that, at least at times, Hayek seems to suggest too great a deference to evolved norms. These aspects of Hayek's thought, I have suggested, are both objectionable in themselves and do not fit well with his liberalism and his faith in the dynamic and self-regulating character of the Great Society. However, I have argued that some basic Hayekean themes allow us to construct an account of evolved morality that grounds an attitude of qualified rational deferral to our current evolved moral rules. Thus we can see how rational and reflective individuals who recognize the complex character of their social order ought to embrace Hayek's dictum that they should forgo expediency and generally rely on the evolved principles of their society.

Notes

1. I am especially grateful to Chandran Kukathas, Julian Lamont, Guido Pincione, and Leif Wenar for their helpful comments and suggestions on earlier versions of this chapter.
2. Friedrich A. Hayek, *Law, Legislation and Liberty,* vol. 1, *Rules and Order* (Chicago: University of Chicago Press, 1973), p. 55.
3. Ibid., p. 38. See also Friedrich A. Hayek, *The Constitution of Liberty* (Chicago: University of Chicago Press 1960), p. 160. Bruce Caldwell reports that the latter is Hayek's first mention of this term. See his *Hayek's Challenge: An Intellectual Biography of F. A. Hayek* (Chicago: University of Chicago Press, 2004), p. 294.
4. Hayek, *Rules and Order,* p. 38.
5. Caldwell correctly argues that Hayek never developed a full-fledged theory of complexity (*Hayek's Challenge,* p. 363). Hayek's writings did, however, display many of the ideas that later crystallized into the complexity theory. J. Barkley Rosser, Jr.'s observation seems more accurate: "Hayek . . . was an early and independent developer of complexity theory in something resembling its current form, albeit without computers" ("On the Complexities of Complex Economic Dynamics," *The Journal of Economic Perspectives,* 13 (Autumn 1999): 169–192 at p. 185n. See also Karen Vaughn's excellent essay, "Hayek's Theory of the Market Order as an Instance of the Theory of Complex, Adaptive Systems," *Journal de Economistes et des Etudes Humaines,* 9 (Juin–Septembre 1999): 241–256. Although Caldwell cites Vaughn in support of his view, her study's conclusions are closer to Rosser's.
6. Friedrich A. Hayek, "The Theory of Complex Phenomena," in *Readings in the Philosophy of Social Science,* eds. Michael Martin and Lee C. McIntyre, (Cambridge, MA: MIT Press, 1994), pp. 55–70 at p. 56. See also Hayek's Nobel Memorial Lecture, "The Pretence of Knowledge," in his *New Studies in Politics, Economics and the History of Ideas* (London: Routledge, 1978), pp. 25–34 at p. 26.
7. See Vaughn, "Hayek's Theory of the Market Order," p. 249.
8. Hayek, "The Pretence of Knowledge," pp. 26–27.
9. Hayek, "The Theory of Complex Phenomena," p. 57. Emphasis added, citation omitted. See Vaughn, "Hayek's Theory of the Market Order," p. 248.

10. This is an example of Hayek's complicated version of methodological individualism; the properties of wholes cannot be reduced to the properties of individuals, though those properties result from individuals in relations. Cf Caldwell, *Hayek's Challenge*, pp. 281ff.

11. See Mitchell Waldrop, *Complexity: The Emerging Science at the Edge of Order and Chaos* (New York: Simon and Schuster, 1992), pp. 81–83.

12. See Edward Tanner, *Why Things Bite Back* (London: Fourth Estate, 1996), p. 16.

13. Hayek, "The Theory of Complex Phenomena," pp. 61–62.

14. This is the so-called "butterfly" effect. See Peter Smith, *Explaining Chaos* (Cambridge: Cambridge University Press, 1998), p. 16.

15. Tanner, *Why Things Bite Back,* p. 16.

16. Smith, *Explaining Chaos,* p. 20.

17. Hayek, *Rules and Order,* p. 40.

18. This is crucial to chaos theory. See Smith, *Explaining Chaos,* p. 13.

19. Hayek, "The Theory of Complex Phenomena," pp. 60ff. See Caldwell, *Hayek's Challenge*, pp. 382ff.

20. Compare Hayek, "The Theory of Complex Phenomena," p. 61, to Smith, *Explaining Chaos,* p. 18.

21. Vaughn, "Hayek's Theory of the Market Order," p. 245.

22. See Hayek, "The Use of Knowledge in Society," in *Individualism and Economic Order* (Chicago: University of Chicago Press, 1948).

23. See Hayek, "The Pretence of Knowledge," p. 27. This is identified as an element of contemporary economic analyses of complexity by Rosser, "On the Complexities of Complex Economic Dynamics," p. 176.

24. Rosser, "On the Complexities of Complex Economic Dynamics," p. 176.

25. Friedrich A. Hayek, "The Meaning of Competition," in *Individualism and Economic Order* (Chicago: University of Chicago Press, 1973), pp. 92–106. See also Israel M. Kirzner, "Discovery, Private Property and the Theory of Justice in Capitalist Society," in *The Meaning of Market Process* (London: Routledge, 1992), pp. 209–227.

26. For a survey see Steven M. Sheffrin, *Rational Expectations,* 2nd ed. (Cambridge: Cambridge University Press, 1996).

27. Ibid., p. 22.

28. Rosser, "On the Complexities of Complex Economic Dynamics," p. 176.

29. Hayek, "The Use of Knowledge in Society." As Israel M. Kirzner observed, "Hayek had no difficulty with the notion, in principle, of a social optimum mapped out by the underlying data of preferences and scarcities. He merely declared that this optimum not to be the relevant criterion for social policy, since the knowledge needed for the formulation of such an optimum is never given or available to a single mind." ("Market Process Theory," in *The Meaning of Market Process,* pp. 3–37 at p. 15).

30. Hayek, "The Use of Knowledge in Society," p. 77. As Chandran Kukathas points out, in comparison to von Mises, Hayek's critique of socialism is not so much that, in the absence of a market, prices could not be calculated but that,

in the absence of a market, the necessary information to determine prices could not be collected (*Hayek and Modern Liberalism* (Oxford: Clarendon Press, 1989), p. 57.

31. Hayek, "The Theory of Complex Phenomena," p. 58.
32. Ibid. See also Rosser, "On the Complexities of Complex Economic Dynamics," pp. 184–185.
33. On the lack on empirical testing of standard economic models, see Roger E. Backhouse, *Truth and Progress in Economics* (Cheltenham, UK: Edward Elgar, 1997), ch. 14. Robert S. Goldfarb concludes that some theoretical propositions are "done in" by the data while, for a significant group of economists, "if the data do not fit the theory, too bad for the data" ("Now You See it, Now You Don't: Emerging Contrary Results in Economics," *Journal of Economic Methodology,* 4 (1997): 221–244 at p. 238).
34. Backhouse, *Truth and Progress in Economics,* p. 113.
35. This is important to chaos theory. See Smith, *Explaining Chaos.*
36. In defending utilitarianism as the basis for public policy Robert E. Goodin (*Utilitarianism as a Public Philosophy* [Cambridge: Cambridge University Press, 1995], p. 63) argues that all this is precisely backwards. He claims that while it is certainly true that policy makers do not have access to micro-level predictive knowledge, they do not need it, and that is why expedient public policy is possible. All that policymakers require is aggregate statistical predictions of the overall consequences of the policies; the individual variations will cancel out. This argument for social scientific knowledge goes back to Durkheim. If we can predict how many suicides will occur in a year, we have the basis for an expedient social policy, even if we cannot predict who will commit suicide. Hayek anticipates this reply, and correctly notes that statistics is "impotent to deal with pattern complexity," because it supposes independence rather than systematic connection:

> Statistics . . . deals with the problem of large numbers essentially by eliminating complexity and deliberately treating the individual elements as if they were not systematically connected. It avoids the problem of complexity by substituting for the information on the individual elements information on the frequency with which their different properties occur in classes of such elements, and it deliberately disregards the fact that the relative position of the different elements in a structure matter.
>
> (Hayek, "The Theory of Complex Phenomena," p. 59)

37. See Tanner, *Why Things Bite Back,* p. 86.
38. I owe this example to Julian Lamont.
39. Tanner, *Why Things Bite Back,* pp. 82–84.
40. Ibid., p. 42.
41. Ibid., p. 272.
42. See Alexander Rosenberg, *Philosophy of Social Science,* 2nd ed. (Boulder, CO: Westview, 1995) and Dierdre McCloskey, "The Rhetoric of Economics," in

The Philosophy of Economics, ed. Daniel M. Hausman (Cambridge: Cambridge University Press, 1994), pp. 395–446.

43. Backhouse, *Truth and Progress in Economic Knowledge,* p. 206.

44. Richard M. Alston, J. R. Kearl, and Michael B. Vaughan, "Is There a Consensus among Economists in the 1990s?" Papers and Proceedings of the 104th Annual Meeting of the American Economic Association, *The American Economic Review* 82, no. 2 (May 1992): 203–209.

45. Ibid., pp. 207ff. This effect was not observed in economists working at the top ten research universities.

46. Goldfarb, "Now You See it, Now You Don't," p. 220.

47. Ibid., p. 237.

48. Philip E. Tetlock, *Expert Political Judgment: How Good Is It? How Can We Know?* (Princeton: University of Princeton Press, 2005), esp. ch. 2.

49. Ibid., pp. 76ff.

50. Tetlock is not himself a skeptic. He is hopeful that we can improve public policymaking, so he focuses on the difference within the expert group, looking at which sorts of experts tend to do better and which do worse.

51. See Rosenberg, *Philosophy of Social Science,* p. 14.

52. Donald Saari, "Mathematical Complexity of Simple Economics," *Notices of the AMA* 42, no. 2 (1995): 222–231, at p. 222. Strange attractors are related to chaos theory; see Smith, *Explaining Chaos,* pp. 142–146.

53. Sarri, "Mathematical Complexity of Simple Economics," p. 229.

54. While we can still identify equilibrium, prices do not always move to equilibrium. Saari, "Mathematical Complexity of Simple Economics," p. 224. On the problems interpreting just what Smith's invisible hand is supposed to be, see William D. Grampp, "What Did Smith Mean by the Invisible Hand?" *Journal of Political Economy,* 108 (January 2000): 441–465.

55. Donald Sarri, *Chaotic Elections! A Mathematician Looks at Voting* (Providence, RI: American Mathematical Association, 2000), p. 152.

56. This constitutes a reply to those who argue that "models of complex systems can incorporate positive feedback and path-dependency that appear to demonstrate inefficient market results that seem to cry out for government remedy." (See Vaughn, "Hayek's Theory of the Market," p. 253.) One of the lessons of public choice theory is that policy recommendations cannot be premised simply on a theory of market failure; a theory of government failure is necessary as well.

57. Hayek, "The Theory of Complex Phenomena," p. 60. See also Douglas Glen Whitman, "Hayek contra Pangloss on Evolutionary Systems," *Constitutional Political Economy,* 9 (1988): 450–466.

58. Hayek, "The Theory of Complex Phenomena," p. 61.

59. Hayek, *Rules and Order,* p. 61.

60. Which will lead to more demands for government action when these costs manifest themselves. See Hayek, *Rules and Order,* pp. 59–60. See also Hayek's *The Road to Serfdom* (1944; Chicago: University of Chicago Press, 1976).

61. Hayek, *The Constitution of Liberty*, Part III.
62. See here Isaac Levi, *The Enterprise of Knowledge* (Cambridge, MA: MIT Press, 1980).
63. The principle of insufficient reason is disputed; in some cases it can lead to counterintuitive results. For a useful defense, see Hans-Werner Sinn, "A Rehabilitation of the Principle of Insufficient Reason," *Quarterly Journal of Economics*, 94 (May 1980): 493–506.
64. See Alan H. Goldman's discussion of "strong rules" in *Practical Rules: When We Need Them and When We Don't* (Cambridge: Cambridge University Press, 2002), p. 15.
65. I shall not distinguish rules and principles here. I am assuming here for sake of simplicity that we have a cardinal scale of strength of reasons. This actually is equivalent to many conceptions of decision value or utility, for example, as used by Nozick (see next note).
66. For the idea of such complex decision value schemes (though not focused on principled reasoning), see Robert Nozick, *The Nature of Rationality* (Princeton: Princeton University Press, 1993). For an application of this idea to principled reasoning, see my "Principles, Goals and Symbols: Nozick on Practical Rationality," in *Robert Nozick*, ed. David Schmidtz (Cambridge: Cambridge University Press, 2002), pp. 105–130.
67. At times Hayek clearly distinguishes the legal rules of common law from moral rules; and at other times his analysis is broader, encompassing the traditions of a society, including its morality. I shall focus here on moral rules and principles. See the quote from Hayek at note 70 below.
68. See my essay "Hayek on the Evolution of Society and Mind," in *The Cambridge Companion to Hayek*, ed. Edward Feser (Cambridge: Cambridge University Press, 2006), pp. 259–286.
69. Friedrich A. Hayek, "Notes on the Evolution of Systems of Rules of Conduct," in *Studies in Philosophy, Politics, and Economics* (Chicago: University of Chicago Press, 1967), p. 68.
70. Ibid., p. 71.
71. Hayek, *The Constitution of Liberty*, p. 37.
72. Hayek, *Rules and Order*, p. 44.
73. Hayek, *The Fatal Conceit: The Errors of Socialism*, ed. W. W. Bartley III (Chicago: University of Chicago Press, 1988), p. 6 (emphasis in original). As Caldwell notes, caution must be exercised when employing this work in interpreting Hayek, as some of the final text seems to reflect the views of Bartley, who finished the manuscript because of Hayek's failing health. See *Hayek's Challenge*, pp. 316ff. One of the limitations of Anthony O'Hear's otherwise interesting analysis of Hayek's account of social evolution is that *Fatal Conceit* is his sole primary source for Hayek. Anthony O'Hear, *Beyond Evolution: Human Nature and the Limits of Evolutionary Explanation* (Oxford: Oxford University Press, 1997), pp. 146ff.
74. And remember that according to Hayek competition is itself a discovery procedure. Hayek, "The Meaning of Competition."

75. Two suppositions are implicit here. First, that an evolutionary account of moral rules provides a *justification* of those rules—it shows that they are sound moral rules. *The Fatal Conceit* (p. 58), however, argues that the rational justification of morality is impossible. The question is whether this is really Hayek's view. Caldwell argues that this position "clearly derives from Bartley" (*Hayek's Challenge*, p. 317; see also note 73 above). Even O'Hear, who takes the *Fatal Conceit* as his sole source for Hayek's views on cultural evolution, ultimately sees Hayek's account as justificatory (*Beyond Evolution*, p. 148). Second, I am supposing in the text that we can provide an answer to the question "why act on justified morality?"—an issue that I consider in the section "Claims (c) and (d): Why We Should Pay Attention to the Results of Social Evolution."

76. Hayek, *The Fatal Conceit*, p. 25.

77. The error of Social Darwinism, he argued, was in thinking that the selection mechanism for social evolution was the same as in Darwin's account of biological evolution (*The Fatal Conceit*, pp. 23–28). Social Darwinists such as Herbert Spencer had a more complicated understanding of evolution than this implies. See Herbert Spencer, *First Principles* (London: Murray, 1862).

78. Hayek is scathing about this "rationalistic" attitude toward our moral principles (*The Constitution of Liberty*, pp. 63ff).

79. Ibid., p. 63.

80. Hayek, *The Constitution of Liberty*, p. 63. Emphasis added.

81. I have examined Hayek's evolutionary account of the development of reason in my "Hayek on the Evolution of Society and Mind."

82. O'Hear, *Beyond Evolution*, p. 214.

83. See Whitman, "Hayek Contra Pangloss on Evolutionary Systems," pp. 49ff.

84. For a nice discussion in the context of cultural evolution, see Whitman, "Hayek Contra Pangloss on Evolutionary Systems," esp. p. 55.

85. See Dennis C. Mueller, *Public Choice III* (Cambridge: Cambridge University Press, 2003), pp. 586–588.

86. See Whitman, "Hayek contra Pangloss on Evolutionary Systems," p. 64.

87. Ibid., p. 51. See also O'Hear, *Beyond Evolution*, pp. 103, 142, 149.

88. See Hayek, *Rules and Order*, pp. 38ff. See also Vaughn, "Hayek's Theory of the Market Order," pp. 250ff.

89. Hayek, *Rules and Order*, p. 43.

90. Hayek, *Law, Legislation and Liberty*, vol. 2, *The Mirage of Social Justice* (Chicago: University of Chicago Press, 1976), p. 5.

91. Hayek, *Rules and Order*, p. 60.

92. Ken Binmore, "Reciprocity and the Social Contract," *Politics, Philosophy and Economics*, 3 (February 2004): 5–35.

93. Note here the similarity to the "precautionary principle" that is popular in environmentalist writing.

94. Hayek, *The Constitution of Liberty*, p. 400. As Virginia Postrel writes, "This faith in spontaneous adjustment, in adaptation and evolution, does indeed separate

dynamists from their fellow conservatives" (*The Future and its Enemies* [New York: Touchstone, 1999], p. 41).

95. Hayek, "The Theory of Complex Phenomena," p. 57.
96. Hayek, *Rules and Order,* p. 63.
97. Vaughn, "Hayek's Theory of the Market Order," p. 244.
98. Hayek's attraction to the Burkean case for traditional morality tempts him to distinguish economic from moral innovation, telling us that the liberal, "especially in the economic field," believes that self-regulation will bring about necessary adaptations, suggesting that the economic order is dynamic while the moral order is fragile. Hayek, *The Constitution of Liberty,* p. 400.
99. David Hume, *A Treatise of Human Nature,* 2nd ed., ed. L. A. Selby-Bigge and P. H. Nidditch (Oxford: Clarendon Press, 1978).
100. See Waldrop, *Complexity,* ch. 1, esp. pp. 44–45.
101. Hayek, *The Constitution of Liberty,* p. 70.

CHAPTER 9

Culture, Order, and Virtue

Michael C. Munger

To understand our civilization, one must appreciate that the extended order resulted not from human design or intention but spontaneously; it arose from unintentionally conforming to certain traditional and largely *moral* practices, many of which men tend to dislike, whose significance they usually fail to understand, whose validity they cannot prove, and which have nonetheless fairly rapidly spread by means of an evolutionary selection—the comparative increase of population and wealth—of those groups that happened to follow them.

F. A. Hayek[1]

For many people, "spontaneous order" seems nonsensical. After all, design implies a designer. Then they turn the argument over: if there is no designer, there cannot be order. Hayek's fundamental insight, not just about market processes but about the evolution of social institutions, is that order can exist without any design whatsoever. Design may by definition imply a designer, but order simply requires regularity, consistency, and coherence in a system. And in the body of work that Hayek produced near the end of his life, he went much further: legitimate and stable social orders are beyond the capacity of human understanding, and can never be created de novo by conscious human agency.

The essence of social spontaneous order is the requirement that individuals, acting of their own volition, will do things that (1) accomplish their ends, and (2) do not violate the expectations of other people in the society. It is tempting to think that spontaneous orders also have good normative properties, but this is by no means obvious. The canonical example of spontaneous order, a well-functioning market, does have good normative properties, in the sense that individual self-interest is consistent with the public good.

But such consistency between individual choices and aggregate consequences is not assured.

Human beings choose actions based on their conceptions of the moral world and their place in it, but they also consider incentives and calculate gains that accrue to one action rather than another. For the purposes of this chapter, I am going to adopt the convention that humans act purposively. I didn't say "rationally," mind you. The claim is only that people choose actions that they believe (rightly or wrongly) will lead to a goal that they consider (rightly or wrongly) desirable.

This impulse, or purpose, on its own, is neither ethically good nor bad. It just is. From what, then, arise our judgments about whether an action is morally laudable, or detestable, or perhaps neutral? The answer given by Hume (for example, in *A Treatise of Human Nature,* Book III) was that these labels are entirely conventional: what is moral in one society might be appalling in another. Manners differ broadly, showing internal consistency (that is, people in a society all recognize good manners, though they may violate them), but may be sharply inconsistent across nations (a person acting according to what his society considers acceptable manners may profoundly offend someone from another society).

So, manners, or more broadly "culture," set a standard of expectation. To repeat, then, culture creates a standard of behavior that allows individuals to accomplish their goals without violating the expectations of the society about acceptable action. It is interesting to note how much further Hayek goes in this regard, compared to Hume. Hume believed that conventions might differ, but that within a culture the sense of convention was shared. Hayek became convinced that the rules themselves had complex properties that conditioned the performance of the society, and that in most cases even those who grew up in the cultural setting itself might resist or resent the moral strictures. Hume believed cultures were self-perpetuating; Hayek believed culture was fragile, with the constant danger that violation of norms would lead to the destruction of the civilization. Hayek adds another step, an evolutionary step, to the argument: some conventions *are* better than others, because of group selection.

It is useful at this point to give a road map to the remainder of the chapter. In the following section, I will consider some more complete definitions of "spontaneous order." Then, in the next section, I will make an argument that the concept of "culture" is in fact a prime example of spontaneous order. In the section following this, I will give two examples of problems of human organization and activity that culture can solve. Finally, in the last section, I will review a conception of spontaneous order in human affairs that unifies the claims that I will be making.

Meaning of Spontaneous Order

Suppose we observe order . . . under what circumstances can we infer that it is "spontaneous"? It is important to emphasize that the form of spontaneous order being considered here is macroscopic and social, a phenomenon quite different from the conception of self-organizing systems in physics, chemistry, or biology. It is much closer to the notion of Krugman than to those of (for example) Dembski and Ruse, Kauffman, Grigoirie Nicolis Prigogine and Ilya Prigogine or Resnick.[2]

But the selection process I will outline is closest, in spirit and in content, to that described by Hayek. I should acknowledge that much of my understanding of this aspect of Hayek's work is indebted to Bruce Caldwell's description and exegesis.[3]

Interestingly, one could argue that the survival of a cultural or moral system is subject to a process of natural selection, no less than is true in natural systems of evolution. Let's pursue this analogy for a moment. Suppose we observe a dog, perhaps a wolf, or a coyote. What inference about origin and survival would we draw? It could be that predators and scavengers fulfill a key part of God's plan, implying design. Or it could be that this morphology (adapted for the environment) and behavior (selected by the censoring of other behaviors through starvation or failure to mate) is sufficiently high on a scale of fitness to survive.

But suppose that now we see a dachshund: what caused this outrage, this offense to dog-shape? Only if God had a truly perverse sense of humor could dachshunds be explained by supernatural design. And dachshunds could not possibly survive, on their own, if they had to compete as predators with wolves and coyotes. It is easy to dismiss the example, of course: obviously human direction and control of breeding brought us wiener dogs. But the reason we like wiener dogs (or, enough humans like them to make them a distinct and recognizable breed) has to do with a much softer selection mechanism: socially constructed taste, or culture. Which is better, a wiener dog or a Chihuahua? They don't compete for food, but their relative proportions in the dog population very much reflect a competition for discretionary income: some people buy dachshund puppies, and others buy Chihuahuas.

So, wolves and coyotes survive because they exhibit one kind of fitness: they can outcompete other predators for resources, in part because of their instinctual pack behaviors. Dachshunds and Chihuahuas survive because they exhibit another kind of fitness: humans from some societies differentially *intentionally* select dachshunds and Chihuahuas as pets. One kind of selection (the natural kind) is Darwinian; the other kind of selection (the cultural kind) is Lamarckian.[4] Dog owners prefer, as a matter of conscious intention, dogs with outlandishly short legs. And so, in Lamarckian terms, the dachshund "wants" to have short legs, and so dachshund legs get shorter.

There is an even larger stage on which survival is important: the survival of the entire society, or culture. My claim is that an emergent process, or spontaneous order of a rather different kind, is likewise observable in the previous step: the formation of preferences. The key difference is the absence of any feedback mechanism by which the merits of the emergent order might be judged, or subjected to modification. Douglass North makes this point quite forcefully:

> Efficient markets are created in the real world when competition is strong enough via arbitrage and efficient information feedback to approximate the Coase zero transaction cost conditions and the parties can realize the gains from trade inherent in the neo-classical argument.
>
> But the informational and institutional requirements necessary to achieve such efficient markets are stringent. Players must not only have objectives but know the correct way to achieve them. But how do the players know the correct way to achieve their objectives? The instrumental rationality answer is that even though the actors may initially have diverse and erroneous models, the informational feedback process and arbitraging actors will correct initially incorrect models, punish deviant behavior and lead surviving players to correct models.[5]

North also makes it clear why the absence of coherent feedback is important, and why societies might have difficulty changing their level of economic performance.[6] He distinguishes two levels of analysis: *institutions* and *organizations*. Institutions are the humanly devised rules of the game, formal (constitutions and laws) or informal (norms, moral systems, manners), but they tend to be long-lived and not easily evaluated, because there is no specific feedback metric for comparison. Organizations are the optimizing responses to the set of incentives and constraints created by institutions.

The reason the distinction is important for North is that organizations are always optimal, in the sense that they maximize the advantage of those who own or control the organization. But transaction costs, both of writing complete contracts and of making changes in institutions, even Pareto-superior changes, may lock organizations into institutional settings that are in some larger sense Pareto inferior. More simply, there may exist alternative rule arrangements that have the potential, through feasible compensation arrangements, to make literally all the citizens in the society better off. Yet these rules are not selected and the existing, inferior rule set is maintained.

My point, of course, is that these sorts of "evolutionary" changes could not be more different from the changes that result from mutation coupled with natural selection. Hayek developed this insight in some very profound ways. His claims are, paradoxically, both under-recognized and controversial. Consider:

> The structures formed by traditional human practices are neither natural in the sense of being genetically determined, nor artificial in the sense of being the product of intelligent design, but the result of a process of winnowing and sifting, directed by the differential advantages gained by groups from practices adopted for some unknown and perhaps purely accidental reasons. . . . Acquired cultural traits may affect physiological evolution—as is obvious in the case of language: its rudimentary appearance undoubtedly made the physical capacity of clear articulation a great advantage, favouring genetic selection of a suitable speech apparatus.
>
> Nearly all writings on this topic stress that what we call cultural evolution took place during the last 1 per cent of the time during which Homo sapiens existed. With respect to what we mean by cultural evolution in a narrower sense, that is, the fast and accelerating development of civilization, this is true enough. Since it differs from genetic evolution by relying on the transmission of acquired properties, it is very fast, and once it dominates, it swamps genetic evolution. But this does not justify the misconception that it was the developed mind which in turn directed cultural evolution . . . *mind and culture developed concurrently and not successively* . . . It is this cultural evolution which man alone has undergone that now distinguishes him from the other animals. . . . To understand this development we must completely discard the conception that man was able to develop culture because he was endowed with reason.[7]

Interestingly, Hayek also recognizes the problem that North takes up, and this is one of the most interesting areas of Hayek's thought (as Caldwell also argues).[8] On the one hand, Hayek argues for something very close to group selection, with "better" moral systems and social conventions out-competing inferior ones. On the other hand, he recognizes that there is no *telos,* no intentionality or infallible human agency in effecting cultural change. In fact, in *The Constitution of Liberty* he clearly makes both points, but there is a tension between them that only a close reading can resolve. First, society's performance is a consequence of its ethical and moral practices:

> It is in the pursuit of man's aims of the moment that all the devices of civilization have to prove themselves; the ineffective will be discarded and the effective retained. But there is more to it than the fact that new ends constantly arise with the satisfaction of old needs and with the appearance of new opportunities. Which individuals and which groups succeed and continue to exist depends as much on the goals that they pursue, the values that govern

their action, as on the tools and capacities at their command. Whether a group will prosper or be extinguished depends as much on the ethical code it obeys, or the ideals of beauty or well-being that guide it, as on the degree to which it has learned or not learned to satisfy its material needs.[9]

Second, and in contrast, changes in ethical or aesthetic norms do not lead predictably to changes for the better. The human capacity for understanding means-ends relations in institutions and socioeconomic performance is very limited. There is no reason to expect that any particular change will result in improvement, in spite of the intentions of the human agents who seek to effect change for positive purposes. This is the same point that North makes later, of course: the feedback mechanisms for institutions, if there are any, are more granular than for market processes. A firm can make more or less profit, depending on its production choices. But a society can either survive, or not, over time. And by the time the society collapses, the information that had inferior institutions is no longer of much value.

Hayek makes another point, one that presages much of the postmodern concerns for the anomic consequences of industrialization and modernity. "Better" institutions, even if they survive, may well not make us happier.

> Though progress consists in part of achieving things we have been striving for, this does not mean that we shall like its results or that all will be gainers. . . . Progress in the sense of the cumulative growth of knowledge and power over nature is a term that says little about whether the new state will give us more satisfaction than the old.[10]

This rather long digression in defining spontaneous orders, and in summarizing Hayek's view of social orders, must now be brought to a close. Caldwell summarizes Hayek's contribution this way:

> In [Hayek's] papers three salient points emerge:
>
> 1) Complex orders occur within a variety of phenomena, from the individual brain all the way on up to a society.
> 2) Orders typically arise when the elements contained in them follow abstract rules.
> 3) Rules are often followed unconsciously; that is, the "agent" following them (even in cases where the "agent" is a human, so is capable of speech) cannot explain what the rule is or why he is following it.[11]

In the following section I turn to my own extensions of Hayek's view of institutions, focusing on stability and change.

Institutional Change and Institutional Evolution

In my earlier work, I defined what I called the "fundamental human problem."[12] It is a problem of institutional design, in the broadest sense. There is a kind of deism in this approach to understanding institutions or mechanism design that should be recognized and might well be criticized. The assumption is that human reactions to incentives and norms can be understood and evaluated after the fact even if they are not always predictable in advance. This view of institutions relies on something like the Hayekian form of spontaneous order in that it is consequentialist, and on the Northian distinction between institutions and organizations. Given a set of institutions, human ingenuity and self-interest will construct organizations that take those institutions as the foundation of the society. If the economic performance or the consistency with transcendent ideas of virtue are better for one set of institutions than another, we can say that those institutions are better, and the others worse.

Fundamental Human Problem The fundamental human problem is the design, or maintenance, of institutions that makes self-interested individual action not inconsistent with the welfare of the larger society.

There are, or so I claimed in my earlier work, two broad means of solving the fundamental human problem:

Project 1—Madisonian Approach: Perfectibility of institutions through mechanism design—Adam Smith, James Madison, John Stuart Mill, F. A. Hayek, Robert Nozick, and others have contributed to this point of view. It works like this: take self-interest as given, with "interests" themselves exogenous. Then try to design mechanisms (with markets being one archetype) where the collective consequences of individual self-interest are not harmful, and may even, "led by an invisible hand," create a better world.

It may not always be recognized that Madison, in discussing the construction of a dynamically stable federal system of divided powers, was relying on the same mechanism:

[T]he great security against a gradual concentration of the several powers in the same department, consists in giving to those who administer each department the necessary constitutional means and personal motives to resist encroachments of the others. The provision for defense must in this, as in all other cases, be made commensurate to the danger of attack. Ambition must be made to counteract ambition. The interest of the man must be connected with the constitutional rights of the place. It may be a reflection on human nature, that such devices should be necessary to control the abuses of government. But what is government itself, but the greatest of all reflections on human nature? If men were angels, no government would be necessary. If angels were to govern men, neither external nor internal controls on government would be necessary. In framing a government which is to be administered by men over men, the great difficulty lies in this: you must first enable the government to control the governed; and in the next place oblige it to control itself.[13]

Now, "Ambition must be made to counteract ambition" means that we can rely on the self-interest of those in power to limit the abuse of power by other branches of government.

Does the U.S. Senate push back when the president asserts power over foreign policy? Yes, it often does, forcefully. Is it out of concern for virtue, or love of the public? Perhaps, but it need not be. The narrow, selfish concern for defense of the powers and prerogatives of the Senate may be sufficient to induce senators to do what citizens would want them to do (prevent the president from becoming king) without any outside direction or control. Thus, the U.S. system of divided powers is a kind of organizational spontaneous order, but only because the Constitution created an institutional context where such an order is stable.

Project 2—Rousseauvian Approach: Perfectibility of humans in societies, through moral education. This is the project that makes culture relevant. We spend much of our time, in schools, churches, and around the dinner table, trying to instill "values" in our children. The reason is that "self-interest" may be malleable, especially in the young. But this is very different from an institutional design that imposes external constraints in the forms of laws and punishments. Moral perfectibility means that laws and morals *cannot* be external constraints. We must inscribe the laws on men's hearts. In this view, the self is reconceptualized intersubjectively, with a focus on the notion that each of us is embedded in a larger context, with ties to one another and to the larger good.

It might be said that once "self-interest" is created as a goal in a young person's mind, then all the other claims about pursuit of self-interest still follow. This might be true, but it renders the idea of pursuit of self-interest tautological (if you did it, it *must* have been in your self-interest) and not terribly interesting as a benchmark for motivation and action.

I should be clear: I am hardly the first, by a long shot, to make the distinction above. Adam Smith led those who recognized clearly the potential for inconsistency between self-interested behavior and the collective good, but we have made considerable progress since then. Riker made a slightly different distinction, but one very much in this spirit. Douglass North doesn't use these names, but clearly recognizes that these two approaches to organizing a society are both important and mutually dependent. Axelrod and Keohane, Heiner, and Schofield have argued that the performance of institutions can be judged by almost exactly the standard I have stated.[14]

The real question, of course, is which approach is better? This leads us to a false dichotomy, since in fact all societies have used elements of both projects in designing institutions. But it is possible to ask the question in an analytic way: Is it better to let people pursue selfish interests and filter these actions through institutions that render the consequences coincident with society's welfare, or is it better to transform people's conceptions of self-interest, accounting for the welfare of others explicitly and limiting both my freedom of thought and the harm I can cause to others?

Each approach has grave dangers. In the case of institutional design, it may simply be the case that conflicting political interests admit to no reconciliation. That is, there may not exist any contracting solution or set of rules that make opposed interests coincide. On the other hand, in the case of moral education, the sacrifice of liberty by the citizen to the "authority" controlling the content of the education may be extreme.

If the primary task of government is to reshape the beliefs and values of citizens, then from what independent base are citizens able to exercise democratic control over government? Yet if moral education is left to parents or religious groups, then the content of the education could easily be pernicious. Race hatred, religious conflict, and bigotry are all belief systems, too. And just these pathologies thrive in many cultures, not because they are in some objective sense true, but because children are taught by their parents, their teachers, or the people they spend time with, to have those beliefs.

Culture as a Hayekian Social Order

The dictionary definition of "culture" is encompassing, because the word is vague. Culture can be taken to have at least the following senses or meanings:

a. The totality of socially transmitted behavior patterns, arts, beliefs, institutions, and all other products of human work and thought

b. These patterns, traits, and products considered as the expression of a particular period, class, community, or population: *Edwardian culture, Japanese culture, the culture of poverty*

c. These patterns, traits, and products considered with respect to a particular category, such as a field, subject, or mode of expression: *religious culture in the Middle Ages, musical culture, oral culture*

d. The predominating attitudes and behavior that characterize the functioning of a group or organization

I think that there is a concept that perfectly illustrates the concept of culture: the word "shibboleth." In fact, the word is often combined with the word "cultural" and its general meaning is *an unspoken but shared understanding of something that identifies insiders, and distinguishes outsiders because they do not share this understanding.*

To be precise, the meaning of the word "shibboleth" was "a small flooding stream, a freshet." But the reason we remember the word is its pronunciation, not its meaning. In the Bible, the book of Judges, there was one tribe, the Gileadites, who could pronounce shibboleth correctly, with the "sh" sound. But the Ephraimites, lacking the "sh" sound, pronounced the word "sibboleth."[15] This distinction mattered, as the following passage illustrates.

> Judg. 12:5–7, *King James Bible*[5] And the Gileadites seized the passages of the Jordan before the Ephraimites; and it was so, that when those Ephraimites who had escaped said, "Let me go over," that the men of Gilead said unto him, "Art thou an Ephraimite?" If he said, "Nay,"[6] then said they unto him, "Say now Shibboleth." And he said "Sibboleth," for he could not frame to pronounce it right. Then they took him and slew him at the passages of the Jordan; and there fell at that time of the Ephraimites forty and two thousand.

Examples abound. In the Battle of the Bulge in December, 1944, during World War II, German infiltrators crept behind American lines dressed as military police. The U.S. troops confronted each other with questions about baseball:

> I asked him if he thought Detroit would win the World Series. He said no, but they put up a bloody good fight. We pulled them out of the Jeep because the World Series had been between the Cardinals and the Browns. It was discovered they were Germans in US uniforms. We sent them back to our G-2 Intelligence group.
> (Personal account, Robert T. Gravlin, 23rd Armored Engineer Battalion)

Woe betide the soldier who didn't follow baseball, who suffered like a Gileadite who happened to speak with a lisp.

But why be concerned about shibboleths and the cultures they delineate? Both of my examples have to do with distinguishing friend from foe in wartime. In war, the idea of the "other" is stark. But even in peacetime, knowing who "we" are may require knowing who "they" are. And the very existence of a "we" may depend on there being a "they." More precisely, what is it about culture and ways of knowing that have to do with shared understandings and differences, that solve larger problems of cooperation? Before continuing, it is useful to specify a definition of culture, at least as I will use it here.

Culture: *The set of "inherited" beliefs, attitudes, and moral strictures that a people use to distinguish outsiders, to understand themselves and to communicate with each other.*

I have put quotations around the word inherited above, not because I am quoting anyone, but because the sense of the word is strained. Hair texture, eye color, general build . . . those sorts of things are inherited. They are hardwired into the genetic structure of humans, and children are directly and entirely the product of their parents. Culture is obviously not inherited like this. We teach it to our children, or they learn it by tacit and perhaps unconscious exposure over time. But it makes sense to think of culture as an inheritance, or legacy, from the past.

To understand the distinction I am trying to make, imagine that twin Ephraemites had been separated at birth, with one being raised by an Ephraemite family and the other raised by a family of Gileadites. The child raised by the Gileadites would be able to pass the "shibboleth" test easily, because she would have had imprinted on her brain the capacity to pronounce the "sh" sound (assuming she had no unusual speech impediment or malformation of her lips or palate). The child raised by the Ephraemite family, by contrast, would be unable to pronounce "shibboleth" correctly.

This inheritance, then, is of an odd kind. You inherit culture from the people who you grow up with, not necessarily from the genes your parents give you. Culture, then, lies entirely on the "nurture" side of the ledger, as against "nature," or truly inherited traits or hardwired instincts selected for over millennia by natural selection and shared by all phenotypes of the human genome.

Let us take stock for a moment, and tie some things together. I want to argue that cultures differ, though I have not said how much two "different" cultures would have to diverge to be distinct. In any case, some are better than others, either on consequentialist grounds or because of their satisfaction of transcendent norms of right and wrong. I also want to argue that the fundamental human problem, ensuring a coincidence between individual action and group welfare, punishes those groups that create pathological institutions, or those groups that fail to sustain good institutions because their culture is inconsistent with self-enforcing obedience to these rules. Finally, let it be clear that what I mean by "self-enforcing obedience" is voluntary and unmonitored adherence to moral codes, because of a belief in right and wrong instilled by ("inherited" from) one's cultural birthplace.

Consider three questions that I hope will illustrate and clarify this argument:

a. In the absence of some central plan or control, will the aggregate consequences of individual human action tend toward order or chaos?

To put it another way, can we think of moral systems as examples of spontaneous orders?

b. What are the moral properties of individual human action? Are self-interested actions moral? Are they ever moral, sometimes moral, always moral?

c. Should the moral properties of acts be judged by their consequences, their intentions, or something else?

If I am right, then the key aspect of a cultural solution to the fundamental human problem is *consequentialist:* right action by and large advances the interests of others, or at least does not harm others, but it is not necessary that each actor specifically intend to promote the public good. And it is at this point that Hayek's argument about group selection is important: a society that solves the fundamental human problem is more likely to survive, in the face of scarcity or attack, than one that does not solve it.

So, one possibility is that what some have called "commercial culture" in fact constitutes a moral system that generates broadly shared prosperity and growth. (For different aspects of this claim, see authors as diverse as Cowen and De Soto).[16] But is there any analogue to political life? That is, is there any institutional arrangement that renders coincident, or at least unopposed, individual interest and group welfare?

Examples of Human Behavior—Culture

I have claimed that spontaneous order, and some notion of "the good," arises in market settings, so long as property rights are secure, exclusively defined, and alienable. But is the same thing ever true for political settings? That is, is it true that each person acting in his/her own best interests results in the best outcomes for the group?

Let us consider how political institutions and culture might reconcile, or fail to reconcile, individual actions and group goals. To start with, it is important to recognize that ideas about the political good (and bad) are viruses. Thomas Hobbes wrote nearly four centuries ago, Jefferson two and a half centuries ago, Marx 150 years ago. They are long, long dead. Yet their ideas come down to us, across the years, in a form that may still be infectious. If I read Jefferson, or Marx, I may be moved to go out and participate in a revolution. It makes no sense, in narrow "rational" terms, for me to sacrifice myself this way. Yet it happens rather often: people fight, and risk, and sometimes suffer death, for things they believe in.

People come up with ideas, and write them down, all the time. I could write "The Mungerist Manifesto," and hope that its precepts (give all your wealth to Munger!) take hold. But it wouldn't persuade anyone. There is an evolutionary pressure, a selection mechanism, at work. Some ideas survive because they are suited for survival. What determines the fitness of some ideas and the unfitness of others? And, more interestingly, why are the ideas that are persuasive in a one nation at one time considered ridiculous, or barbaric, in another place or time?

Let's be clear what the "gene," or perhaps "meme" is: suppose a religious idea (doctrine) requires celibacy. Can the religion survive? Believing in the idea of celibacy kills off the host, at least in the sense that a celibate person is a biological dead end. But the religion itself is a different entity. If the religious establishment attracts resources and new adherents faster than old ones die off, then that doctrine prospers. In fact, if adherents leave their estates to the religious establishment, the religion may do very well. An often-cited example is Pennsylvania's "Shakers": a religion that thrived for more than a century, but which rendered each adherent's DNA dead because of the celibacy requirement.

To repeat, then: ideative, moral viruses can kill the host, yet still be a successful virus. For ideas, it is the propagation of the "meme," not the happiness or survival of the human host, that matters. This means that the first metric for judging a society and the moral ideas that animate it is survival. Survival has two aspects: (1) Does the society face down foreign aggressors? (2) Is the governing ideology stable? Only if the answers to these two questions are "yes" do we get to the question most of us are interested in: Is the moral sense of the society consistent with more general principles of justice and virtue?

The disturbing thing is that it is by no means obvious that justice and virtue are qualities that ensure military survival or constitute a moral system that is self-perpetuating in the face of self-interested action by citizens. And there is the reason that people study culture: we want to know why some peoples are susceptible to the classical ideas of democracy, liberty, and virtue, while others are much less so. The difference is probably not genetic, but is inherited through the mental process of acculturation.

The answer that I offer is simple, correct, and useless: Not everyone is persuaded (susceptible) to the same idea. But as a consequence of cultural differences, the capacity of groups of people to solve collective action problems differs widely. Nations differ fundamentally, and persistently, in ways that make it literally impossible to compare them directly. When the World Bank, or the International Monetary Fund, attempts to impose a "one size fits all" market solution under the assumption that Western conceptions of right and wrong, and the legitimacy of self-interest, are already in place, disaster often ensues.

The nature of these differences, and the strong persistence of these differences, arises from the basic human need to solve problems of commitment, information, and transactions cost in political dealings. Douglass North has written widely on this subject, and I can but touch on it here.[17] Still, it is useful to give an example of the problem, and the possible solution.

The fundamental problem for politics is illustrated best by the simple "Prisoner's Dilemma" (PD). The problem here is that if each individual acts in his self-interest, without an ability to extract commitments from or make commitments to others, then the result for all participants is inferior to a feasible alternative. Consider table 1, which depicts the situation of two prisoners who are being interrogated about a crime they may or not have committed.

Table 1 Example of two-person Prisoner's Dilemma

		Jones Confess	Don't confess
Smith	Confess	20, 20	0, Death
	Don't confess	Death, 0	5, 5

The state has evidence sufficient to convict on a lesser charge if neither confesses. If one prisoner turns the state's evidence and the other prisoner is unrepentant (i.e., does not confess), the squealer goes free and the other prisoner is sentenced to death.

The numbers in the table represent years served in prison. We need to make an assumption about what the prisoners perceive as their self-interest: less prison time is preferred to more, but a death sentence is worse than any prison sentence. If the prisoners cannot make, or extract, credible commitments ("I promise not to tell, if you don't tell, either!"), then the ideal (from the group's perspective) outcome of no confessions, each serve five years, will never be observed. The reason is that each prisoner is tempted to confess by the prospect *either* of getting off free if the other prisoner remains silent, or at least serving only 20 years instead of getting the death sentence if the other prisoner also confesses.

The problem with this outcome, and all of the other situations for which it is an apt analogy, is that a feasible better alternative (five years each) is passed up for a worse alternative (20 years each) just because there is no means of making or enforcing agreements. The pursuit of narrow self-interest (confess) leads to a worse outcome for both people. More simply, the entire group is worse off because they act in their self-interest. This PD problem is often cited as the reason that spontaneous order does not work in politics.

But the fact is that our beliefs and preferences are not the simple egoistic views of homo economicus. Most humans grow up in a culture. Most humans also have only a limited understanding of just how important our cultural heritage is. The key point to recognize is that culture often makes us act irrationally, from the perspective of outsiders. In some cultures (perhaps uniquely in some Western countries), a group of people waiting for some service will line up, in the order of their arrival, and wait their turn. No one has to order them to do so, and no third party enforces the rules against butting in line. If someone tries to cut in front of you in line, you might react indignantly, and the prospect of being publicly labeled a noncooperator may be sufficient to ensure obedience. That is not to say that queuing always works perfectly, but it works surprisingly often. But there are other cultures where the idea of a line is decidedly foreign. If you try to queue up, you will literally never get to the front of the line.

Not surprisingly, since the PD is a classic problem, there is also a classic answer. The Sicilian mafia invokes a norm, "omerta," which literally means "silence," but which in practice describes a whole code of behavior. The keys to omerta are of two types, which make its success at solving the PD problem of interest to us. One thing omerta accomplishes is a swearing of allegiance and brotherhood. An initiate in La Cosa Nostra pledges to protect and care about others in the gang. He promises never to give evidence, or cooperate in any way, with the police or the authorities. The rationale is that one internalizes the welfare of the group, rather than caring only about oneself. The payoffs are the same, but now the prisoner values them differently. Since the preference ordering is different (I prefer death to squealing, and I know you do, too, so neither of us will ever talk), the problem is solved.

The other aspect of interest in omerta is the credible promise of third-party enforcement. If someone breaks omerta, the organization promises to hunt them down and kill them, by torture if possible, and also to kill all the members of the squealer's immediate family. Notice that this changes the payoffs in the PD matrix, so that it no longer describes a PD game, though for a different reason: naked self-interest now leads the prisoner to keep mum rather than confess.

Societies, and cultures, put internal constraints on the way that people act publicly and collectively. There are two possibilities that may be difficult to distinguish, but which are fundamentally different in terms of the kinds of spontaneous order they describe. The first is to assume that people always act self-interestedly, but are subject to political institutions that direct their self-interest in a way that is not harmful, or even helpful. In this sort of culture, an act is virtuous because of its consequences, not its intent. We judge the quality of a person by how much value they create in the society.

The second possibility is to inscribe the law on men's hearts, rather than write the law in books and hire police to enforce it. In this sort of culture, to the extent that it does exist, people act in a way that is directly consistent with the welfare of others, and care about it directly. In this second view, the virtue of the act lies in its intent. We judge the quality of a person by how selflessly they act. Are these rules of judging the product of reason, or cultural evolution? Hayek would argue that reason is almost an afterthought:

> Thus a tradition of rules of conduct, existing apart from any one individual who had learnt them, began to govern human life. It was when these learnt rules, involving classifications of different kinds of objects, began to include a sort of model of the environment that enabled man to predict and anticipate in action external environments, that what we called reason appeared. There *was then probably much more "intelligence" incorporated in the system of rules of conduct than in man's thoughts about his surroundings.*[18]

Let me emphasize this point, since it is the core of my argument: people cooperate not because they rationally solve the PD problem. People cooperate because prerational social rules of culture are "designed" to do so. This design is evolutionary rather than conscious, and it is all the more effective as a result.

Cooperation Is the Problem, Culture Has Many Different Answers

What actions will be chosen by citizens who find themselves in a strategic situation, where the "best" choice for me depends on what I expect you to do, and vice versa? If we know that each citizen chooses the action that is best for her, given her preferences and her beliefs about the other players' actions, we still don't know very much. Most social interactions do not take place in a laboratory setting where the informational and behavioral assumptions of the PD are valid. Instead, citizens interact in a cultural context, with a shared set of beliefs about the things that counts as right action.

How do people form these beliefs about each other? Direct experience and communication may play some important role. But culture is the dominant answer, because it both economizes on the costs of gathering information and reduces the expectation of defecting from the implicit cooperative agreements.

If I know you are an American, I can reasonably expect that you will accept the norm that governs rationing service: first come, first served, form a line. If I go into a McDonalds in Beijing, it is not obvious that this norm will be accepted there. Which set of norms is better? We have no basis for saying, though most people seem to prefer their own culture rather strongly.

It is well known that if a PD game is repeated, there are cooperative solutions. But suppose you and I are only going to "play" once. Can I count on you to obey the norms of cooperation, meaning that if I cooperate I won't be taken advantage of? Quite possibly, if the two of us share a cultural background, and so have a common set of understandings of right and wrong, and also share an identity that makes cooperation more likely, we may cooperate even in one-shot dealings.

There may be a cooperative equilibrium, then. The difficulty is that, as for any cooperative game, there are many equilibriums. There are many divisions of payoffs that could, in principle, support a stable outcome both of us prefer to noncooperation. But which? Again, culture provides the answer. The coordination problem (should we drive on the left or the right) may simply require a focal-point solution. Culture identifies salient events in our shared history, important ideas or claims about virtue, that allow us to simplify and prune the otherwise very bushy cooperative game tree. Culture goes a long way toward satisfying the rather strict "common knowledge" assumption of game theory, even if you and I cannot communicate or commit. And we may understand neither the problem nor the solution, and yet be served by the spontaneous social order of culture better than if we did try to understand the problem and solve it through reason. As Hayek put it:

> A self-generating or spontaneous order and an organization are distinct, and [their] distinctiveness is related to the two different kinds of rules or laws that prevail in them. . . . What today is generally regarded as "social" or distributive justice has meaning only within the second of these kinds of order, the organization; but that it is meaningless in, and wholly incompatible with, that spontaneous order which Adam Smith called "the Great Society", and Sir Karl Popper called "the Open Society."[19]

Rational choice theory applies well, but should only be understood as applying, to the formal rules and choice of organizations. Larger societal rules, practices, and norms are products of a spontaneous order that narrowly focused rational choice theory has little prospect of deciphering.

Notes

Helpful comments were offered by Peter McNamara and Randy Simmons. All errors in what remains are entirely the responsibility of the author.

1. Friedrich A. Hayek, *The Fatal Conceit: The Errors of Socialism* (Chicago: University of Chicago Press, 1988), p. 6, emphasis in original.

2. See Paul Krugman, *The Self-Organizing Economy* (Cambridge, MA, and Oxford: Blackwell, 1996); William Dembski and Michael Ruse, ed., *Debating Design: From Darwin to DNA* (New York: Cambridge University Press, 2004); Stuart Kauffman, *Origins of Order: Self-Organization and Selection in Evolution* (New York: Oxford University Press, 1993); Grigoirie Nicolis and Ilya Prigogine, *Self-Organization in Non-Equilibrium Systems* (Indianapolis: JohnWiley, 1997); Mitchell Resnick, *Turtles, Termites and Traffic Jams: Explorations in Massively Parallel Microworlds,* Complex Adaptive Systems Series (Boston: MIT Press, 1997).

3. See Bruce Caldwell, "The Emergence of Hayek's Ideas on Cultural Evolution," *Review of Austrian Economics* 13 (2000): 5–22 and *Hayek's Challenge: An Intellectual Biography of F. A. Hayek* (Chicago: University of Chicago Press, 2004).

4. Jean-Baptiste Lamarck, *Philosophie Zoologique* (1809) contrasted with Charles Darwin's *Origin of Species* (1859). I had believed that this distinction in discussing culture was original to me, but in fact it appears verbatim in Caldwell's discussion of Hayek's thought in "The Emergence of Hayek's Ideas on Cultural Evolution," p. 6. I am indebted to Caldwell for the Hayek citation on genetic evolution, as well as most of the other Hayek references in the remainder of the chapter.

5. Douglass C. North, "Economic Performance through Time," *American Economic Review* 84, no. 3 (June 1994): 360.

6. Douglass C. North. *Institutions, Institutional Change, and Economic Performance* (New York: Cambridge University Press, 1990).

7. Friedrich A. Hayek, *Law, Legislation and Liberty,* vol. 3, *The Political Order of a Free People* (Chicago: University of Chicago Press, 1979), pp. 155–156.

8. Bruce Caldwell, "The Emergence of Hayek's Ideas on Cultural Evolution," and Bruce Caldwell, "Hayek and Cultural Evolution," in *Fact and Fiction in Economics: Models, Realism, and Social Construction,* ed. Uskali Maki (New York: Cambridge University Press, 2002), pp. 285–303.

9. Friedrich Hayek, *The Constitution of Liberty* (Chicago: University of Chicago Press, 1960), p. 36.

10. Ibid., p. 41.

11. Caldwell, "The Emergence of Hayek's Ideas on Cultural Evolution," p. 13.

12. Michael C. Munger, "Political Science and Fundamental Research," in "The Public Value of Political Science Research," ed. Arthur Lupia, special issue, *PS: Political Science and Politics* 33 (2000): 25–33.

13. Alexander Hamilton, James Madison, and John Jay, *The Federalist Papers,* No. 51 (New York: Random House, Modern Library, 1937).

14. William Riker *Liberalism against Populism: A Confrontation between the Theory of Democracy and the Theory of Social Choice* (San Francisco: W. H. Freeman, 1982); Douglass C. North, *Structure and Change in Economic History* (New York: W. W. Norton, 1981) and "Economic Performance through Time"; Robert Axelrod and Robert O. Keohane, "Achieving Cooperation under Anarchy: Strategies and Institutions," *World Politics* 37, no. 1 (October 1985): 226–254; Ronald Heiner, "The Origin of Predictable Behavior," *American Economic Review* 73 (1983): 560–595; Norman Schofield, "Anarchy, Altruism, and Cooperation," *Social Choice and Welfare* 2 (1985): 207–219.

15. How did they get people to be quiet in the grade school library?
16. Tyler Cowen, *In Praise of Commercial Culture* (Cambridge: Harvard University Press, 1998); Hernando De Soto, *The Mystery of Capital: Why Capitalism Triumphs in the West and Fails Everywhere Else* (New York: Basic Books, 2000).
17. Douglass C. North, "Economic Performance through Time," and "Institutional Change: A Framework of Analysis," in *Institutional Change: Theory and Empirical Findings,* ed. S.-E. Sjöstrand (Armonk, NY: M. E. Sharpe, 1994), pp. 35–48.
18. Hayek, *Law, Legislation and Liberty,* vol. 3, p. 157, emphasis in original.
19. Friedrich A. Hayek, *Law, Legislation and Liberty,* vol. 1, *Rules and Order* (Chicago: University of Chicago Press, 1973), p. 2.

CHAPTER 10

The Limits of Spontaneous Order: Skeptical Reflections on a Hayekian Theme

Jerry Z. Muller

One of Friedrich Hayek's most penetrating works was a small book published in 1973, *The Mirage of Social Justice.* In it, Hayek suggested that the term "social justice" was on many lips, and had become a sort of ideological trump card, though its precise meaning was difficult to define. Three decades later, much the same might be said of Hayek's notion of "spontaneous order." This chapter does not mean to suggest that the term is analytically useless, but that its explanatory scope is more limited than its devotees imagine, and that its potential for leading us astray is greater than they are aware.

As with so many of his ideas, Hayek formulated the concept of "spontaneous order" in his critical confrontation with socialism. Like many thinkers who develop their views primarily in response to some looming ideological foe, Hayek's work has a tendency to overshoot the mark, to one-sidedness, and exaggeration. That is why his work needs to be assimilated critically, and with a grain of salt. Hayek's conceptual powers were exceptional, but he had a propensity to tunnel vision; he missed so much because his focus was so narrow. We ought not to be so blinded by Hayek's brilliance as to lose sight of his limitations. These limitations apply above all to his notion of "spontaneous order."

Hayek asserted that capitalist society was best understood as an example of "spontaneous order," which occurs "when order is achieved among human beings by allowing them to interact with each other on their own initiative—subject only to the laws which uniformly apply to all of them."[1] He distinguished a "spontaneous order" from an organization, a system deliberately created to attain some particular purpose.[2] By "spontaneous order," Hayek meant several things (which he tended to conflate, but which are actually distinct). First, he thought of the market order as "spontaneous" in that it coordinated human purposes by appealing to existing motives of self-interest, rather than requiring the ideological coordination of society toward some common set of goals. Second, the concept was supposed to cast light on the *genesis* of modern liberal society, based upon the capitalist market: in referring to a *spontaneous* order Hayek meant that the market order had not come about in a planned, deliberate fashion to conform to a set of ideals. It had developed over time, through a process of trial and error, and had been retained because it was found to be useful to a wide range of individuals. In that sense, it had developed—and was still developing—by a process of cultural evolution. From the fact that it had not been created deliberately or rationally, Hayek concluded that it could not be fully understood, nor could it be altered by rational, deliberate action.[3]

Hayek's genetic or historical account of modern liberal capitalist society as a "spontaneous order" is at once insightful and distortive. Insightful because it is true that what we call "capitalism" was not conceived in advance by anyone. "Socialism" did arise as a deliberate intellectual construct of what a good society ought to look like: the problem, for socialists, was to discover the institutional mechanisms through which this ideal could be actualized in the real world—a problem that proved insoluble. What we think of as "capitalism" by contrast, is a model of political and economic relations that was derived by intellectuals such as Adam Smith from reflection upon historical experience and existing institutions. After explaining the economic growth that arose from the division of labor, made possible by market exchange, Smith wrote that "it is not originally the effect of any human wisdom, which foresees and intends that general opulence to which it gives occasion."[4]

Yet Hayek's characterization of the origins and development of capitalism as one of "spontaneous order" is misleading. It ignores the fact that when thinkers such as Smith devoted themselves to analyzing the market and the institutions that make it possible, they did so with an eye to making them function more effectively, more justly, and with more benefit to the population as a whole. Smith's legacy was one of showing how rational insight into the functions and malfunctions of institutions can lead to their modification, in order to improve the lives of those living under such them.[5] Hence, *An Inquiry into the Nature and Causes of the Wealth of Nations* is replete with suggestions for institutional reform, many of them quite radical (such as the abolition of entails). Indeed, if *The Wealth of Nations* shows anything, it is that the powerful, well-connected, and well-placed "spontaneously" pursue their self-interest at the expense of the other members of society, attempting whenever possible to circumvent the very mechanisms of the competitive market that Smith thought necessary to advance public welfare.

Another way in which Hayek's characterization of the development of modern liberal society as "spontaneous" is distortive is that it glosses over what every historian knows, or ought to know: that in most places, the market order came about not "spontaneously" but through the deliberate policy of rulers and their bureaucratic advisers, who learned about the market either from their experiences abroad or from reading social scientists such as Adam Smith. In almost every such case, introducing the market meant vast and deliberate institutional change, which included using the power of the central government to break down existing hierarchies of political and economic power that inhibited free trade. That deliberate, planned, nonspontaneous introduction of the legal institutions was necessary to create a freer, more productive, and more capitalist economy was as true in late eighteenth-century Germany as in late nineteenth-century Japan, or late twentieth-century China.[6]

Hayek also tried to characterize *traditions* as examples of spontaneous order. That too was a half-truth at best. A secularist, he came to regard religious traditions as usefully conveying modes of behavior that were necessary complements to the institutions of the market and the rule of law, even if those traditions were based on premises that were untrue or mythical.[7] Here there are several problems. First, Hayek's rhetorical warmth toward traditions seems to be in tension with his emphasis on the progressive role of social and economic innovators, who set an example to be emulated by others precisely by breaking with tradition.[8] Second, the "tradition" that Hayek defended was that of the modern West, which acts as a solvent of those moralities that Hayek calls "tribal" but which others regard as "traditional."[9] Third, the notion that traditions are unitary and linear is the illusion of conservative traditionalists, an illusion achieved by retroactive smoothing out (and selective forgetting) of the past. As Nietzsche put it, "There is no more important proposition for all kinds of historical research than . . . that anything in existence, having somehow come about, is continually reinterpreted anew, requisitioned anew, transformed and redirected to a new purpose by [the will to power, which functions by] reinterpretation and adjustment, in the process of which earlier meanings and purposes are necessarily obscured or completely eliminated."[10] Traditions develop, that is to say, in ways that are often far from "spontaneous." As Leo Strauss noted, "The typical mistake of the conservative . . . consists in concealing the fact that the continuous and changing tradition which he cherishes so greatly would never have come into being through conservatism, or without discontinuities, revolutions, and sacrileges committed at the beginning of the cherished tradition and at least silently repeated in its course."[11] Discontinuities, revolutions, sacrileges: that is a long way from tradition as "spontaneous order."

Hayek's notion of "spontaneous order" is his reworking of the concept of the unintended consequences of social action, one of the most central concepts in social science, as Robert K. Merton showed in a famous article of 1937.[12] Nowhere is that concept more central than in *The Wealth of Nations*. But it is instructive to compare what Smith has to say about the subject with Hayek's use of the term.

Hayek regarded himself as the legatee of the Scottish Enlightenment, and especially of David Hume and Adam Smith. But his divergence from his chosen ancestors is instructive, and by no means to Hayek's credit. Hayek played the role not only of economist and political theorist, but also of historian of ideas. But Hayek's work in the history of ideas, as those who have examined it closely have discovered, needs to be treated with caution. For Hayek looked to thinkers of the past primarily for echoes of ideas that he already held.[13] His history of ideas is less a telescope, bringing great thinkers of the past closer to us, than a mirror, in which he saw his own reflection. That holds true for his idea of spontaneous order as well.

The theme of the unintended consequences of human action appears with many variations in *The Wealth of Nations*. Smith explores the myriad ways in which the outcomes of intentional actions are different from those anticipated, in directions sometimes positive and sometimes negative, or positive from the perspective of society but not from that of the actor. Smith is perhaps best known for his explication of unintended consequences that are beneficial for the actor and for society at large. The most striking version of this theme comes in Smith's critique of the arguments made by manufacturers who favored government duties and prohibitions on the importation of goods that could be made in Britain. They argued that such protective measures would benefit the nation at large by providing both employment and economic growth. Smith's analysis was that while such measures might indeed help the growth of particular industries, they would do so at the expense of investment in other industries where such investment would be more productive. Government attempts to direct investment might not only be counterproductive, he argued, they were also unnecessary, since by and large individuals were most inclined to invest close to home, from where they could keep an eye on their investments. He concluded:

> Every individual is continually exerting himself to find out the most advantageous employment for whatever capital he can command. It is his own advantage, indeed, and not that of the society, which he has in view. But the

study of his own advantage naturally, or rather necessarily leads him to prefer that employment which is the most advantageous to the society. . . .[14] He generally, indeed, neither intends to promote the public interest, nor knows how much he is promoting it. By preferring the support of domestic to that of foreign industry, he intends only his own security; and by directing that industry in such a manner as its produce may be of the greatest value, he intends only his own gain, and he is in this, as in many other cases, led by an invisible hand to promote an end which was no part of his intention. Nor is it always the worse for the society that it was no part of it. By pursuing his own interest he frequently promotes that of the society more effectually than when he really intends to promote it.[15]

The image of the "invisible hand" in this passage is a metaphor for the socially positive unintended consequences of the institution of the market that through the profit motive and the price mechanism channels the self-interest of individuals into collective benefits. Notice that Smith does *not* dismiss the possibility of deliberately promoting the public interest. Nor does he believe that the pursuit of self-interest always and inevitably leads to socially positive outcomes. What he does assert is that under proper institutional conditions, actions motivated by individual self-interest *may* lead to outcomes that are positive for society, in a way that the social scientist can explain and help the legislator to anticipate. Smith is of course correct—but notice, again, how far this is from a claim that social orders can be explained as "spontaneous order."

For Smith, moreover, maintaining, perfecting, and protecting the market, and compensating for its negative effects, required the visible hand of government. Smith's views on the functions of the modern state followed from his analysis of the anticipatable *negative* consequences of the market. If the spread of the market was the source of or at least the precondition for much of what was best about modern civilized society, it was also the root of a number of intrinsic dangers that it was the role of the social scientist to anticipate and of the legislator to obviate.

One of these was the problem of national defense. The need for national defense grew more urgent with the progress of economic development. The record of history showed that as a society grew richer, it became a more attractive object of attack by its poorer neighbors. Moreover, the division of labor upon which opulence depended left most men less fit to be soldiers. Fortunately, the division of labor and the growth of affluence that exacerbated the problem of national defense also provided their potential solution—if legislators put the proper mechanisms into place, at increasing expense to the state.

In the current stage of history—that of commercial society, characterized by a market economy, urbanization, and an intensive division of labor—as the likelihood of being attacked increased, so too did the difficulty and expense of war. Yet Smith believed that the very advance of the division of labor and opulence made it possible for liberal societies to avoid defeat. Like other human activities, he reasoned, the art of war became more complex with the division of labor, and its mastery required the same specialization as did other fields. Yet it could not be in the interest of private individuals to devote themselves fully to the art of war, which brought no profit in time of peace. It was only the wise policy of the state that could attract some individuals to devote themselves fully to military matters—a wisdom often lacking in past advanced societies.[16]

Because of its greater wealth, an opulent society, which necessarily required military protection, was better positioned to provide it, since it could afford to devote a portion of its superior resources to a professional army. The development of modern firearms made preparation for warfare evermore expensive, giving wealthy nations an additional advantage, Smith claimed.[17] Smith's acute historical awareness of the link between national defense and the preservation of civilization led him to characterize the art of war as "certainly the noblest of the arts," and to insist on the primacy of defense over economic considerations in trade policy. Here was another case in which the legislator, aided by rational social scientific reflection, could foresee and forestall the negative unanticipated consequences of social developments.

Next to providing for the national defense against other sovereign states, the most important function of government was to provide justice and security under the law. An essential prerequisite for national opulence, Smith believed, was legal and political institutions that maintained peace, protected liberty and property, and allowed for market exchange among independent producers. It was to the security of property provided and enforced by law that Smith attributed much of his nation's increasing wealth, since only that security made it worthwhile for every individual to make "the natural effort . . . to better his own condition."[18] Without a regular and reliable system of justice it was impossible for merchants and manufacturers to enforce contracts and the payments of their debts.[19] Just as the scale of expenditures for military expenditures rose as society became more advanced, so Smith thought did the costs of administering justice that assured each individual the possession of property he had acquired by legitimate means. It was only the state that protected property and hence made "private" property possible.

Now, compare all of this to Hayek's treatment of these subjects. Together, his later works, *The Constitution of Liberty* and *Law, Legislation and Liberty,* are almost one thousand pages in length. In those one thousand pages, there is only a single, one-sentence mention of national defense.[20] Moreover, in books ostensibly devoted to the issue of law, there is no mention whatsoever of law enforcement as a function of government: the term "police" occurs only once, in connection with the term "police state."[21] While there is some discussion of government bureaucracy, there is no discussion of its necessity in making the rule of law possible. Yet, without the armed forces, the police, and the civil service, there is no rule of law, and without the rule of law, there is no "spontaneous order." That the rule of law rests upon such organizations as the armed forces, the police, and the civil service is eclipsed in Hayek's discussion, as it never was in the works of Adam Smith. Indeed, the thrust of Hayek's contrast between "spontaneous order" and "organization" is to make us forget how much of the well-being of free societies depends not only on organizations such as the armed forces, police, and civil service, but also on organizations such as zoning boards, which set the necessary limits without which the uncoordinated pursuit of self-interest results in unintended negative consequences. In short, Hayek's work marginalizes the discussion of public goods and of the governmental organizations and restrictions that make self-interested market activity more likely to result in socially beneficent outcomes.

Similarly, in his enthusiasm for spontaneous order, Hayek overlooks the issue of negative externalities, again in contrast to Adam Smith, his purported intellectual forebear. Smith devoted substantial parts of *The Wealth of Nations* to pointing out the negative effects of even a well-functioning market, and to suggesting remedies for them. Think, for example, of his famous description of the negative effects of the division of labor on many workers:

> The man whose whole life is spent in performing a few simple operations has no occasion to exert his understanding. He naturally loses, therefore, the habit of such exertion, and generally becomes as stupid and ignorant as it is possible for a human creature to become. The torpor of his mind renders him, not only incapable of relishing or bearing a part in any conversation, but of conceiving any generous, noble, or tender sentiment, and consequently of forming any just judgment concerning many even of the ordinary duties of private life. Of the great and extensive interests of his country he is altogether incapable of judging. . . . His dexterity at his own particular trade seems, in this manner, to be acquired at the expense of his intellectual, social, and martial virtues. But in every improved and civilized society this is the state into which the labouring poor, that is, the great body of the people, must necessarily fall, unless government takes some pains to prevent it.[22]

One can, I believe, read through the 20 volumes of Hayek's collected works and never come upon a similar passage. He was so committed to defending the spontaneous order of the market from its opponents that he rarely stopped to consider that it was the responsibility of those who defend the market to point out its shortcomings, and to try to develop remedies. The weaknesses of Hayek as a thinker come from his propensity to exaggerate the scope of his very real insights. His was the crystal clear vision of the one-eyed man. Hayek's opposition to the use of government to enshrine any single culture led him to deny that there could be any shared cultural standards for the sake of which the market might be restrained. As a result, he had no criteria by which to evaluate the negative effects of the market, or to suggest a principled reason to try to remedy them. Here, too, he proved far more one-sided than his chosen predecessor, Adam Smith.

It is not that Hayek's thought about the role of markets, of initiative, of experimentation and entrepreneurship is *intrinsically* at odds with recognizing the unintended but anticipatable *negative* effects of the market. The fact that Hayek devoted so little attention to the negative consequences of the spontaneous order of the market testifies not to the weakness of his analytic categories but to his one-sidedness. One can certainly believe that there are negative effects of the market, and yet come up with solutions compatible with Hayek's description of a liberal society. But one is unlikely to do so if one becomes accustomed to thinking of the market or of modern liberal society only as a "spontaneous order." The concept of "spontaneous order" is an important half-truth that becomes dangerous only when it is taken to be the whole truth. The concept is like a flashlight beam, illuminating a significant portion of reality, but also leaving much of reality in the shadows.

The largest slice of reality that it leaves in the shadows is of course government. That is not because Hayek was an anarchist: on the contrary, he stressed time and again that the rule of law, enforced by government power, was a necessary prerequisite, without which no spontaneous order was possible. He stressed that the Scottish Enlightenment tradition of social thought with which he identified "was never antistate as such, or anarchistic . . . [but rather] accounted both for the proper functions of the state and the limits of state action." The term "laissez-faire," he noted, did not stem from the Scottish Enlightenment tradition.[23] Hayek was clear that liberty existed only when protected by the state, which enforced the rule of law, a set of rules that applied equally to all and that assured each individual "a known sphere of unimpeded action." These laws included "a right to privacy and secrecy, the conception that man's house is his castle and nobody has a right even to take cognizance of his activities in it."[24] They also included the right to property, which Hayek regarded not as some eternal and unchanging essence, but as in need of redefinition in keeping with changing social needs.[25] Hayek was not against government as such. Yet the thrust of his work was to suggest, in the words of one of his acolytes, Ronald Reagan, that "government is the problem." Again, this is a half-truth: there are times when government *is* the problem, and other times when it is the solution. Most often, in advanced societies such as ours, the problem is how to have enough government, without having too much government, and how to deliberately build mechanisms of self-interest into solutions to the problems that require government for their attainment, because the market does not solve them "spontaneously."

From time to time, Hayek had interesting and important things to say about this. He was not, contrary to what many people imagine, opposed to the welfare state as such. He acknowledged that "there are common needs that can be satisfied only by collective action," and asserted that as society grows richer, "that minimum of sustenance which the community has always provided for those not able to look after themselves, and which can be provided outside the market, will gradually rise, and that government may, usefully and without doing any harm, assist or even lead in such endeavors."[26] Nor was he opposed in principle to government regulation of working conditions, building codes, and so on.[27] Hayek's criticism of proposals for the welfare state lay not so much with the aims as with the methods of government action.[28] He was suspicious above all of government monopolization of the provision of social, medical, or educational services, since that eliminated the competitive process by which new and possibly better means could be discovered. Yet those possibilities remain marginal in Hayek's work.

A lamentable propensity of ideological thought, much in evidence in Hayek's work, is the tendency to cast all choices in terms of polar opposites. In *The Fatal Conceit,* Hayek describes the contemporary conflict of ideologies as between the advocates of "the spontaneous order created by a competitive market" versus "those who demand a deliberate arrangement of human interaction by central authority based on collective command over available resources." But is the unrestrained market really the only alternative to a centrally planned and owned economy? Surely not.[29] Yet Hayek's rhetoric makes us forget that one can have a market-based economy, restrained by government, and influenced by considerations of public policy arrived at through rational analysis, much as *The Wealth of Nations* influenced public policy in its own day and after.

Hayek took the themes of the uses of self-interest, of the unintended consequences of action, and of cultural evolution from Hume and Smith, but gave them a far more conservative turn than it had had for the Scots whom he annexed to his intellectual family tree.[30] He increasingly stressed that the major institutions he sought to conserve—the free market and the legal structure that made it possible—were the products not of rational deliberation but of the unintended results of human action. Though Hayek clearly thought that the market order had increased human well-being, he was wary of judging it by any specific criterion. Taken to the extreme to which Hayek sometimes took it, his emphasis on our inability to fully comprehend the market order amounted to a counsel of passive acceptance and resignation.[31]

Here Hayek's tendency to exaggerate his own insights led to self-contradiction, as some of his sympathetic critics have pointed out. His emphasis on the limits of human knowledge led him to a distrust of all rational institutional design. But this was at odds with his suggestions for institutional reform based upon a rational analysis of the malfunctions of contemporary democratic institutions. Some of these suggestions were quite radical: think of Hayek's argument for the denationalization of money. Hayek's antagonism to planning—what he called "the error of constructivism"— made it impossible for him to make a principled argument for the sort of "piecemeal social engineering" that was both possible and desirable in a liberal society, as his friend Karl Popper recognized.[32]

Ideas have consequences, and that includes the idea of spontaneous order. The problem with a striking half-truth such as the idea of spontaneous order is that, like its mirror twin, the idea of a planned economy, it can have negative consequences in the real world. One example is the fate of Russia in the post-Soviet era. Those Americans who believed that "government is the problem" advised the Russians to fix their problems by radically diminishing the power of their government. But the Russians soon found that without a government strong enough to enforce the rule of law, protect property, and maintain infrastructure, commerce was difficult and expensive. Without the means to enforce the rule of law, the contraction of government ownership led less to capitalism than to kleptocracy.[33] And without an adequate bureaucracy for tax collection, necessary state services collapsed: without an adequately funded public health system, the mortality rate rose quickly, while life expectancy declined.[34] So too, the lack of American planning for maintaining order in post-Saddam Iraq was due in some part to the tacit assumption that freed from the shackles of the Baathist regime, the people of Iraq would spontaneously order themselves.[35] The consequences of this assumption proved disastrous, and demonstrated an "appalling ignorance of the elementary preconditions of political stability."[36] But does not the concept of "spontaneous order" have a propensity to lead to such ignorance?

One can accept a great deal of what Hayek has to say without subscribing to his Manichean view. Consider the sentiments in the following quotation:

Individualism, if it can be purged of its defects and its abuses, is the best safeguard of personal liberty in the sense that, compared with any other system, it greatly widens the field for the exercise of personal choice. It is also the best safeguard of the variety of life, which emerges precisely from this extended field of personal choice, and the loss of which is the greatest of all the losses of the homogeneous or totalitarian state. For this variety preserves the traditions which embody the most secure and successful choices of former generations; it colors the present with the diversification of its fancy; and being the handmaid of experiment as well as of tradition and of fancy, it is the most powerful instrument to better the future.

Much of this sounds like Hayek. But in fact, it comes from John Maynard Keynes's *General Theory*, in which Keynes defended the expansion of the role of government "as the only practicable means of avoiding the destruction of existing economic forms in their entirety and as the condition of the successful functioning of individual initiative."[37] This is not meant to suggest a blanket endorsement of Keynes over Hayek: only that we should keep in mind that there is much more to liberty, freedom, and well-being than spontaneous order. Or, to put it another way, those who value spontaneous order most should reflect on its limits and prerequisites.

Notes

1. Friedrich A. Hayek, *The Constitution of Liberty* (Chicago: University of Chicago Press, 1960), p. 160 (hereafter cited as *CL*). Hayek is quoting Michael Polanyi.
2. Friedrich A. Hayek, *Law, Legislation and Liberty,* vol. 1, *Rules and Order* (Chicago: University of Chicago Press, 1973), p. 2.
3. For a useful recent discussion of Hayek's conception of "spontaneous order" see Christina Petsoulas, *Hayek's Liberalism and Its Origins: His Idea of Spontaneous Order and the Scottish Enlightenment* (London: Routledge, 2001), chapter 1.
4. Adam Smith, *An Inquiry into the Nature and Causes of the Wealth of Nations,* ed. R. H. Campbell and A. S. Skinner (Indianapolis: Liberty Fund, 1981) (hereafter cited as *WN*), I, ii. 1.
5. See on this Jerry Z. Muller, *Adam Smith in His Time and Ours: Designing the Decent Society* (Princeton: Princeton University Press, 1995).
6. For the German case, see the chapters on Justus Möser and on Hegel in Jerry Z. Muller, *The Mind and the Market: Capitalism in Modern European Thought* (New York: Knopf, 2002).
7. See for example, *CL*, pp.61ff; and Friedrich A. Hayek, *The Fatal Conceit: The Errors of Socialism* (Chicago: University of Chicago Press, 1988), pp. 135–140. Readers of the latter work should be aware that the issue of how much of it was actually written by Hayek and how much by his editor, W. W. Bartley III, remains an open question among scholars.
8. On this Schumpetrian element of Hayek's thought see Muller, *The Mind and the Market,* p. 358.

9. A point made by Alain de Benoist, "Hayek: A Critique," *Telos,* 110 (Winter 1998): 71–104, 92. For similar criticisms by James Buchanan and Stefan Böhm, see Hans Jörg Hennecke, *Friedrich August von Hayek: Die Tradition der Freiheit* (Düsseldorf: Verlag Wissenschaft und Finanzen, 2000), p. 374.

10. Friedrich Nietzsche, *Nietzsche: 'On the Genealogy of Morality' and Other Writings,* Essay 2, part 12, revised student, ed. Keith Ansell-Person, trans. Carol Diethe (Cambridge: Cambridge University Press, 1994).

11. Leo Strauss, preface to *Spinoza's Critique of Religion* (New York: Schocken, 1965), p. 27.

12. Robert K. Merton, "The Unanticipated Consequences of Purposive Social Action," *American Sociological Review* 1, no. 6 (December 1936): 894–904.

13. See on this Peter J. Boettke, "F. A. Hayek as Intellectual Historian of Economics," in *Historians of Economics and Economic Thought: The Construction of Disciplinary Memory,* ed. Steven G. Medema and Warren Samuels (London: Routledge, 2001); also www.gmu.edu/departments/economics/working/Pages/0003.html; and Petsoulas, *Hayek's Liberalism and Its Origins,* passim.

14. Smith, WN, IV. ii. 4, p. 454.

15. Ibid., IV. Ii. 9, p. 456.

16. Ibid., V, i. a. 14, p. 697.

17. Ibid., V. i. a. 44, p. 708.

18. Ibid., IV. v. b. 44, p. 540.

19. Ibid., V. iii. 7, p. 910.

20. Hayek, *CL,* p. 143.

21. Hayek, *CL,* p. 237.

22. Smith, *WN,* V. i. f 50, p. 782.

23. Hayek, *CL,* p. 60.

24. Ibid., pp. 141–142.

25. Friedrich A. Hayek, *The Road to Serfdom* (Chicago: University of Chicago Press, 1944, reprinted with a new preface, 1976), pp. 36–39; *Law, Legislation and Liberty,* vol. 1, pp. 108–109.

26. Hayek, *CL,* pp. 257–258. Similarly, *Road to Serfdom,* pp.120–121; Friedrich A. Hayek, *Law, Legislation and Liberty,* volume 3, *The Political Order of a Free People* (Chicago: University of Chicago Press, 1979), pp. 41, 44, 61–62.

27. Hayek, *CL,* pp. 220ff.

28. Ibid., pp. 257–258.

29. See on this Jeffrey Friedman, "What's Wrong with Libertarianism," *Critical Review* 11, no. 3 (1997), and "Hayek's Political Philosophy and His Economics," *Critical Review* 11, no. 1 (1997).

30. See on this Hennecke, *Friedrich August von Hayek,* p. 386, and Emma Rothschild, *Economic Sentiments: Adam Smith, Condorcet, and the Enlightenment* (Cambridge: Harvard University Press, 2001), pp. 146–153.

31. This point has been made by many of Hayek's critics, including de Benoist, "Hayek: A Critique," p. 90; and Richard Epstein, "Hayekian Socialism," *Maryland Law Review,* 58 (1999).

32. For a thoughtful recent critique see Petsoulas, *Hayek's Liberalism*, chapter 2; on the divergences between Hayek and Popper, see Malachi Haim Hacohen, *Karl Popper: The Formative Years 1902–1945* (Cambridge: Cambridge University Press, 2000).

33. David Satter, "The Rise of the Russian Criminal State," *Hoover Digest*, no. 3 (Summer 2003) (An excerpt from his *Darkness at Dawn: The Rise of the Russian Criminal State* [New Haven: Yale University Press, 2003]).

34. Paul Demeny, "Population Policy Dilemmas in Europe at the Dawn of the Twenty-First Century," *Population and Development Review* 29, no. 1 (March 2003): 1–28.

35. On the absence of such planning for the maintenance of order see for example Thomas E. Ricks, *Fiasco: The American Military Adventure in Iraq* (New York: Penguin, 2006), pp. 109–111.

36. Stephen Holmes, "Neo-Con Futurology," *London Review of Books* 28, no.19 (October 5, 2006).

37. John Maynard Keynes, *The General Theory of Employment, Interest and Money* (London: Macmillan, 1973), p. 380.

Bibliography

Alexander, Richard. *The Biology of Moral Systems.* Hawthorne, NY: Aldine de Gruyter, 1997.

Alston, Richard M., J. R. Kearl, and Michael B. Vaughan, "Is There a Consensus among Economists in the 1990s?" Papers and Proceedings of the 104th Annual Meeting of the American Economic Association. *The American Economic Review* 82, no. 2 (May 1992): 203–209.

Amadae, S. M. *Rationalizing Capitalist Democracy: The Cold War Origins of Rational Choice Liberalism.* Chicago: University of Chicago Press, 2003.

Anastaplo, George. *The Constitution of 1787: A Commentary.* Baltimore, MD: Johns Hopkins University Press, 1989.

Arnhart, Larry. *Aristotle on Political Reasoning: A Commentary on the "Rhetoric."* DeKalb: Northern Illinois University, 1981.

_____. "Assault on Evolution." *Salon.com,* February 28, 2001. www.salon.com/books/feature/2001/02/28/idt/print.html.

_____. "Conservatives, Darwin, and Design." *First Things,* no. 107 (November 2000): 23–31.

_____. *Darwinian Conservatism.* Exeter, UK: Imprint Academic, 2005.

_____. *Darwinian Natural Right: The Biological Ethics of Human Nature.* Albany: State University of New York Press, 1998.

_____. "Evolution and the New Creationism." *Skeptic* 8, no. 4 (2001): 46–52.

_____. "The Incest Taboo as Darwinian Natural Right." In *Incest, Inbreeding, and the Westermarck Effect,* ed. Arthur Wolf and William Durham. Stanford, CA: Stanford University Press, 2004. 190–218.

_____. *Political Questions: Political Philosophy from Plato to Rawls.* 3rd ed. Prospect Heights, IL: Waveland Press, 2003.

_____. "Thomistic Natural Law as Darwinian Natural Right." In *Natural Law and Modern Moral Philosophy,* ed. Ellen Frankel Paul, Fred D. Miller, and Jeffrey Paul. New York: Cambridge University Press, 2001. 1–33.

Auspitz, Lee. "Individuality, Civility, and Theory: The Philosophical Imagination of Michael Oakeshott." *Political Theory* 4 (August 1976): 261–294.

Axelrod, Robert. *The Complexity of Cooperation: Agent-Based Models of Competition and Collaboration.* Princeton: Princeton University Press, 1997.

_____. *The Evolution of Cooperation.* New York: Basic Books, 1984.

Axelrod, Robert, and Robert O. Keohane. "Achieving Cooperation under Anarchy: Strategies and Institutions." *World Politics* 37, no. 1 (October 1985): 226–254.

Backhouse, Roger E. *Truth and Progress in Economics.* Cheltenham, UK: Edward Elgar, 1997.

Barkow, Jerome H., Leda Cosmides, and John Tooby, eds. *The Adapted Mind: Evolutionary Psychology and the Generation of Culture.* New York: Oxford, 1992.

Barry, Norman. *Hayek's Economic and Social Philosophy.* London: Macmillan, 1979.

de Benoist, Alain. "Hayek: A Critique." *Telos* 110 (Winter 1998): 71–104.

Benson, Bruce L. "Customary Law as a Social Contract: International Commercial Law." *Constitutional Political Economy* 3 (1992): 1–27.

_____. *The Enterprise of Law: Justice without the State.* San Francisco, CA: Pacific Research Institute for Public Policy, 1990.

Binmore, Ken. *Game Theory and the Social Contract.* Vol. 1, *Playing Fair.* Cambridge, MA: MIT Press, 1994.

_____. *Natural Justice.* New York: Oxford University Press, 2005.

_____. "Reciprocity and the Social Contract." *Politics, Philosophy and Economics* 3 (February 2004): 5–35.

Boettke, Peter. "Economic Calculation: The Austrian Contribution to Political Economy." In *Calculation and Coordination.* London and New York: Routledge, 2001. 29–46

_____. "F. A. Hayek as Intellectual Historian of Economics." In *Historians of Economics and Economic Thought: The Construction of Disciplinary Memory,* ed. Steven G. Medema and Warren Samuels, London: Routledge, 2001.

Boettke, Peter, and Karen Vaughn. "Knight and the Austrians on Capital, and the Problem of Socialism." *History of Political Economy* 34, no. 1 (2002): 155–176.

Bonner, John T. *The Evolution of Culture in Animals.* Princeton: Princeton University Press, 1980.

Boyd, Richard. "Michael Oakeshott on Civility, Civil Society, and Civil Association." *Political Studies* 52 (October 2004): 603–622.

Boyd, Robert, and Peter Richerson. "Culture and Cooperation." In *Beyond Self-Interest,* ed. Jane J. Mansbridge. Chicago: University of Chicago Press, 1990.

Brown, Donald. *Human Universals.* Philadelphia: Temple University Press, 1991.

Bryce, James. *The American Commonwealth.* 2 vols. 1888. Reprint, New York: G. P. Putnam's Sons, 1959.

Buchanan, James M. *Why I, Too, Am Not a Conservative: The Normative Vision of Classical Liberalism.* Cheltenham, UK: Edward Elgar, 2005.

Burke, Edmund. *Reflections on the Revolution in France.* Indianapolis: Hackett, 1987.

Caldwell, Bruce. "The Emergence of Hayek's Ideas on Cultural Evolution." *Review of Austrian Economics* 13 (2000): 5–22.

————. "Hayek and Cultural Evolution." In *Fact and Fiction in Economics: Models, Realism, and Social Construction,* ed. Uskali Maki. New York: Cambridge University Press, 2002. 285–303.

————. "Hayek and Socialism." *Journal of Economic Literature* 35 (December 1997): 1856–1890.

————. *Hayek's Challenge: An Intellectual Biography of F. A. Hayek.* Chicago: University of Chicago Press, 2004.

Capaldi, Nicholas. "The Preservation of Liberty." In *Liberty in Hume's History of England,* ed. Nicholas Capaldi and Donald Livingston. Amsterdam: Kluwer, 1990.

Capaldi, Nicholas, and Donald Livingston, eds. *Liberty in Hume's History of England.* Amsterdam: Kluwer, 1990.

Chwe, Michael Suk-Young. *Rational Ritual.* 2nd ed. Princeton: Princeton University Press, 2003.

Coase, Ronald. *The Firm, the Market, and the Law.* Chicago: University of Chicago Press, 1990.

Cohen, Avi J. "The Hayek/Knight Capital Controversy: The Irrelevance of Roundaboutness, or Purging Processes in Time?" *History of Political Economy* 35, no. 3 (2003): 469–490.

Cowen, Tyler. *In Praise of Commercial Culture.* Cambridge, MA: Harvard University Press, 1998.

Damasio, Antonio. *Descartes's Error: Emotion, Reason, and the Human Brain.* New York: G. P. Putnam's Sons, 1994.

Danford, John W. *David Hume and the Problem of Reason: Recovering the Human Sciences.* New Haven: Yale University Press, 1990.

Danielson, Peter. "Competition among Cooperators: Altruism and Reciprocity." *Proceedings of the National Academy of Science* 99, no. 3 (May 14, 2002): 7237–7242.

Darwin, Charles. *The Descent of Man, and Selection in Relation to Sex.* 2 vols. London: J. Murray, 1871.

————. *On the Origin of Species.* Cambridge, MA: Harvard University Press, 1964.

————. *The Origin of Species.* 1859. Reprint, New York: Gramercy, 1979.

Demeny, Paul. "Population Policy Dilemmas in Europe at the Dawn of the Twenty-First Century." *Population and Development Review* 29, no. 1 (March 2003): 1–28.

Dembski, William, and Ruse, Michael, ed. *Debating Design: From Darwin to DNA.* New York: Cambridge University Press, 2004.

Deutscher, Guy. *The Unfolding of Language: An Evolutionary Tour of Mankind's Greatest Invention.* New York: Henry Holt, 2005.

Duffy, Eamon. *Stripping of the Altars: Traditional Religion in England 1400–1580.* New Haven, CT: Yale University Press, 1992.

Ebenstein, Alan. *Hayek's Journey: The Mind of Friedrich Hayek*. New York: Palgrave Macmillan, 2003.

Emmett, Ross B. "The Economist and the Entrepreneur: Modernist Impulses in Frank H. Knight's *Risk, Uncertainty and Profit*." *History of Political Economy* 31 (Spring 1999): 29–52.

Epstein, Richard. "Hayekian Socialism." *Maryland Law Review* 58 (1999).

Erreygers, Guido, ed. *Economics and Interdisciplinary Exchange*. London: Routledge, 2001.

Ferguson, Adam. *An Essay on the History of Civil Society*. Edited by Fania Oz-Salzberger. Cambridge: Cambridge University Press, 1995.

Flathman, Richard. *Pluralism and Liberal Democracy*. Baltimore: Johns Hopkins University Press, 2005.

_____. *Reflections of a Would-be Anarchist: Ideals and Institutions of Liberalism*. Minneapolis: University of Minnesota Press, 1998.

Fleischacker, Samuel. *A Third Concept of Liberty: Judgment and Freedom in Kant and Adam Smith*. Princeton, NJ: Princeton University Press, 1999.

Frank, Robert H. *Passions within Reason*. New York: Norton, 1988.

Frei, Christopher, and John Nef, eds. *Contending with Hayek: On Liberalism, Spontaneous Order, and Post-Communist Transitions*. New York: Peter Lang, 1994.

Friedman, Jeffrey. "Hayek's Political Philosophy and His Economics." *Critical Review* 11, no. 1 (1997).

_____. "What's Wrong with Libertarianism." *Critical Review* 11, no. 3 (1997).

Gadamer, Hans-Georg. *Truth and Method*. New York: Continuum, 1993.

Gazzaniga, Michael S., Richard B. Ivry, and George R. Mangun. *Cognitive Neuroscience: The Biology of the Mind*, 2nd ed. New York: Norton, 2002.

Gaus, Gerald. "Hayek on the Evolution of Society and Mind." In *The Cambridge Companion to Hayek*, ed. Edward Feser. Cambridge: Cambridge University Press, 2006.

_____. "Principles, Goals and Symbols: Nozick on Practical Rationality." In *Robert Nozick*, ed. David Schmidtz. Cambridge: Cambridge University Press, 2002.

Glimcher, Paul. *Decisions, Uncertainty, and the Brain: The Science of Neuroeconomics*. Cambridge, MA: MIT Press, 2003.

Goldberg, Steven. *Why Men Rule: A Theory of Male Dominance*. LaSalle, IL: Open Court, 1993.

Goldfarb, Robert S. "Now You See It, Now You Don't: Emerging Contrary Results in Economics." *Journal of Economic Methodology* 4 (1997): 221–244 at p. 238.

Goldman, Alan H. *Practical Rules: When We Need Them and When We Don't*. Cambridge: Cambridge University Press, 2002.

Gonce, Richard A. "The Role of Pessimism in Frank H. Knight's Political Economy." Paper presented at History of Economics Society, College of Charleston, South Carolina, June 22, 1997.

Goodin, Robert E. *Utilitarianism as a Public Philosophy.* Cambridge: Cambridge University Press, 1995.

Grady, Mark F., and Michael T. McGuire. "The Nature of Constitutions." *Journal of Bioeconomics* 1 (1999): 227–240.

Grampp, William D. "What Did Smith Mean by the Invisible Hand?" *Journal of Political Economy* 108 (January 2000): 441–465.

Gray, John. *Hayek on Liberty.* 3rd ed. London: Routledge, 1998.

Hacohen, Malachi Haim. *Karl Popper: The Formative Years 1902–1945.* Cambridge: Cambridge University Press, 2000.

Hamilton, Alexander, James Madison, and John Jay. *The Federalist Papers.* New York: Random House, Modern Library, 1937.

Hamowy, Ronald. "F. A. Hayek and the Common Law." *The Cato Journal* 23 (Fall 2003): 241–264.

_____. *The Political Sociology of Freedom: Adam Ferguson and F. A. Hayek.* Cheltenham: Edward Elgar, 2005.

_____. *The Scottish Enlightenment and the Theory of Spontaneous Order.* Carbondale: Southern Illinois University Press, 1987.

Hartwell, R. M. *A History of the Mont Pelerin Society.* Indianapolis: Liberty Fund, 1995.

Hayek, Friedrich. A., ed. *Collectivist Economic Planning: Critical Studies on the Possibilities of Socialism.* London: Routledge, 1935.

_____. *The Constitution of Liberty.* Chicago: University of Chicago Press, 1960.

_____. *The Counter-Revolution of Science.* 1952. Reprint, Indianapolis: Liberty Press, 1979.

_____. *The Fatal Conceit: The Errors of Socialism,* ed. W. W. Bartley III. Chicago: University of Chicago Press, 1988.

_____. *Individualism and Economic Order.* Chicago: University of Chicago Press, 1948.

_____. "Individualism: True and False." In *Individualism and Economic Order.* Chicago: University of Chicago Press, 1948. 1–32.

_____. "The Intellectuals and Socialism." *University of Chicago Law Review* 16 (Spring 1949): 417–433.

_____. *Law, Legislation and Liberty.* Vol. 1, *Rules and Order.* Chicago: University of Chicago Press, 1973.

_____. *Law, Legislation and Liberty.* Vol. 2, *The Mirage of Social Justice.* Chicago: University of Chicago Press, 1976.

_____. *Law, Legislation and Liberty.* Vol. 3, *The Political Order of a Free People.* Chicago: University of Chicago Press, 1979.

_____. "The Meaning of Competition." In *Individualism and Economic Order.* Chicago: University of Chicago Press, 1948. 92–106.

_____. Nobel Memorial Lecture. "The Pretence of Knowledge." In *New Studies in Politics, Economics and the History of Ideas.* London: Routledge, 1978. 25–34.

———. "Notes on the Evolution of Systems of Rules of Conduct." In *Studies in Philosophy, Politics, and Economics.* Chicago: University of Chicago Press, 1967.

———."On the Relationship between Investment and Output." *Economic Journal* 44 (June 1934): 207–231.

———. "Origins and Effects of Our Morals." In *The Essence of Hayek,* ed. Chiaki Nishiyama and Kurt R. Leube. Stanford, CA: Hoover Institution Press, 1984. 318–330.

———. *The Road to Serfdom.* 1944. Reprint, Chicago: University of Chicago Press, 1976.

———. *The Sensory Order.* Chicago: University of Chicago Press, 1952.

———. *Studies in Philosophy, Politics, and Economics.* Chicago: University of Chicago Press, 1967.

———. "The Theory of Complex Phenomena." In *Readings in the Philosophy of Social Science,* ed. Michael Martin and Lee C. McIntyre. Cambridge, MA: MIT Press, 1994. 55–70.

———. "The Use of Knowledge in Society." In *Individualism and Economic Order.* Chicago: University of Chicago Press, 1948. 77–91.

Heiner, Ronald. "The Origin of Predictable Behavior." *American Economic Review* 73 (1983): 560–595.

Hennecke, Hans Jörg. *Friedrich August von Hayek: Die Tradition der Freiheit.* Düsseldorf: Verlag Wissenschaft und Finanzen, 2000.

Hocutt, Max. *Grounded Ethics: The Empirical Bases of Normative Judgments.* New Brunswick: Transaction, 2000.

Holloway, Carson. *The Right Darwin?* Dallas: Spence Publishing, 2006.

Holmes, Stephen. "Neo-Con Futurology." *London Review of Books* 28, no. 19 (October 5, 2006).

Hume, David. "Dialogues Concerning Natural Religion." In *Writings on Religion,* ed. Antony Flew. La Salle, IL: Open Court, 1992.

———. *Enquiry Concerning the Principles of Human Understanding.* Edited by L.A. Selby-Bigge. 3rd ed. Rev. P. H. Nidditch. Oxford: Clarendon, 1975.

———. *Enquiry Concerning the Principles of Morals.* Edited by L. A. Selby-Bigge. 3rd ed. Rev. P. H. Nidditch. Oxford: Clarendon, 1975.

———. *Essays, Moral, Political, and Literary.* Edited by Eugene F. Miller. Indianapolis: Liberty Fund, 1985.

———. *History of England.* 6 volumes. Indianapolis: Liberty Fund, 1983.

———. *The Natural History of Religion.* Edited by H. E. Root. Stanford, CA: Stanford University Press, 1957.

———. *A Treatise of Human Nature.* 2nd ed. Edited by L. A. Selby-Bigge and P. H. Nidditch. Oxford: Clarendon Press, 1978.

Hunt, Louis. "Principle and Prejudice: Burke, Kant and Habermas on the Conditions of Practical Reason." *History of Political Thought* 23, no. 1 (Spring 2002): 130–132.

Infantino, Lorenzo. *Ignorance and Liberty.* London: Routledge, 2003.

Ingrao, Bruna. "Economic Life in Nineteenth-Century Novels: What Economists Might Learn from Literature." In *Economics and Interdisciplinary Exchange,* ed. Guido Erreygers. London: Routledge, 2001.

Jacobs, Struan. "Michael Polanyi's Theory of Spontaneous Orders." *Review of Austrian Economics* 11, nos. 1–2 (1999): 111–127.

Johnson, Gary. "The Evolutionary Origins of Government and Politics." In *Human Nature and Politics,* ed. Joseph Losco and Albert Somit. Greenwich, CT: JAI Press, 1995. 243–305.

Johnson, Steven. *Emergence: The Connected Lives of Ants, Brains, Cities, and Software.* New York: Scribner, 2001.

Kauffman, Stuart. *Origins of Order: Self-Organization and Selection in Evolution.* New York: Oxford University Press, 1993.

Keller, Rudi. *On Language Change: The Invisible Hand in Language.* London: Routledge, 1994.

Keynes, John Maynard. *The General Theory of Employment, Interest and Money.* London: Macmillan, 1973.

Kirzner, Israel M. *The Meaning of Market Process.* London: Routledge, 1992.

Kley, Ronald. *Hayek's Political and Social Thought.* Oxford: Oxford University Press, 1995.

Knight, Frank H. "The Case for Communism: From the Standpoint of an Ex-Liberal." In *Research in the History of Economic Thought and Methodology, Archival Supplement,* ed. W. J. Samuels. 1932. Reprint, Stamford, CT: JAI Press, 1991. 57–108.

———. "Economic Man and Human Being." Paper presented at University of Virginia, Charlottesville, May 1963. Box 6, Folders 17 and 20, Frank H. Knight Papers, University of Chicago Archives.

———. "Economics and Human Evolution." Paper presented at Man in Transition—An Anthropological Study, Antioch College Office of Continuing Education, Yellow Springs, Ohio, February 1961. Box 12, Folder 23, Frank H. Knight Papers, University of Chicago Archives.

———. *The Economic Organization.* Chicago: University of Chicago, 1933.

———. "Human Nature and World Democracy." In *Freedom and Reform: Essays in Economics and Social Philosophy.* 1944. Reprint, Indianapolis: Liberty Press, 1982. 358–384.

———. *Intelligence and Democratic Action.* Cambridge: Harvard University Press, 1960.

———. "Laissez-Faire: Pro and Con." In *Selected Essays by Frank H. Knight, 2: Laissez-faire: Pro and Con,* ed. Ross B. Emmett. 1967. Reprint, Chicago: University of Chicago Press, 1999. 435–453.

———. "Philosophy and Social Institutions in the West." In *Selected Essays by Frank H. Knight, 2: Laissez-faire: Pro and Con,* ed. Ross B. Emmett. 1962. Reprint, Chicago: University of Chicago Press, 1999. 411–434.

————. "The Planful Act: The Possibilities and Limitations of Collective Rationality." In *Freedom and Reform: Essays in Economics and Social Philosophy.* 1947. Reprint, Indianapolis: Liberty Press, 1982. 398–439.

————. "The Rights of Man and Natural Law." In *Selected Essays by Frank H. Knight, 2: Laissez-faire: Pro and Con,* ed. Ross B. Emmett. 1944. Reprint, Chicago: University of Chicago Press, 1999. 209–242.

————. *Risk, Uncertainty and Profit.* Boston: Houghton Mifflin, 1921.

————. "The Role of Principles in Economics and Politics." In *Selected Essays by Frank H. Knight, 2: Laissez-faire: Pro and Con,* ed. Ross B. Emmett. 1951. Reprint, Chicago: University of Chicago Press, 1999. 361–391.

————. "Science, Society, and the Modes of Law." In *Selected Essays by Frank H. Knight, 2: Laissez-faire: Pro and Con,* ed. Ross B. Emmett. 1956. Reprint, Chicago: University of Chicago Press, 1999. 392–410.

————. The Sickness of Liberal Society. In *Selected Essays by Frank H. Knight, 2: Laissez-faire: Pro and Con,* ed. Ross B. Emmett. 1946. Reprint, Chicago: University of Chicago Press, 1999. 284–313.

————. "Social Science." In *On the History and Method of Economics: Selected Essays.* 1941. Reprint, Chicago: University of Chicago Press, 1956. 121–134.

————. "World Justice, Socialism, and the Intellectuals." *University of Chicago Law Review* 16 (Spring 1949): 434–443.

Knight, Frank H., and Thornton W. Merriam. *The Economic Order and Religion.* New York: Harper & Bros., 1945.

Krugman, Paul. *The Self-Organizing Economy.* Cambridge, MA, and Oxford: Blackwell, 1996.

Kukathas, Chandran. *Hayek and Modern Liberalism.* Oxford: Clarendon, 1989.

Lal, Deepak. *Reviving the Invisible Hand: The Case for Classical Liberalism in the Twenty-First Century.* Princeton: Princeton University Press, 2006.

————. *Unintended Consequences: The Impact of Factor Endowments, Culture, and Politics on Long-Run Economic Performance.* Cambridge, MA: MIT, 2001.

Lange, Oskar. "On the Economic Theory of Socialism." In *On the Economic Theory of Socialism,* ed. Benjamin Lippincott. New York: McGraw-Hill, 1964.

Lavoie, Don. "Computation, Incentives, and Discovery: The Cognitive Function of Markets in Market Socialism." *Annals of the American Academy of Political and Social Science* 507 (1990): 72–79.

————. *Rivalry and Central Planning: The Socialist Calculation Debate Reconsidered.* Cambridge: Cambridge University Press, 1985.

Levi, Issac. *The Enterprise of Knowledge.* Cambridge, MA: MIT Press, 1980.

Locke, John. *Two Treatises of Government.* Cambridge: Cambridge University Press, 1989.

Ludwig, Arnold. *King of the Mountain: The Nature of Political Leadership.* Lexington: University Press of Kentucky, 2002.

Lutz, Donald S. *The Origins of American Constitutionalism.* Baton Rouge: Louisiana State University Press, 1988.

Maki, Uskali. *Fact and Fiction in Economics: Models, Realism, and Social Construction.* New York: Cambridge University Press, 2002.

Marx, Karl. *Capital.* Vol. 1. Translated by Ben Fowkes. New York: Vintage Books, 1977.

McCloskey, Dierdre. "The Rhetoric of Economics." In *The Philosophy of Economics,* ed. Daniel M. Hausman. Cambridge: Cambridge University Press, 1994. 395–446.

McGrew, William C. *The Cultured Chimpanzee: Reflections on Cultural Primatology.* Cambridge: Cambridge University Press, 2004.

McNamara, Peter. *Political Economy and Statesmanship: Smith, Hamilton, and the Foundation of the Commercial Republic.* DeKalb: Northern Illinois University Press, 1998.

Merton, Robert K. "The Unanticipated Consequences of Purposive Social Action." *American Sociological Review* 1, no. 6 (December 1936): 894–904.

Miller, Eugene F. "Hume on Liberty." In *Liberty in Hume's History of England,* ed. Nicholas Capaldi and Donald Livingston. Amsterdam: Kluwer, 1990.

Mises, Ludwig von. *Socialism: An Economic and Sociological Analysis.* Translated by J. Kahane. Indianapolis: Liberty Classics, 1981.

Mueller, Dennis C. *Public Choice III.* Cambridge: Cambridge University, 2003.

Muller, Jerry Z. *Adam Smith in His Time and Ours: Designing the Decent Society.* Princeton: Princeton University Press, 1995.

———. *The Mind and the Market: Capitalism in Modern European Thought.* New York: Knopf, 2002.

Murphy, James Bernard. *The Moral Economy of Labor: Aristotelian Themes in Economic Theory.* New Haven, CT: Yale University Press, 1993.

———. "Nature, Custom, and Reason as the Explanatory and Practical Principles of Aristotelian Political Science." *The Review of Politics* 64 (2002): 469–495.

———. "Nature, Custom, and Stipulation in Law and Jurisprudence." *Review of Metaphysics* 43 (June 1990): 751–790.

Nardin, Terry. *The Philosophy of Michael Oakeshott.* University Park: Penn State University Press, 2001.

Nietzsche, Friedrich. *Nietzsche: 'On the Genealogy of Morality' and Other Writings.* Revised student ed. Edited by Keith Ansell-Person. Translated by Carol Diethe. Cambridge: Cambridge University Press, 1994.

North, Douglass C. "Economic Performance through Time." *American Economic Review* 84 (1994): 359–368.

———. "Institutional Change: A Framework of Analysis." In *Institutional Change: Theory and Empirical Findings,* ed. S.-E. Sjöstrand. Armonk. NY: M. E. Sharpe, 1994. 35–48.

———. *Institutions, Institutional Change, and Economic Performance.* New York: Cambridge University Press, 1990.

———. *Structure and Change in Economic History.* New York: W. W. Norton, 1981.

Nozick, Robert. *The Nature of Rationality.* Princeton: Princeton University Press, 1993.

Oakeshott, Michael. *Experience and Its Modes.* Cambridge: Cambridge University Press, 1933.

———."On Being Conservative." In *Rationalism in Politics and Other Essays.* Indianapolis: Liberty Press, 1991. 407–437.

———. *On Human Conduct.* Oxford: Clarendon Press, 1991.

———. *Rationalism in Politics and Other Essays.* Indianapolis: Liberty Press, 1991.

———. "Rational Conduct." In *Rationalism in Politics and Other Essays.* Indianapolis: Liberty Press, 1991. 99–131.

———. "Rationalism in Politics." In *Rationalism in Politics and Other Essays.* Indianapolis: Liberty Press, 1991. 5–42.

———. "Political Education." In *Rationalism in Politics and Other Essays.* Indianapolis: Liberty Press, 1991. 43–69.

———. "The Voice of Poetry in the Conversation of Mankind." In *Rationalism in Politics and Other Essays.* Indianapolis: Liberty Press, 1991. 488–541.

O'Driscoll, Gerald P., Jr., and Mario J. Rizzo. *The Economics of Time and Ignorance.* London and New York: Routledge, 1996.

Ofek, Haim. *Second Nature: Economic Origins of Human Evolution.* Cambridge: Cambridge University Press, 2001.

O'Hear, Anthony. *Beyond Evolution: Human Nature and the Limits of Evolutionary Explanation.* Oxford: Oxford University Press, 1997.

Ottenheimer, Martin. *Forbidden Relatives: The American Myth of Cousin Marriage.* Urbana: University of Illinois Press, 1996.

Otteson, James R. *Actual Ethics.* Cambridge: Cambridge University Press, 2006.

———. "Adam Smith und die Objektivität moralischer Urteile: Ein Mittelweg." In *Adam Smith als Moralphilosoph,* ed. Christel Fricke and Hans-Peter Schuett. Berlin: DeGruyter, 2005.

———. *Adam Smith's Marketplace of Life.* Cambridge: Cambridge University Press, 2002.

———. *Adam Smith.* London: Continuum, forthcoming.

Patinkin, Don. "Frank Knight as Teacher." In *Essays on and in the Chicago Tradition.* Durham: Duke University, 1981. 23–51.

Petsoulas, Christina. *Hayek's Liberalism and Its Origins: His Idea of Spontaneous Order and the Scottish Enlightenment.* London: Routledge, 2001.

Pinker, Steven. *The Blank Slate: The Modern Denial of Human Nature.* New York: Viking, 2002.

Pipes, Richard. *Property and Freedom.* New York: Alfred A. Knopf, 1999.

Polanyi, Michael. "The Growth of Thought in Society." *Economica* 8 (November 1941): 428–456.

————. *The Logic of Liberty: Reflections and Rejoinders*. Chicago: University of Chicago Press, 1951.

————. *The Tacit Dimension*. Garden City, NY: Doubleday, 1966.

Postrel, Virginia. *The Future and Its Enemies*. New York: Touchstone, 1999.

Prigogine, Grigoire Nicolis, and Ilya Prigogine. *Self-Organization in Non-Equilibrium Systems*. Indianapolis: John Wiley, 1997.

Purcell, Edward A., Jr. *The Crisis of Democratic Theory: Scientific Naturalism and the Problem of Value*. Lexington: University Press of Kentucky, 1973.

Reed, Leonard. 1958. "I, Pencil." http://209.217.49.168/vnews.php?nid=316.

Resnick, Mitchell. *Turtles, Termites and Traffic Jams: Explorations in Massively Parallel Microworlds*. Complex Adaptive Systems Series. Cambridge, MA: MIT Press, 1997.

Richerson, Peter J., and Robert Boyd. *Not by Genes Alone: How Culture Transformed Human Evolution*. Chicago: University of Chicago Press, 2005.

Ricks, Thomas E. *Fiasco: The American Military Adventure in Iraq*. New York: Penguin, 2006.

Ridley, Matt. *The Origins of Virtue*. New York: Penguin, 1996.

Riker, William. *Liberalism against Populism: A Confrontation between the Theory of Democracy and the Theory of Social Choice*. San Francisco: W. H. Freeman, 1982.

Ritchie, David. *Darwinism and Politics*. New York: Charles Scribner's Sons, 1901.

Robertson, D. H. *The Control of Industry*. London: Nisbet, 1928.

Rosenberg, Alexander. *Philosophy of Social Science*. 2nd ed. Boulder, CO: Westview, 1995.

Rosser, J. Barkley, Jr. "On the Complexities of Complex Economic Dynamics." *The Journal of Economic Perspectives* 13 (Autumn 1999): 169–192.

Rothschild, Emma. *Economic Sentiments: Adam Smith, Condorcet, and the Enlightenment*. Cambridge: Harvard, 2001.

Rousseau, *The Discourses and Other Early Political Writings*. Edited and translated by Victor Gorevitch. Cambridge: Cambridge University Press, 1997.

Rubin, Paul. *Darwinian Politics: The Evolutionary Origins of Freedom*. New Brunswick, NJ: Rutgers University Press, 2002.

Satter, David. "The Rise of the Russian Criminal State." *Hoover Digest*, no. 3 (Summer 2003) (An excerpt from his *Darkness at Dawn: The Rise of the Russian Criminal State* New Haven: Yale University Press, 2003).

Saari, Donald. *Chaotic Elections! A Mathematician Looks at Voting*. Providence, RI: American Mathematical Association, 2000.

————. "Mathematical Complexity of Simple Economics." *Notices of the AMA* 42, no. 2 (1995): 222–231.

Schabas, Margaret. Review of *Economics and Interdisciplinary Exchange*, ed. Guido Erreygers. *History of Political Economy* 35, no. 3 (September 2003): 602–603.

Schelling, Thomas C. *Micromotives and Macrobehavior*. New York: Norton, 1978.

Schofield, Norman. "Anarchy, Altruism, and Cooperation." *Social Choice and Welfare* 2 (2005): 207–219.

Schultz, Walter J. *The Moral Conditions of Economic Efficiency.* Cambridge: Cambridge University Press, 2001.

Schumpeter, Joseph. *History of Economic Analysis.* New York: Oxford University Press, 1954.

Searle, John. *The Construction of Social Reality.* New York: Free Press, 1997.

Sheffrin, Steven M. *Rational Expectations.* 2nd ed. Cambridge: Cambridge University Press, 1996.

Singer, Peter. *A Darwinian Left: Politics, Evolution and Cooperation.* New Haven, CT: Yale University Press, 1999.

———. *The Expanding Circle: Ethics and Sociobiology.* New York: Farrar, Straus, and Giroux, 1981.

Sinn, Hans-Werner. "A Rehabilitation of the Principle of Insufficient Reason." *Quarterly Journal of Economics* 94 (May 1980): 493–506.

Skyrms, Brian. *The Stag Hunt and the Evolution of Social Structure.* Cambridge: Cambridge University Press, 2004.

Smith, Adam. *Essays on Philosophical Subjects.* Edited by W. P. D. Wightman and J. C. Bryce. Indianapolis: Liberty Classics, 1982.

———. *An Inquiry into the Nature and Causes of the Wealth of Nations.* Edited by R. H. Campbell and A. S. Skinner. Indianapolis: Liberty Classics, 1981.

———. *Lectures on Jurisprudence.* Edited by R. L. Meek, D. D. Raphael, and P. G. Stein. Indianapolis: Liberty Classics, 1982.

———. *The Theory of Moral Sentiments.* Edited by D. D. Raphael and A. L. Macfie. Indianapolis: Liberty Classics, 1982.

Smith, Barry. "The Connectionist Mind: A Study in Hayekian Psychology." In *Hayek: Economist and Social Philosopher: A Critical Retrospective,* ed. S. F. Frowen. London: Macmillan, 1976.

Smith, Peter. *Explaining Chaos.* Cambridge: Cambridge University Press, 1998.

Smith, Vernon. *Bargaining and Market Behavior: Essays in Experimental Economics.* 2nd ed. Cambridge: Cambridge University Press, 2005.

Sober, Elliot, and David Sloan Wilson. *Unto Others: The Evolution and Psychology of Unselfish Behavior.* Cambridge: Harvard University Press, 1998.

de Soto, Hernando. *The Mystery of Capital: Why Capitalism Triumphs in the West and Fails Everywhere Else.* New York: Basic Books, 2000.

Sowell, Thomas. *A Conflict of Visions: Ideological Origins of Political Struggles.* New York: Basic Books, 2002.

Spencer, Herbert. *First Principles.* London: Murray, 1862.

Stigler, George J. *Memoirs of an Unregulated Economist.* New York: Basic Books, 1988.

Stiglitz, Joseph E. *Whither Socialism?* Cambridge, MA: MIT Press, 1994.

Strauss, Leo. *Spinoza's Critique of Religion.* New York: Schocken, 1965.

Strogatz, Steven. *Sync: The Emerging Science of Spontaneous Order.* New York: Hyperion Books, 2003.

Sunstein, Cass. *Free Markets and Social Justice.* New York: Oxford University Press, 1997.

Tanner, Edward, *Why Things Bite Back.* London: Fourth Estate, 1996.

Tetlock, Philip E. *Expert Political Judgment: How Good Is It? How Can We Know?* Princeton: Princeton University Press, 2005.

Thach, Charles. *The Creation of the Presidency, 1775–1789.* Baltimore, MD: Johns Hopkins University Press, 1969.

Thomsen, Esteban F. *Prices and Knowledge: A Market-Process Perspective.* London and New York: Routledge, 1992.

Tocqueville, Alexis de. *Democracy in America.* Translated by Harvey C. Mansfield and Delba Winthrop. Chicago and London: University of Chicago Press, 2000.

Vanberg, Viktor J. *Rules and Choice in Economics.* London: Routledge, 1994.

Vaughn, Karen I. "Hayek's Theory of the Market Order as an Instance of the Theory of Complex, Adaptive Systems." *Journal de Economistes et des Etudes Humaines* 9 (Juin–Septembre 1999): 241–256.

———. "Can Democratic Society Reform Itself? The Limits of Constructive Change." In *The Market Process: Essays in Contemporary Austrian Economics,* ed. Peter Boettke and David Prychitko. Cheltenham: Edward Elgar, 1994. 229–243.

Vernon, Richard. "The 'Great Society' and the 'Open Society': Liberalism in Hayek and Popper." *Canadian Journal of Political Science* 9, no. 2 (June 1976): 261–276.

Waal, Frans de. *The Apes and the Sushi Master.* New York: Basic Books, 2001.

Waldrop, Frans de. *Complexity: The Emerging Science at the Edge of Order and Chaos.* New York: Simon and Schuster, 1992.

Walton, Craig. "Hume's *History of England* as a Natural History of Morals." In *Liberty in Hume's History of England,* ed. Nicholas Capaldi and Donald Livingston. Amsterdam: Kluwer, 1990.

West, John G. *Darwin's Conservatives: The Misguided Quest.* Seattle: Discovery Institute Press, 2006.

Westermarck, Edward. *The Origin and Development of the Moral Ideas.* 2 vols. London: Macmillan, 1908.

Whiten, A., J. Goodall, W. C. McGrew, T. Nishida, V. Reynolds, Y. Sugiyama, C. E. G. Tutin, R., W. Wrangham, and C. Boesch. "Cultures in Chimpanzees." *Nature* 399 (1999): 682–685.

Whitman, Douglas Glen. "Hayek contra Pangloss on Evolutionary Systems." *Constitutional Political Economy* 9 (1988): 450–466.

Wilson, Edward O. *Consilience: The Unity of Knowledge.* New York: Knopf, 1998.

Wilson, James Q. *The Moral Sense.* New York: Free Press, 1997.

Wright, Robert. *The Moral Animal: Why We Are the Way We Are.* London: Abacus, 1994.

Yenor, Scott. "Between Rationalism and Postmodernism: David Hume's Political Science of 'Our Mixed Condition.'" *Political Research Quarterly* 55, no. 2 (June 2002): 329–350.

Young, H. Peyton. *Individual Strategy and Social Structure: An Evolutionary Theory of Institutions.* Princeton: Princeton University Press, 2001.

Contributors

Larry Arnhart is professor of political science at Northern Illinois University. He is the author of *Aristotle on Political Reasoning: A Commentary on the "Rhetoric"* (Northern Illinois University Press, 1982); *Political Questions: Political Philosophy from Plato to Rawls* (Waveland Press, 2002); *Darwinian Natural Right: The Biological Ethics of Human Nature* (State University of New York Press, 1998); and *Darwinian Conservatism* (Imprint Academic 2005).

Richard Boyd is associate professor of government at Georgetown University. He has also taught at the University of Chicago, University of Pennsylvania, University of Wisconsin-Madison, and Deep Springs College. He is the author of *Uncivil Society: The Perils of Pluralism and the Making of Modern Liberalism* (Rowman & Littlefield, 2004), as well as journal articles and book chapters on various thinkers and themes in classical liberalism. He is completing a book-length manuscript titled "Membership and Belonging: On the Boundaries of Liberal Political Theory."

Ross B. Emmett is associate professor and codirector of The Michigan Center for Innovation and Economic Prosperity, James Madison College, Michigan State University. A historian of the Chicago School of economics, he also has research interests in classical economics, constitutional political economy, and institutional analysis related to innovation and economic development. He is the editor of the *Biographical Dictionary of American Economists* (Thoemmes Continuum, 2006), *Selected Essays of Frank H. Knight* (University of Chicago Press, 2000), *The Chicago Tradition in Economics, 1892–1945* (Routledge, 2002), and *Great Bubbles: Reactions to the South Sea Bubble, the Mississippi Scheme and the Tulip Mania Affair* (Pickering & Chatto, 2000). *Did the Chicago School Reject Frank Knight?* a collection of his essays, is forthcoming from Routledge in 2008. He is among the editors of the annual *Research in the History of Economic Thought and Methodology.*

Gerald F. Gaus is the James E. Rogers Professor of Philosophy at the University of Arizona. Among his books are *On Philosophy, Politics and Economics* (Wadsworth, 2008); *Contemporary Theories of Liberalism: Public Reason as a Post-Enlightenment Project* (Sage, 2003); *Justificatory Liberalism* (Oxford, 1996); and *Value and Justification* (Cambridge, 1990). He is the coeditor, with Chandran Kukathas, of the *Handbook of Political Theory* (Sage, 2004). He is the founding editor, along with Jonathan Riley, of *Politics, Philosophy and Economics*. He is currently completing a book on *The Order of Public Reason* (Cambridge University Press).

Louis Hunt is associate professor in political theory and constitutional democracy at James Madison College, Michigan State University. His research and publications deal with Kantian and Hegelian political philosophy, the Scottish Enlightenment, and the problems of modern civil society.

Peter McNamara teaches political science at Utah State University. He is the author of *Political Economy and Statesmanship: Smith, Hamilton and the Foundation of the Commercial Republic* (Northern Illinois University Press, 1998), and the editor of *The Noblest Minds: Fame, Honor and the American Founding* (Rowman and Littlefield, 1999). He is currently working on the topic of liberalism and the problem of human nature.

James Ashley Morrison is a PhD candidate in political science at Stanford University. His dissertation compares the theories of money developed by John Locke, Adam Smith, and J. M. Keynes in their systems of political economy.

Jerry Z. Muller is professor of history at the Catholic University of America in Washington, D.C. His works include *Adam Smith in His Time and Ours: Designing the Decent Society* (Free Press, 1993); *Conservatism: An Anthology of Social and Political Thought from David Hume to the Present* (Princeton, 1997); and *The Mind and the Market: Capitalism in Modern European Thought* (Knopf, 2002).

Michael C. Munger teaches political science and serves as chair of the political science department at Duke University. He is currently the editor of the journal *Public Choice*. His work includes *Ideology and the Theory of Political Choice* (University of Michigan Press, 1994) and *Analytical Politics* (Cambridge University Press, 1997) with Melvin Hinich, as well as *Analyzing Policy* (W. W. Norton, 2000). His interests combine the study of rational choice methods in the investigation of political behavior and institutions, and political theory. His work in progress is a book on racism and the economics of slavery in the American south before 1835.

James R. Otteson is associate professor and chair of the Department of Philosophy and a fellow of the College of Arts and Sciences Leadership Board at the University of Alabama. He is the author of *Adam Smith's Marketplace of Life* (Cambridge, 2002) and *Actual Ethics* (Cambridge, 2006).

Scott Yenor is an associate professor of political science at the Boise State University, where he teaches political philosophy. He has written on the Scottish Enlightenment, the political import of revealed religion, and Tocqueville, and is currently working on a manuscript about the family's place in modern political thought. He lives in Boise with his wife, Amy, and their four children.

Index